Protestants in a Catholic State

Protestants in a Catholic State

Ireland's Privileged Minority

KURT BOWEN

McGill-Queen's University Press
Kingston and Montreal

Gill and Macmillan

Legal deposit 3rd quarter 1983
Bibliothèque nationale du Québec

Printed in Canada

First published in Ireland 1983 by Gill and Macmillan Ltd, Goldenbridge, Dublin 8
with associated companies in London, New York,
Delhi, Hong Kong, Johannesburg, Lagos, Melbourne, Singapore, Tokyo

7171 0928 3

Canadian Cataloguing in Publication Data
Bowen, Kurt Derek.
   Protestants in a Catholic state
   Bibliography: p.
   Includes index.
   ISBN 0-7735-0412-5
   1. Protestants – Ireland – History – 20th century. 2. Christianity – Ireland.
   3. Ireland – Social conditions. I. Title.
   HN400.3.A8B68   305.6'3'0417   C83-098104-7

Contents

Tables

Acknowledgments

This book has been published with the help of a grant from the Social Science Federation of Canada using funds provided by the Social Sciences and Humanities Research Council of Canada. Publication has also been assisted by the Canada Council under its block grant program. The Canada Council and the Institute of Social and Economic Research at Memorial University of Newfoundland both provided fellowships which made my research possible.

I am especially indebted to Dr Bryon Wilson, my thesis adviser at Oxford University, for his patient support and always trenchant comments. Later, in Canada, I also benefited greatly from discussions with Rod Beaujot, Mervin Chen, Sam Clark, and Tom Regan.

In Ireland I received invaluable assistance from many academics, librarians, and officials at Trinity College Dublin, the Economic and Social Research Institute, the Church of Ireland Divinity Hostel, the Church of Ireland Board of Education, and the Representative Church Body Library. I also owe more than I can adequately convey to the clergy, teachers, and laypeople of the Church of Ireland community who so graciously endured the innumerable questions of a young academic learning his trade. I shall never forget their generosity, which often extended to providing food and shelter after I had taken up so much of their time. Unfortunately, I cannot identify them individually as some of what follows is based on their personal experiences. They are not, of course, responsible for my interpretations and conclusions, but I hope I have done justice to the trust they so freely gave.

Lastly, I want to record my greatest debt of all, namely, to my wife, Dale. My debt goes well beyond such matters as typing, proofreading, and toleration of an absent spouse which are so essential for the completion of any manuscript. From beginning to end, Dale was my constant alter ego, always questioning my judgments and offering insights of her own. I look forward to continuing our partnership in the years ahead.

Protestants in a Catholic State

CHAPTER ONE

Introduction

This book traces the changing fortunes of the small Protestant community in the southern twenty-six counties of Ireland after independence was achieved in 1922. Unlike the enduring conflict between Protestants and Catholics in Northern Ireland (which has remained a part of Great Britain), relations between the two communities in the South have been relatively peaceful since the founding of the state. Their centuries-old traditions of opposition and segregation continued for some time, but after 1945 a new era began to emerge, so that by the end of the 1970s as many as 40 per cent of the southern minority may have been marrying Catholics. This dominant and growing trend might be described as either assimilation or integration. If assimilation is the more appropriate description, it suggests that Protestants will eventually disappear by being absorbed into the larger Catholic community. Integration, on the other hand, implies that Protestants will survive as their differences with Catholics decline in social importance and become matters of personal and private choice. Since the old divisions have only recently started to crumble, it is still far from certain whether assimilation or integration best describes the Protestant experience after 1922. Nevertheless, this is the central question that underlies the present study. It is obviously of greatest concern to southern Protestants for whom it is a matter of life and death. However, it is also an issue that must surely concern all Irishmen since it addresses the fundamental fears of northern Protestants over the treatment they might receive in a united Ireland.

Up to the end of the 1970s, when this study comes to a close, the basic communal division in the South was between Protestants and Catholics. But we will be primarily concerned with the approximately 80 per cent of all Protestants who were members of the

Church of Ireland. Apart from small numbers of Methodists, Baptists, and Quakers, Presbyterians are the one significant body of southern Protestants that tend to be ignored. Presbyterians were largely concentrated in the South's portion of the province of Ulster. These three border counties of Cavan, Donegal, and Monaghan were something of a transitional zone between the North and the South, but even here Catholics outnumbered Protestants and the Church of Ireland was the largest Protestant denomination. In the three other provinces of Leinster, Munster, and Connacht, a full 90 per cent of all Protestants were members of the Church of Ireland. Their numerical predominance ensured that their religion, their leaders, and their institutions shaped the basic outlook and style of the Protestant community in the South. For the most part, the community boundaries that will be described here tend to encompass, rather than exclude, these other smaller Protestant denominations. However, by focusing on Irish Anglicans, we are better able to grasp the essential and distinctive features of the southern minority.

In addition to the usual documentary sources, a considerable amount of information is based on my own enquiries and interviews during 1973 and 1974 within six parishes selected to represent the economic and regional diversity of the community. To honour a promise of anonymity, pseudonyms will be used for parish names where necessary. Three of the parishes were in large urban areas. One was in a provincial city; another was a large and quite prosperous parish in the suburbs of Dublin; and the third was chosen because it contained a strong working and lower middle-class element. Like most other rural parishes, two of the three in this category encompassed small towns as well as their surrounding rural areas. At one extreme was a relatively large parish in Ulster; in between was a midlands parish where the Protestant community was smaller but still quite strong; and the last was typical of the many tiny and struggling parishes in the remote western and southern parts of the country. Preliminary enquiries were made in at least two parishes of each type before a final selection was made. Through the clergy and other key informants, basic social information was gathered on families enumerated in parish lists. On this basis I conducted extensive interviews with a small representative sample of eighty-three adults. Additional interviews were also conducted with teachers and officers of other organizations that were part of the community. Many of my later comments concerning mixed marriages, occupational segregation, and community life are derived from these sources.

The initially strong sense of separate identity among Irish

Anglicans was based on three fundamental divisions of religion, class, and ethnicity. Religious and economic differences need no elaboration at this point, but that involving ethnicity may not be quite so clear. In using this term I refer to the fact that the minority regarded itself – and was so regarded by others – as having a separate ancestry from the Gaelic and Catholic majority. In a broad sense, the minority might be considered to be an ethnic group which came to employ religion as the principal symbol of its separate "people-hood." However, ethnicity is used here in the narrower sense of referring to the secular, British traditions of Irish Anglicans which derived from their close links with England. On its own, no one of these three divisions can fully explain the original tensions between the two communities. To a certain extent, each of them operated independently of the others, and each of them showed varying degrees of vitality in the post-independence years. Nonetheless, these three divisive forces were closely interrelated, for they all had their origin in the English conquest of Ireland during the seventeenth century, when what was to become the Church of Ireland community emerged with all the trappings and privileges of a colonial minority. In order to understand the complex character of communal divisions after 1922, we must first delve briefly into Ireland's colonial past.

Although the nationalist canon speaks of some 700 years of British rule, the initial conquest by the Normans or Old English cannot be compared to the massive incursions of the sixteenth and seventeenth centuries. At the height of their power, the Old English had acquired nominal control over two-thirds of the country, but their very success proved to be the cause of their downfall. Because of their small numbers, they were inclined to intermarry with the Gaelic leadership, and their English feudal customs usually failed to make much impression on the Gaelic peasantry and lesser chiefs whom they ruled. Gaelic influence then began to revive in the fourteenth century. In much of the country the Old English, who still retained control of their estates, found themselves increasingly isolated both from each other and from the mother country. By the end of the Middle Ages a proper English colony could be said to exist only in an ever smaller strip of land around Dublin known as "the Pale." Even within its borders efforts to prohibit intermarriage and to prevent the use of the Irish language were not always successful, and England showed little interest in the affairs of its dwindling colony. The most prominent of the Old English nobles still acknowledged the English monarch as "Lord of Ireland," but for all practical purposes they were independent rulers who were as suspicious of the English of England as they were of the "mere Irish."[1]

England's neglect of Ireland was brought to an abrupt halt by Henry VIII. As his struggles with France, Spain, and the Papacy intensified, he grew ever more fearful that his enemies would exploit his unguarded back door in Ireland. For many years the Old English earls of Kildare continued to serve as his lord deputy, but with their Yorkist leanings and independent ways it was a rather strained marriage of convenience. In 1534 Henry found the pretext he needed when Thomas FitzGerald, the son of the earl of Kildare, broke into sudden revolt upon being falsely informed that his father had been executed in London. By 1540 Henry had crushed the FitzGeralds of Kildare, and their supporters had wisely decided to submit. They and most of the other leading nobles were then persuaded to surrender their lands and receive them back under royal grant in the hope that this would pacify the country. Henry also managed to have his church reformation legislation passed by the Irish parliament, and in 1541 he was proclaimed King of Ireland. For a time the country seemed peaceful, but hope of a lasting peace was to prove illusory, since the bulk of the population beyond the Pale had yet to be subdued militarily. And with the rejection of the indirect rule of the Kildares, England was now committed to playing an active role in the entirety of its new kingdom.

From this point on, the Old English in the Pale grew increasingly resentful as control of the central administration began to be transferred to a new body of loyal and Protestant Englishmen. Following the introduction of visible changes in doctrine and liturgy under Edward VI, it also became evident that neither Gael nor Old English would accept Elizabeth's reformation legislation of 1560. In practice, many of the ancient churches of the country remained under Catholic control, but from this point on all the privileges of the established and now reformed Church of Ireland were to fall into Protestant hands as soon as English law could be exercised. In the Pale and in the towns where English traditions were well established, the Old English remained grudgingly loyal, since Elizabeth showed no interest in persecuting Catholics solely for their religion. But elsewhere the slow advance of the English provoked repeated revolts. In Munster, for instance, questionable land claims by English adventurers were backed by the government out of fear that this southern province was especially vulnerable to Spanish intervention. After a series of rebellions by the Old English in which they eventually sought support from Spain and the papal nuncio in order to defend their threatened estates, their lands were confiscated and then distributed to new English settlers. Not long after, a much more widespread rebellion broke out in the Gaelic stronghold of Ulster. It too was proclaimed as a war against the heretical English, although the rebel leaders, O'Neill and O'Donnell, were primarily concerned with preserving their political independence and Gaelic traditions. Once again they were defeated after a long and bloody struggle which left virtually all of Ireland in a state of uneasy subjugation. In this conflict, Gaelic hatred of the English and of their Protestant religion soon became indistinguishable, although for a little longer the strained loyalty of the Old English continued to obscure the importance of the religious division.[2]

Once the war was over, England returned to its policy of colonization in the hope of pacifying the country. Its first major success was in Ulster where the flight of O'Neill and O'Donnell in 1607 enabled the government to confiscate their lands on the ground of treason. But in the rest of the country the advance of the new English settlers was blocked by the Old English, who still held about half of all Irish land and were a powerful force in commerce and government. Although their strength deterred England from applying its own harsh laws against Catholics, it was not prepared to meet the demand of the Old English for official religious toleration. Its distrust of the Old English was further evidenced when they were stripped of their majority in the lower house of the Irish parliament through the creation of a large number of new seats for Protestants. To fill the administration's coffers and to make possible further plantation schemes, the government also began to revive old royal claims to large estates as a means of extracting land from those who had not actually rebelled. The strategy did not especially disturb the Old English as long as it was applied solely to the native Irish, but their loyalty was stretched to the limit when their own large estates in Connacht were threatened in the 1630s. Encouraged by the Scottish rebellion and fearing the anti-Catholicism of the English parliament, the Gaelic chiefs in Ulster were the first to rebel when they saw the opportunity presented by the mounting tensions between crown and parliament in England. The Old English wavered, but they too were soon convinced that their only hope of survival lay in joining the rebels in support of Charles I. With this act, religion, rather than national origin, became the fundamental badge of loyalty, and the fate of the Old English was sealed.[3]

After a decade of war Cromwell and his Puritan parliament emerged as victors. The rebels' initial victories in the Protestant areas in the North became enshrined in Protestant mythology as their great massacre at the hands of the Catholic hordes; and tales of Cromwell's savagery during his later invasion became equally entrenched in the folk memory of the Catholic majority. Unlike its royal predecessors, Cromwell's administration subjected the Catholic church and its adherents to a ruthless policy of repression. Its most lasting influence, however, lay in the Act of Settlement, which led to a massive transfer of Catholic lands to Cromwell's soldiers, previous Protestant settlers, and the English adventurers who had advanced money to subsidize the reconquest of the country. Even the towns, which had once been such an important Old English stronghold, fell under Protestant control. When combined with the land already held by Protestants before 1641, the power and wealth of Ireland now shifted irretrievably into the hands of Protestants.[4]

Nevertheless, another thirty years were to elapse before Catholics received their final defeat. Although Charles II eased the persecution of Catholics and returned some land to Catholic royalists, he did not alter the Cromwellian settlement in any substantial way. When his Catholic brother, James II, ascended the throne in 1685, Catholic hopes soared for the last time, and Protestants once again feared that they might lose all that they had gained. In a short space of time the lord lieutenancy, the army, and finally the Irish parliament passed under Catholic control. But by then William and Mary had already been established as king and queen of England under a Protestant banner. James fled to Ireland where he, his French allies, and his Irish Catholic supporters were decisively defeated at the Battle of the Boyne on 1 July 1690. The war dragged on for another year, but the Protestant victory was no longer in serious doubt. In the aftermath, further confiscations were added to those that had gone before. The result was that no more than a seventh of Irish land was now under Catholic control, and this proportion was to decline even further in the next century. On this firm economic basis was built the Protestant Ascendancy which was to rule Ireland for some 200 years.[5]

The new ruling class was now a Church of Ireland body, for the vast majority of large landlords from other Protestant denominations had joined the established church. After the recurring turmoil and insecurity of the previous century, they were determined to cement their newly acquired privileges as firmly as possible. In some cases the penal laws passed by the Irish parliament were directed against Dissenters as well as Catholics, but it was the latter who were subject to the more oppressive and extensive set of restrictions. Politically, Catholics were denied the vote, access to public office, and the right to bear arms. Economically, their right to obtain new land was restricted to leases of no more than thirty-one years; inheritance by gavelkind (i.e., equal distribution to all sons) was imposed upon them; they were prevented from inheriting land from Protestants by marriage or descent; and a converted eldest son was entitled to inherit the family estate, regardless of the wishes of the remainder of the family. In addition, Catholic schools were prohibited; Catholic bishops and all but secular clergy were banished from the country; and mixed marriages were banned. Interestingly enough, Catholic worship was not prohibited, and the supply of clergy was not seriously threatened, since the laws banning bishops and foreign education were never effectively implemented. As the Church of Ireland showed little missionary zeal, it would appear that the framers of the penal laws were less concerned with extinguishing Catholicism than with keeping Catholics in a state of political, economic, and social subordination. In effect, the penal laws represented an Irish form of apartheid in which religion served as the fundamental determinant of all privileges – and hence of colonist and colonized.[6]

Although population figures for this period are notoriously unreliable, estimates for 1732 and 1759 suggest that Protestants had grown from their extremely tiny numbers in the early 1600s to approximately 27 per cent of the total Irish population.[7] Since the great majority of Catholics remained loyal to their faith, the Protestant community was principally derived from the new settlers who had been established by the preceding waves of conquest and colonization. The most successful efforts were in Ulster which attracted a substantial body of Scottish Presbyterians, who quickly became the largest single Protestant denomination in the province. Their Scottish and Calvinistic traditions soon gave northern Protestantism a character all of its own, which was later accentuated by the development of an industrial economy. However, their most distinctive feature was that they soon outnumbered the Catholics, and by 1911 they comprised a solid 66 per cent of the population of the six counties that were to become Northern Ireland.[8]

From the beginning, the southern minority found itself in a very different position. The most obvious difference was that efforts at colonization in the South were never as successful as in the North. Even under Cromwell's settlement, many of his ordinary soldiers sold their allotted lands to larger Protestant landlords who then made use of Catholics as their tenants. This also occurred in Ulster, but the consequences were far more severe in the South. By 1732 Protestants were probably less than 17 per cent of the population, and by the time of the first reliable census in 1861 they were only 12 per cent of the twenty-six counties that became independent in 1922. Outside the border counties of Cavan, Donegal, and Monaghan, they were largely free from the Scottish and Presbyterian influence of the North. Being predominantly members of the Church of Ireland, they tended to identify more closely with the Ascendancy, and their small numbers made it easier for them to take advantage of their religious bond with the country's ruling class. Although not all Irish Anglicans were members of the middle and upper classes, in general they fitted much more closely to the classical picture of a small and privileged colonial minority that depended on external support for the preservation of its dominant position.

Throughout the lengthy period of British rule, the colonial character of the minority was strengthened by a steady trickle of Englishmen in pursuit of privilege and advancement. As in any colony, they were attracted by the careers available in the military, the established church, and the various branches of the civil administration. Others were enterprising businessmen drawn by the close commercial links between the two countries, and some were skilled farm workers or tenant farmers brought over by Protestant landlords in the hope of improving their estates. However, this preponderantly English influence was not the only source of southern Protestantism. In the seventeenth and eighteenth centuries the South was settled with French Huguenot and German Palatine refugees whose descendants were often absorbed into the Church of Ireland. Whereas the typical colony was based on racial differences, Ireland was unique in that the option of conversion was always available to the oppressed Catholic majority. By all accounts, only a tiny percentage of Catholics did convert, but owing to the pressure of the penal laws the practice was by no means unknown, especially among the remaining Catholic gentry who wished to retain what little wealth they still possessed. Later, when the disabilities attached to marriage with a Catholic were removed, it is likely that a small degree of intermarriage occurred. Although none of these accretions seriously weakened the division between Protestant and Catholic, they did mean that the British heritage of the minority soon became a matter of social and cultural allegiance rather than of literal descent.[9]

Like the Old English before them, Protestants during the eighteenth century began to accentuate the Irish dimension of their identity. The growing disaffection of the new "Patriots" was fuelled by Britain's commercial restrictions on the Irish economy, by its control of the Irish parliament, and by its predilection for appointing Englishmen to key positions in the Irish administration. In 1782 the British government acceded to some of their demands, although it retained the not unimportant right to veto all Irish legislation. For a brief period of less than twenty years, Protestants became ardent defenders of the rights of the Irish nation. But the Irish nation to which they now attached themselves was still in their eyes a Protestant entity in which Catholics would play at best a subordinate role. Although the bulk of the penal laws were rescinded, there was no thought of allowing Catholic representation in parliament. In 1793 a limited franchise was extended to Catholics, but this was enacted only at the insistence of the British government, which hoped to counter the spread of more extreme demands made popular by the French and American revolutions. These revolutionary sentiments had also taken hold among some Protestants who had been frustrated by their failure to achieve voting rights for their own middle class within the ascendancy-dominated parliament. In this climate, the more radical Protestants joined Wolfe Tone's party of United Irishmen, which called for a broadly based form of government in which Irishmen of all creeds would be represented. But when Catholics began to rally to Wolfe Tone's call, the division between Protestant and Catholic reasserted itself in the formation of the Orange Lodge. While some Protestants did participate in the eventual rebellion of 1798, the sectarian character of the rising in the South soon extinguished their revolutionary instincts. And within two short years a combination of British bribes and the great shock of the rising drove the still wholly Protestant parliament to agree to legislative union with Britain.[10]

Despite their initial discontent over the Union, the great majority of Protestants soon became its most ardent supporters. The reason was obvious for they were now a part of the United Kingdom with its Protestant majority at Westminster. As such, their security and privileged position appeared to have been strengthened, but from a slightly longer perspective it is evident that the Union was a vital turning point in their history. Previously the presence of an Irish parliament had enabled Irish Protestants to dissociate themselves from England and to regard themselves as in some way Irish, while still actively defending their interests against Catholics. But with the loss of their own parliament, they were forced to ally themselves ever more closely with England as their only means of protection. Increasingly, they came to conceive "of themselves as an English garrison,"[11] although it would be more accurate to describe their heightened sense of ethnicity as British, since it involved feelings of loayalty to the crown and British traditions rather than a sense of English nationality. The driving force behind this development was, of course, the steady rise of the Catholic majority, which now laid exclusive claim to the mantle and rights of Irish nationalism. In the process, the institutionalized privileges of the minority were everywhere eroded.

In the religious sphere, the last 120 years of British rule saw a marked growth in the temporal power and organizational strength of the Catholic church. As a result of the penal laws, the church at the beginning of the nineteenth century was still weak, understaffed, and financially straitened. With approximately 3,000 members of the laity for every cleric in 1840, weekly mass attendance in most parts of the country ranged from 30 to 60 per cent, while in the west it dropped to as low as 20 per cent. Yet within a space of fifty years attendance had risen to rates of 90 per cent or more. This "devotional revolution" was made possible by a huge increase in the number of professional religious and by a massive building campaign which extended the church's influence into every facet of the nation's life. The founding of Maynooth and the later arrival of Archbishop Cullen in 1849 brought about a great improvement in the discipline and education of the clergy. Retreats, missions, and devotional exercises of all sorts were everywhere introduced; the full panoply of religious ritual and episcopal grandeur was established as a counterweight to the pomp of the Ascendancy; and the bishops were welded by Cullen into a united body whom neither the British government nor Irish nationalists could afford to ignore.[12]

Ironically, the great tragedy of the famine played a major role in this renewal. After the initial havoc, there was a period of sustained economic growth which enabled the laity to subsidize the expansion of their church, and the subsequent drop in population helped to improve the ratio of laity to clergy. Moreover, the famine and its aftermath of emigration had its greatest impact on the Gaelic-speaking peasantry, whose numbers fell from 50 per cent of the population in 1845 to 23 per cent in 1851, leaving only 5 per cent unable to speak English.[13] Although other factors were at work in the decline of Gaelic culture, Emmet Larkin has argued that it created an "identity crisis" which made Catholicism all the more attractive as "a substitute ... cultural heritage with which they could identify and be identified."[14]

Of course, it must not be forgotten that the penal laws' use of religion to distinguish colonist and colonized had already firmly linked religious and national identity. As has been frequently noted, the genius and legacy of O'Connell lay in his harnessing of the Catholic church to the nationalist movement which impelled the English in 1829 to allow Catholic representation in Parliament. In later years the alliance was by no means total or automatic for the ultramontanist leanings of the bishops made them distrustful of the more extreme and violent element among the nationalists. However, the bulk of the lesser clergy were more openly sympathetic to all nationalist efforts. By the 1880s the bishops and Parnell's nationalist party had reached an unofficial understanding whereby the church gave its support to home rule in return for recognition of its special place as the moral arbiter and spiritual leader of the nation. Eventually, even the much more radical policies of Sinn Fein received the cautious approval of the church, when the party's electoral victory had been secured and it had shown its willingness to support the established concordat between Catholicism and nationalism. Under these conditions, the emotionally charged labels of Catholic and Irish became virtually equivalent. Had it been otherwise, it is still questionable whether Protestants would have embraced the nationalist movement, but as it was their alienation was all the more complete.

Nowhere was the strengthening of communal boundaries more evident than in the field of education. This was not the intent of the British government when in 1831 it introduced a new system of state-funded primary schools in which both pupils and management were to be drawn from all denominations. However, the endeavour soon foundered in the face of widespread opposition. The Church of Ireland refused to give its support on the ground that its position as the established church entitled it to sole control of the nation's education; while the Presbyterians were so enraged that some were driven to burn their schools in protest. With their far more limited resources, Catholics were actually the major participants during the 1830s, but their attitude hardened when the National Board later attempted to extend its administrative powers. In 1844 the board was forced to alter its rules and regulations so that by 1852 only 175 of the 4,795 schools in operation were under joint religious management. After this experience, the private and equally denominational character of secondary education was left intact, and even at the university level the religious divide was maintained.[15]

The major Protestant institution was Trinity College Dublin which had been an integral part of the Protestant Ascendancy ever since its founding in 1591. Before 1793 only Anglicans were permitted to receive its degrees, and it was not until 1873 that scholarships and senior positions were opened to all denominations. Any hopes that Trinity might now become a national institution were dashed two years later when the Catholic hierarchy condemned it as a danger to the faith and morals of their laity. In fact, Catholic nationalists and the hierarchy had already been successful some thirty years earlier in boycotting the "godless colleges" established by the government in Belfast, Cork, and Galway. In 1854 the bishops created their own Catholic university in Dublin, but they continued to agitate for a university of their own with full state support. Their demand was finally met in 1908 when the National University was formed, comprising the three colleges in Dublin, Cork, and Galway. Although its charter made no mention of any formal links with the Catholic church, the ready acquiescence of the hierachy made it clear that for all practical purposes the state was now committed to supporting a Catholic university. Needless to say, few Protestants were pleased, but at least they could console themselves that the Trinity had retained its independence.[16]

The rising power of the Catholic church had an equally profound effect on the Church of Ireland. At the beginning of the century, it was little more than a corrupt and extremely wealthy arm of the state. Its numerous higher clergy were often justifiably reviled as profligate, absentee place-seekers; its working curates were usually underpaid; and not a few parishes lacked the basic amenities of either a rectory or a church. This state of affairs was slow to change, but over the following decades administrative reforms were introduced and the worst excesses of the clergy were curbed. Under the influence of English evangelicals, efforts were also made to reach out to the Catholic laity. During the famine, in particular, there were some spectacular results, but most converts emigrated and the evangelical crusade soon faded, since few of the resident clergy welcomed the tensions created by such endeavours. Encouraging as these early signs of renewal may have been, Irish Anglicans tended to be far more disturbed by the constant protest of Catholics at the establishment privileges of their church. To the Catholic church it was an outrageous anomaly that the state should support a church that could claim the allegiance of only 12 per cent of the population, and the Catholic laity were equally incensed that they should be forced to pay tithes in support of an alien religion. Although this popular tithe grievance was effectively reduced in 1838 by transferring responsibility for payment from tenant to landlord, there still remained the underlying issue of state support for a minority church. Eventually, in 1869, a combination of pressures from the Catholic hierarchy, nationalists, and English nonconformists induced an already sympathetic Gladstone to secure the passage of a bill at Westminster disestablishing the Church of Ireland.[17]

Gladstone was roundly condemned, but the terms of the act

proved to be far more beneficial to the Church of Ireland than many had expected. The severing of all state financial support was accompanied by an extremely generous severance award which was then augmented by the still affluent and secure landed gentry. By 1885 the church had built up a capital fund of £6,475,005, of which over four million had been acquired from the government. Had disestablishment occurred much later, it is likely that the changing political climate and the declining fortunes of the gentry would have made it much more difficult to achieve such a substantial reendowment. Full autonomy was also restored to the church in all matters of doctrine, organization, and worship. In effect, the Church of Ireland was transformed from a colonial appendage into an independent church that was now much more responsive to the needs and pressures of its laity. Its discipline, its insularity, and its anti-Catholic leanings were intensified; and with the termination of its English connections, the church found it much easier to argue – at least in addressing its own members – that it was now a genuinely Irish institution unsullied by the taint of colonialism. The Church of Ireland continued to encompass all of the thirty-two counties of Ireland. Within this larger unit, the shrinking southern dioceses tended to develop their own advisory bodies and distinctive policies, but to some extent the links across the border helped to reinforce the divisive outlook of the church in the South. In short, the relatively early imposition of disestablishment and the form that it took did much to ensure that the Church of Ireland would emerge after 1922 as the most influential and enduring institution within southern Protestantism.[18]

By 1922 Catholics had also made considerable headway in overcoming their subordinate position within the economy. Their first successes occurred during the penal law era when restrictions on owning land drove them into trade and commerce. After the removal of formal disabilities, their influence in these two fields continued to grow, and they began to penetrate the professions. Protestants in 1861 still retained a marked though diminished superiority in most sectors of the economy, but over the next fifty years their dominance was substantially eroded within the southern twenty-six counties. According to the last British census of 1911, Catholics had come to outnumber Protestants in all occupations except for the military and the higher levels of the banking world. Catholic dominance in urban areas was still less than secure for they amounted to only 57 per cent of secular professionals, and in the tiny industrial sector a small number of Protestant firms continued to dominate the export trade. Economic differences were to play a part in communal divisions for some time after independence, but taken by themselves these illustrations give a rather misleading impression of the overall trend.

As is well known, the most dramatic reversal occurred on the land, which remained under the control of the Protestant Ascendancy as late as the 1870s. Although the official statistics for this period do not tell us a great deal, the census commissioners in 1871 were agreed that "the acreage of land in protestant episcopalian ownership exceeds so largely the surface under all other proprietorship as to constitute the landed proprietory of the country."[19] The economic discontent of the Catholic majority at being a community of tenants in their own country was soon directed into the nationalist movement. Between 1870 and 1909 the British government was pressured into enacting a series of land acts which transferred over 13,000,000 acres from large landlords to their tenants and left Ireland "a country of peasant proprietors."[20] In the short term, the sale of their large estates often proved to be of considerable financial benefit to many landlords, and we shall see shortly that other political developments contributed to the eventual demise of the Ascendancy. Nonetheless, the economic dominance of Protestants in the South had been broken by 1922, since they had lost control of the country's major productive base – namely the land.

In spite of their fading fortunes and their growing suspicions that Britain could no longer be trusted, only a handful of Protestants were prepared to embrace the nationalist movement. When the Liberal home rule bills were introduced in 1886, 1893, and 1912, special meetings of the Church of Ireland's General Synod were immediately called. For the archbishop of Armagh, the only acceptable response to this "criminal enactment" was "to use every legitimate effort to resist it." At the meetings held in 1886 and 1893, unanimous resolutions were passed condemning home rule; in 1912 the consensus was marred by the opposition of only five members to the various loyalist resolutions.[21] The *Gazette* and *Irish Times* were equally adamant in their opposition, while Trinity's attitude may be gathered from the short-lived proposal of its governing body that an amendment should be passed to the home rule bill of 1912 exempting the college from its provisions.[22] The spokesmen for these organizations were drawn from the middle and upper classes, but pro-British sentiment was apparent throughout the entire community. Thus when the Standing Committee of the Church of Ireland sent a protest to all parishes concerning the 1893 home rule bill, all but twenty of the 1,218 polled immediately affirmed their support.[23]

As one elderly clerk whom I interviewed in the 1970s recalled, he and his peers prior to 1922 had been "brought up drawing Union Jacks" and were "mad for royalty." On the surface, it might seem that such individuals had little to lose or to fear. But their intense suspicions of Catholicism, their segregated social life, and their economic bonds with their more affluent coreligionists were enough to convince even the poorest Protestants that their only salvation lay in retaining the Union.

What they feared was that adequate constitutional safeguards could not and would not be devised to protect either their "civil and religious liberties" or the "security of their property and life."[24] To the archbishop of Dublin, home rule agitation was a thinly disguised demand for an "advanced form of socialism,"[25] and Lord Iveagh of the Guinness family was convinced that the nationalists would immediately "increase the income tax out of all knowledge and tax us out of existence."[26] In its extreme form, the parallel religious concern was that independence might lead to the suppression of the Protestant faith, while others expected that they might be forced to hand over some of their ancient church buildings to the Catholic church. Not all Protestants anticipated such dire consequences, but very few doubted that the close alliance of Catholicism and nationalism would effectively exclude them from the nation's public life.[27] Like other colonial minorities, they were convinced that not only their own interests but those of the entire nation would be bound to suffer if the guiding hand of their experienced leadership was removed. Moreover, many were deeply concerned at the growing force of the movement to revive the country's Gaelic heritage which emerged during the last decades of the nineteenth century. As was true of the nationalist movement, a few Protestant played a prominent part in the Gaelic revival, but the great majority regarded it with hatred and suspicion. For the corollary of Gaelic pride was increased animosity to the British traditions cherished by Protestants, who were well aware that the narrow tenets of Irish nationalism called into question their very right to consider themselves as Irishmen.[28] In essence, they feared retribution for the sins of their fathers, and they looked forward with trepidation to a state of exclusion similar to that which they had imposed on the Catholic majority some 200 years earlier.

The capacity of southern Protestants to resist the nationalist movement and to preserve their political power within Ireland grew steadily weaker. This was not immediately apparent, for Catholic Emancipation in 1829 did little to weaken the control of landlords over the small and easily intimidated electorate.[29] But in the second half of the nineteenth century successive extensions of the franchise finally broke the power of the landlords. After the crucial reforms of 1884 the frightened Ascendancy in the South initiated what was to become known as the Irish Unionist Alliance. At the election of 1885 it set up a well-organized propaganda machine and provided considerable financial backing for a full slate of unionist candidates, but none were returned in any of the fifty-two southern constituencies with the exception of the three uncontested seats for Trinity. In 1898 the influence of the Ascendancy was further undermined by the abolition of the local administrative powers of the grand juries which had been largely controlled by landlords. In the new and democratic system of county councils, representation by unionists and by Protestants in the South virtually disappeared. Then in 1911 the last obstacle to the successful passage of a home rule bill was removed when the veto power of the British House of Lords was reduced to a two-year right of delay. Although the Home Rule Act of 1914 was not to be implemented until the end of World War I, southern Protestants were now isolated and defenceless. In theory, their one remaining hope lay in joining forces with the far larger and stronger body of northern Protestants, but in practice armed resistance was an impossible option for the small and scattered southern minority. Moreover, unionist organizations in the North had long been separate from those in the South, and by 1916 northern Protestants were resolved to accept partition if that was the price required for avoiding home rule.[30]

After the Easter Rebellion of 1916, the nationalist movement entered its final stage, when the much more radical demands of Sinn Fein came to supersede those of the Irish Nationalist party and the country erupted into open warfare. Faced with this radically changed situation, southern unionism was split in 1919 by the formation of the Unionist Anti-Partition League, which rejected the more intransigent stance of the older IUA that any form of home rule was unthinkable. In their hearts, the leaders of the UAPL were equally attached to the Union, but they argued that some sort of compromise with nationalist opinion was necessary if peace and the future security of their minority interests were to be achieved. Indeed, as the war intensified, some began to believe that it might be better to live with Sinn Fein "rather than face the continuance of the chaos of the last fifteen years."[31] In these last hectic years, a few of the more moderate unionist leaders were heavily involved in the various efforts to achieve a negotiated settlement, but as a group unionists were weakened by their internal disunity and by their lack of any real power. Thus even at the last negotiations that led to the signing of the treaty in December 1921, the IUA repudiated the three prominent members of the Church of Ireland who were invited to take part. (Lord Middleton was an extensive landowner; Archbishop Bernard had recently been appointed provost of Trinity after serving as archbishop of Dublin; and Andrew Jameson, the distiller, was an acknowledged leader of the Protestant business community.) While they did not achieve the special privileges they sought in a strong upper house for the new legislature, they did gain promises of proportional representation and guarantees of civil and religious liberties. Given the state of the country, these were not insignificant achievements. But the essential objective of unionism was now a lost cause, and after another brief flurry of consultations a year later organized unionist activity in the South ceased.[32]

All this meant that the Church of Ireland community found itself in vastly changed circumstances by the time independence was declared. Wherever they looked, their once secure and legally established position of dominance had been broken over the last 100 years. Although they remained economically privileged and highly segregated, their confidence had been especially shaken by the loss of the ascendancy leaders who had been emasculated by political and economic reforms and then driven from the country during the last years of violence. They could no longer hope to rely on Britain for their protection, and with their colonial past they were less than certain what the future might hold. Thus they faced their newly independent country weakened and intimidated by the events of recent years, bereft of their traditional leadership, and deeply conscious that their "attitude of criticism and detachment has hardly made friends for us among those from whom we differ."[33]

CHAPTER TWO

Demographic Trends

As Catholics steadily reasserted their political, economic, and cultural hold over the country, the already small Church of Ireland community found that its fading social influence was accompanied by an equally disturbing trend of population decline. For much of the nineteenth century, Irish Anglicans may have gained some solace from the knowledge that Catholics were declining at much the same rate. But with the increasing momentum of the nationalist movement, the minority's rate of decline rapidly accelerated. For the first forty years after independence, the number of Irish Anglicans and their proportion of the total population continued to fall. Then, in the 1960s and 1970s, a few hopeful signs emerged suggesting that the century-old experience of decline was finally slowing and might soon be reversed. This exceptional demographic history serves as a useful starting-point for a detailed study of the post-1922 era. Inevitably, the small, scattered, and diminishing character of the Protestant population heavily influenced their relations with the Catholic community. And as emigration and mixed marriages were the root causes of their decline, these trends cast much light on their response to their newly subordinate status within independent Ireland.

THE TRANSITIONAL YEARS

The rate of Church of Ireland decline reached its peak in the census period of 1911 to 1926, which encompassed the final, violent stage of the nationalist struggle, the advent of independence, and the ensuing Civil War. In all, the number of Irish Anglicans fell from 249,535 in 1911 to 164,215 in 1926 – a decline of 34 per cent.[1] Their ranks were heavily depleted in all parts of the country, but the

TABLE 1
Denominational Trends, 1861–1971

	% Total population		% Population change at end of census period	
	C. of I.	R.C.	C. of I.	R.C.
1861	8.5	89.4	—	—
1871	8.4	89.2	−9.1	−8.1
1881	8.2	89.5	−6.2	−4.2
1891	8.3	89.3	−9.7	−10.6
1901	8.2	89.3	−7.9	−7.1
1911	7.9	89.6	−5.6	−2.3
1926	5.5	92.6	−34.2	−2.2
1936	4.9	93.4	−11.7	+0.8
1946	4.2	94.3	−13.9	+0.4
1961	3.7	94.9	−16.7	−4.0
1971	3.3	95.1	−6.1	+4.6

decrease was not evenly distributed. With a 23 per cent decline, Ulster was least affected by the transition; Leinster and Connacht were closer to the national average; and Munster, with a fall of 44 per cent, proved to be the most inhospitable of all the provinces. On the whole, Irish Anglicans in rural areas (−29 per cent) were less inclined to leave than were their urban counterparts (−40 per cent). But since their number declined by 31 per cent in the capital city of Dublin, this rural-urban differential was largely due to the very high decline of approximately 50 per cent in the provincial cities and smaller towns. However, the most striking contrast was with the parallel Catholic decrease of only 2 per cent which was lower at any time since the famine.

The exceptional size of the minority's decline suggests that the causes were different in kind and intensity from those that characterized the post-1926 era. Two distinctive sets of pressures at work at this time deserve special mention. The first involved the establishment of the Irish Free State and its new administrative structures. In some cases the exodus of Irish Anglicans was a direct result of the 1921 treaty. Under its terms, the British armed forces were withdrawn, and the Royal Irish Constabulary and the Dublin Metropolitan Police were disbanded. The minority's involvement in the armed forces was particularly high. According to the British census of 1911, 63 per cent of all ranks in the twenty-six counties and 81 per cent of the officers were Anglicans. In addition, six Irish regiments were disbanded in 1922, although it is impossible to ascertain the number who were Irish Anglicans as these regiments sometimes recruited from Britain.[2] With their longstanding tradition of service within the British Empire, it is likely that a good number were also scattered throughout the rest of the British armed forces. No doubt many continued to follow their careers within the empire after 1922, but after this date their links with Ireland became all the more tenuous. The total loss brought about by the severing of the imperial connection cannot be accurately calculated. It has, however, been estimated that the withdrawal of the armed forces and their dependents serving in Ireland accounted for a quarter of the total Protestant decline.[3]

The proportion of Anglicans in the police and civil service were at the much lower levels of 24 and 13 per cent respectively. Unlike the military, their departure was not mandatory, and an effort was made to maintain a continuity of staff in the new police force and civil service. Nonetheless, the administrative disruptions involved in the transition, uncertainty regarding the reliability of the new government, unwillingness to serve the new regime, and concern over pension privileges caused many to transfer to Britain and Northern Ireland.[4] In all, 65 per cent of the minority in these occupations departed between 1911 and 1926. Again, the loss to the community would be considerably increased if their accompanying dependents were included.

Intimidation and violence also played a part in prompting the exodus of the minority. As the Anglo-Irish War of 1919 to 1921 intensified, and during the Civil War which continued until 1923, members of the Church of Ireland suffered raids, attacks on property, eviction notices, and murder. The local Church of Ireland gentry were subject to a particularly concentrated campaign of terror and persecution with neither the British nor the Free State government could prevent. With their ostentatious loyalism, their ascendancy backgrounds, and their isolated residences in the countryside, they stood out as helpless symbols and as convenient targets for anti-British sentiment. Some probably did assist the British and pro-treaty forces, but for the most part their small numbers deterred them from taking an active part in either conflict. Nevertheless, they were often raided for arms and provisions by the Irish Republican Army, and some of their houses were burned as reprisals for acts of both governments which had no connection with the houses and families attacked. Moreover, age-old economic resentments were at work. Not all tenants had taken advantage of the land acts, and many members of the Ascendancy retained a quite sizeable acreage of untenanted land. With the general spread of lawlessness and the return of many landless men after World War I, economic tensions mounted. Once again, not a few Protestant landlords found that they were subject to cattle driving, vandalism, and illegal expropriation of their land by their remaining tenants and the landless in the hope that "if they wait a little longer they will get their lands free."[5] Faced with this situation, seventy of the eighty landed Protestant families in County Clare emigrated after 1919.[6] Although Clare was an extreme case, *The Morning Post* listed 192 Irish residences and clubs that were burned during the Civil War.[7] At a local level, Lionel Flemming found that of the four "big houses" in Timoleague, one had been burned and two others abandoned by the end of the Civil War.[8] Indeed, even Sir Horace Plunkett, who had founded the Irish Co-operative Movement and had long been a disciple of conciliation, had his house burned to the ground.[9] The eventual result was both the wholesale departure of the Ascendancy and their final destruction as a distinguishable national class within Ireland.

The Church of Ireland gentry may have absorbed the bulk of the violence directed against Protestants, but ordinary members of the community – small shopkeepers and farmers – were also threatened and killed. West Cork appears to have been a particularly troubled area, for various reports indicated that murders of Protestants were a regular and frequent occurrence between 1919 and 1921. One of them, John Good, was suspected of having informed on the IRA, but local Protestants feared that his death was part of a calculated land war aimed at driving them off the land.[10] Later in 1922 seven Protestants were killed in the area around Dunmanway, and the same fears were again rekindled. If this was the intent, it was partly successful, for the *Irish Times* reported that "over 100 persons ... left the district ... for various destinations across the channel."[11] However, activities of this sort were not confined to West Cork. In Mullingar, "the business premises of nearly all the Protestant residents were attacked by the usual armed men."[12] At Ballinasloe, a manager of a local boot store, an agent for Guinness's, a widow, a linesman, and the station-master – all Protestants – were advised to leave.[13] Around Westmeath, "Protestant residents in the country part" were "served with the same orders,"[14] and in Leitrim, a number of Protestants were given notice to quit, and their school and teacher's residence were destroyed by fire.[15]

Minority fears were sufficiently aroused for J.A.F. Gregg, the archbishop of Dublin, to lead a deputation from the General Synod to the provisional government, enquiring "if they were to be permitted to live in Ireland or if it was desired that they should leave the country."[16] Arthur Griffith did his best to reassure the deputation, as he had done earlier at the time of the treaty.[17] At least in public, Gregg appeared willing to support this view, for at the Dublin diocesan synod he stressed that the violence against Protestants did not have "the moral support of the general body of Irish opinion, nor ... the support of the government of Ireland."[18] The *Irish Times* echoed similar opinions when it argued that there were "no signs" of a systematic campaign against Protestants, although it acknowledged that "ex-Unionists" were "the chief victims because their local isolation and their relatively high standard of prosperity made them easy marks for lawlessness and greed."[19] After Griffith died in 1922, O'Higgins, who emerged as one of the strongest men in the new government, again reassured the minority in a speech in the Dail in which he declared that "These people are part and parcel of the nation, and we being the majority and strength of the country ... it comes well from us to show that these people are regarded, not as alien enemies, not as planters, but that we regard them as part and parcel of the nation, and that we wish them to take their share of its responsibilities."[20]

Despite the soothing and evidently sincere character of these public statements, the circumstances of the country insured that the reality of day to day life was often a very different matter. In the heat of the Civil War, the pro-treaty forces could not and did not control a large part of the country. Even in Foxrock, a suburb of Dublin, the home of Sir Henry Robinson was looted, and he and his son were threatened with courtmartial "for 'resisting the soldiers of the Irish Republic in the execution of their duty'." On behalf of the pro-treaty forces, Michael Collins arrived at the Robinsons' house the next day, but all he could do was advise that they should "'clear out, and come back later when things had settled down'."[21] In a similar vein, the leaders of the Clare Volunteers during the earlier Anglo-Irish War did what they could to suppress activities directed specifically against Protestants, but they were not always successful in restraining the deeply rooted hatred of their men. On at least three occasions, the officers could do no more than make amends after the fact by bringing in their men to extinguish fires that had been set in local Protestant churches.[22] It would be wrong to infer from these examples that the life and the property of the minority were under constant threat. Just as the state of the conflict fluctuated from month to month and from county to county, so did the degree of intimidation of the minority vary enormously. The general outlook of the emerging national leadership also augured well for the future treatment of the minority in independent Ireland. However, there can be little doubt that events of the sort just described go a long way to explain the unprecedented flight of the minority during these transitional years.

POPULATION TRENDS

In the years that followed the Civil War, peace was restored and a stable system of government was established. In this more settled atmosphere (as tables 1 and 2 show), the rate of Church of Ireland decline fell to roughly half that of the previous period. Nevertheless, the population trends of the two communities did not grow appreciably closer. For the next thirty-five years, the number of Irish Anglicans continued to diminish by approximately 1 per cent a year, while Catholics managed to hold their own for a time, and then they too underwent a small decline. This far from happy state of affairs persisted until 1961, but thereafter there were signs of a marked change. Between 1961 and 1971, Catholics recorded their first substantial increase since the famine, and the Anglican decline finally appeared to be levelling off. For the first time since independence, seven counties and the entire province of Munster saw their previously dwindling Church of Ireland communities actually begin to grow. In the 1970s this revival accelerated, with the preliminary results of the 1979 census indicating that the total Irish population had increased by an unprecedented 386,633 or 13 per cent.[23] Although information on the Church of Ireland population in 1979 is still not available at the time of writing, it seems likely that Irish Anglicans were infused with a new measure of stability by this general reversal of old trends.

The character and extent of this revival is open to question. It is possible that the slowed rate of Church of Ireland decline was due to an influx of English immigrants who were enumerated in the census as members of the Church of Ireland. According to longstanding census practice, any individual who claimed to be Church of England or Anglican was listed as Church of Ireland. This procedure makes it impossible to estimate the number of Irish-born Anglicans, since the foreign-born were not classified by religion in any census. This does not create a serious problem before 1945, when the small English population of about 35,000 was declining, but the number of English and Welsh suddenly rose from 45,463 in 1961 to 75,189 in

TABLE 2
Church of Ireland Trends by County, 1926–1971

County	Population 1926	Population 1971	% Change 1926–71	% Population 1926	% Population 1971
Total	164,215	97,741	−40.5	5.5	3.3
Leinster	92,899	60,117	−35.3	8.1	4.0
Carlow	2,719	1,858	−31.7	7.9	5.4
Dublin City	27,186	21,991	−19.1	7.4	2.9
Dublin	26,623	12,917	−51.4	16.1	6.4
Kildare	3,193	2,415	−24.4	5.5	3.4
Kilkenny	2,342	1,324	−43.5	3.3	2.2
Laoighis	4,193	2,701	−35.6	8.1	6.0
Longford	1,973	880	−55.4	5.0	3.1
Louth	2,295	1,164	−49.3	8.7	1.6
Meath	2,884	1,800	−37.6	4.6	2.5
Offaly	3,409	1,979	−41.9	6.5	3.8
Westmeath	2,301	1,193	−48.2	4.0	2.2
Wexford	5,119	3,432	−33.0	5.4	4.0
Wicklow	8,662	6,463	−25.8	15.0	9.7
Munster	28,614	17,807	−37.8	3.0	2.0
Clare	883	772	−7.3	0.9	1.0
Cork Co.	16,893	10,457	−38.1	4.6	3.0
Kerry	2,051	1,407	−31.0	1.4	1.2
Limerick City	1,285	665	−48.2	3.2	1.2
Limerick	1,691	935	−44.7	1.7	1.2
Tipperary N.R.	2,188	1,498	−31.5	3.6	2.8
Tipperary S.R.	1,559	778	−50.1	1.9	1.2
Waterford	2,114	1,295	−38.7	2.7	1.7
Connacht	12,417	6,084	−51.0	2.2	1.6
Galway	1,673	1,253	−25.1	1.0	0.8
Leitrim	3,286	1,093	−66.7	5.9	3.9
Mayo	2,066	953	−53.9	1.2	0.9
Roscommon	1,147	461	−60.1	1.4	0.9
Sligo	4,245	2,324	−45.3	6.0	4.6
Ulster	30,285	13,733	−54.7	10.1	6.6
Cavan	10,102	4,513	−55.3	12.2	8.6
Donegal	13,774	6,818	−50.1	9.0	6.3
Monaghan	6,409	2,402	−62.3	9.8	5.2

1971. It would, however, be unwise to assume that most of the English and Welsh in 1971 were Anglicans. Despite the predominance of Anglicanism in England, a substantial proportion may have been Catholics of Irish ancestry who had returned to Ireland as a result of the greater prosperity of the 1960s. Indeed, no other explanation is possible. If the very modest assumption is made that 25 per cent of the English and Welsh in 1971 were recorded as Church of Ireland, it would still imply that Irish-born Anglicans declined by 15 per cent – i.e., at a higher annual rate than at any time since 1926. Such an assumption would also imply that a quarter of Anglicans in Dublin were really English or Welsh. Even if this unlikely assumption was true, clergy and Irish-born Anglicans were agreed that Englishmen accounted for far less than a quarter of the membership of their churches and other organizations. Given the lack of hard information on the topic, further speculation is pointless. All that can be safely concluded is that the rate of decline among Irish Anglicans in the 1960s was probably greater than the census indicates.

As early as 1926, Irish Anglicans clearly deserved to be described as a minority since they amounted to only 7 per cent of the total population. While two-thirds of the much smaller Presbyterian community resided in the three border counties, this was true of only 18 per cent of Irish Anglicans. Another third lived in the Dublin area, and the remaining 54 per cent were widely scattered throughout the country. In Dublin itself, only a small proportion were Church of Ireland, although they rose to almost 30 per cent in some suburbs, and Greystones, a nearby resort and retirement centre, still retained a slim Protestant majority. As might be expected, the combination of Presbyterians and Irish Anglicans in Ulster created exceptional concentrations of as high as 40 to 60 per cent within a few very small rural communities, but for the province as a whole Catholics were still the predominant force with 82 per cent of the total population. Further south, in parts of the midlands, Wexford, and West Cork, it was still possible to find the occasional pocket of Protestants who accounted for as much as 25 per cent of their small local communities. Yet even in these areas of notable Protestant concentration, Protestants never exceeded 15 per cent of the population at the rural district level. Moreover, these are the extreme examples. In the remainder of both the midlands and the west, the minority was much more widely dispersed (see table 2). In general, it would be fair to say that the small and scattered Church of Ireland community rarely possessed the unconscious insularity of residential and geographic segregation which was so characteristic

TABLE 3
Rural-Urban Trends by Denomination, 1926–1971

	1926	1936	1946	1961	1971
% Urban[a]					
C. of I.	42.5	44.2	44.4	49.3	51.2
R.C.	30.1	34.9	37.3	45.9	53.8
% Change Urban[b]					
C. of I.	−40.1	−8.1	−13.4	−7.5	−2.5
R.C.	+8.5	+14.0	+7.0	+18.3	+22.7
% Change Rural[b]					
C. of I.	−29.6	−13.4	−13.6	−24.0	−9.5
R.C.	−6.2	−4.5	−2.8	−17.8	−10.8

[a]Towns of 1,500 population and over.
[b]Since last census period.

of the North. This, in turn, implies that Irish Anglicans have long been forced to rely upon essentially social means of maintaining their separateness.

The strong sense of isolation and insecurity created by their small numbers intensified in the years after 1926 as they saw their community diminish by a further 41 per cent. Tables 2 and 3 reveal that they experienced substantial declines in all parts of the country and in both rural and urban areas, although their heaviest losses tended to occur in the rural and remote counties of the west. Even in Ulster, the former Protestant strongholds were never less than 70 per cent Catholic by 1971. Similarly, the other old pockets of Irish Anglicans in the Dublin suburbs, West Cork, and the midlands were now diluted to approximately 10 per cent of their local communities, and in the rest of the country Irish Anglicans were often below their national average of 3.3 per cent. As these trends developed, they were also undergoing a progressive aging as a community. In fact, by the early 1960s, the 18 per cent of their membership over the age of sixty-five was a greater proportion than in all but one other country in the world. In short, the combination of extensive population decline, marked aging, particularly heavy losses in the periphery, and widespread reductions in population density – all suggest a dying community.

More substantial support for such an interpretation is to be found in table 4 which summarizes the major determinants of the falling Church of Ireland population. As the figures are estimates rather than precise calculations, they must be viewed as no more than

TABLE 4

Annual Average Birth, Death, and Migration Rates by Denomination, 1926–1971[a]

	Church of Ireland				Roman Catholic			
	1926–36	1936–46	1946–61	1961–71	1926–36	1936–46	1946–61	1961–71
Birth rate	12.6	13.2	14.4	13.5	20.1	20.9	22.4	22.0
Death rate	17.0	18.7	17.7	17.3	13.9	14.3	12.4	11.4
Rate of natural increase	−4.4	−5.5	−3.3	−3.8	+6.2	+6.6	+10.0	+10.6
Actual rate of population change	−12.4	−15.0	−12.1	−6.2	+0.8	+0.4	−2.7	+4.5
Net migration rate	−8.0	−9.5	−8.8	−2.4	−5.4	−6.2	−12.7	−6.1

[a]per 1,000 average population of each intercensal period.

rough approximations.[24] Bearing this in mind and leaving aside the topic of emigration for the moment, the most striking feature of table 4 is its suggestion that the Church of Ireland population was undergoing a process of natural decrease after 1926. In other words, even without the influence of continuing emigration, the Church of Ireland population would still have fallen during each census period because their number of deaths exceeded their number of births. Had there been no loss whatsoever from migration during the 1960s, three-quarters of the Church of Ireland decline actually recorded by the census would still have occurred because of this ingrained propensity to diminish naturally. In contrast, Catholics underwent a natural increase of 11 per cent during the same period, despite the fact that their rate of emigration was higher.

Clearly any community is in serious difficulty when it cannot compensate for the inevitable losses of mortality. The immediate cause of this extremely rare state of affairs was the minority's abnormally low birth rate which was lower than that in all but one other European country until the 1960s. Although comparisons of nations and small communities can be misleading, it is tempting to conclude that Irish Anglicans were suffering from something akin to a death wish in the face of the conditions they confronted within independent Ireland. Tempting as this notion may be, it is difficult to sustain, once the birth rate (normally called the crude birth rate) has been broken down into its constituent parts. A more precise and widely accepted measure of individual willingness to bear children is the fertility rate, the number of legitimate live births per 1,000 married women aged 15–44. By international standards, the Church of Ireland fertility rate in 1946 (175) was not exceptionally low, although it was only 60 per cent of the very high Catholic rate which was greater than that of all other European countries at this time. Denominational estimates cannot be obtained for the prewar years, but in 1946 the Church of Ireland rate was marginally higher than the rates for France, Sweden, and Switzerland, and it was considerably higher than the American or British.[25] It was also much the same as the fertility rates for Protestants in Northern Ireland.[26] In other words, in comparison with both Northern Ireland and the rest of Europe, there is no evidence to suggest that the Church of Ireland community's status as a political and cultural minority had an adverse effect on its adherents' fertility. By 1971 their fertility had fallen to a rate of 147 and for Catholics it had dropped to 238, but as this decline was occurring throughout the western world the Church of Ireland rate remained unexceptional. All that can be safely said is that their privileged economic standing helped to depress their overall level of fertility, since relatively few Irish Anglicans were in the more productive lower classes. Even so, the rate can be considered low only in comparison with the remarkably high fertility of Catholics.

At first glance, it would appear that the marriage practices of the Irish Anglicans were the major cause of their abnormally low birth rate. While religious differences in this respect are not available before 1946, Ireland as a whole in the 1930s was a rather extreme case of the general European tendency to marry late and infrequently.[27] Thereafter, these practices began to diminish elsewhere, but the Irish were much slower to follow suit – and hence grew all the more distinctive. In 1946, for instance, the average age of marriage for Church of Ireland women was 30, although it had declined to 25 by 1972. Church of Ireland nuptiality (i.e., the percentage of married women in the crucial child-bearing age group of 25–34) also rose considerably from 55 per cent in 1946 to 78 per cent in 1971, but in the later 1960s Church of Ireland women were still slightly less likely to be married than were most other European women.[28] Looking somewhat closer to home, the proportion of married women among Northern Protestants was somewhat higher in both 1946 and 1961.[29] These various comparisons suggest that the low nuptiality of Irish Anglicans in the South was in part due to their small and scattered numbers, the consequent lack of suitable marriage partners, and their unwillingness to marry Catholics. However, we must not push such notions too far because every census since 1946 has shown Catholics to have been even more reluctant to marry than have Irish Anglicans. At least in this regard, a common Irish identity appears to have transcended religious differences. What enabled Catholics to sustain their high rate of population increase was their extremely high fertility, whereas the minority lacked this balancing mechanism. Thus it is only by international standards that the marriage customs of Irish Anglicans can be viewed as contributing to their distinctive pattern of natural decrease.

Taken together, these various considerations suggest that the natural decrease of the minority was largely due to emigration. We shall see shortly that emigration was highest among those aged fifteen to forty-four. Since it is this sector of the community which is mainly responsible for child bearing, the especially rapid depletion of their ranks ensured that those who remained after 1926 were incapable of producing an adequate rate of births. The low birth rate and the emigration of young adults also account for the growing proportion of Irish Anglicans in the older age categories – and thus for their collectively high death rate. Although the Church of Ireland fertility rate does not lend support to the idea of a communal death wish, their low nuptiality and high average age of marriage clearly accentuated the basic trend brought about by emigration. With the acceleration of urbanization and industrialization after 1946, mortality rates declined throughout the country and Irishmen of all creeds became much less prone to celibacy and late marriage. These developments should have strengthened the Church of Ireland population, but persisting emigration, diminishing fertility, and continuous aging guaranteed that their death rate remained substantially higher than their birth rate. Even with the radical decline in emigration during the 1960s, the natural decrease of the minority showed little sign of improvement.

In spite of all this, it would be dangerous to draw too sombre a conclusion. Since emigration was the fundamental cause of this downward spiral, the persistence of low emigration throughout the 1970s suggests that we may see signs of a delayed revival when the 1979 census figures are released. Such a prospect seems all the more likely in the light of the recent increase of English immigrants, the marked growth in nuptiality, and the ever lower age of marriage. Of course, the one neglected element in this projection is the influence of mixed marriages.

EMIGRATION

A few brief comments are in order on the possibility of spiritual migration or conversion to other faiths. Within the Protestant fold, switching from one church to another was not uncommon when a marriage or the lack of a suitable church in the area made it convenient. Although denominational allegiances were usually quite strong, systematic efforts at poaching were rare, and the exchanges that did occur rarely caused social comment or friction. What did cause far greater concern was the fear that fellow Protestants might be duped or coerced into the Catholic faith. But by all accounts, conversion to Catholicism was an infrequent occurrence. As "converted baronets," Sir Shane Leslie and Sir Henry Pellingham found themselves regarded as "white elephants." Leslie quickly discovered that converts "are not wanted by their Catholic neighbours unless they change their politics as well."[30] Complete absorption into the Catholic world may well have been especially difficult for those with ascendancy backgrounds, although it should be added that few had any interest in taking this step. In fact, throughout the Church of Ireland community, material advantages, British loyalties, and an intense commitment to Protestantism combined to create a deeply rooted opposition between the two communities. Both sets of clergy tended to portray the other side as wilful and arrogant heretics who should be avoided in most circumstances. The laity, for their part, saw conversion as a betrayal of family and community, and not a few were convinced that such wrong-headed behaviour could only be interpreted as a sign of impending insanity.

In the antagonistic atmosphere that prevailed before the 1960s, conversions were largely confined to the few mixed marriages that occurred. Even then, conversion was far from universal, although it was facilitated by the tendency of Irish Anglicans to reject any of their faith who succumbed to the very considerable pressure they encountered to raise their children as Catholics. The one other context where a few conversions may have occurred was in the small number of "conversion scandals" recorded in the pages of the *Gazette*. According to its letter page, a few unsuspecting, semi-delirious, and elderly Protestants were pressured into death-bed conversions when sudden illness forced them to enter hospitals run by religious orders.[31] However, such incidents have no demographic significance, and they probably aroused more communal resistance than anything else. With the recent growth of mixed marriages, the whole question of the religious upbringing of the children of such marriages has become a much more pressing issue. But outside of this context there was still little evidence in the 1970s of much conversion among adults of either faith.

Turning to the major theme of emigration, we find from tables 4 and 5 that it was the chief cause of the decline in the minority's

TABLE 5
Church of Ireland Net Migration by Age
Group, 1926–1971[a]

Age	1926–36	1936–46	1946–61	1961–71
0–14	−1.7	−0.4	−5.1	+4.6
15–24	−10.8	−20.2	−15.3	−12.4
25–34	−18.9	−26.5	−23.2	−13.6
35–44	−9.6	−11.6	−9.8	+4.0
45–54	−5.0	−8.8	−4.6	+1.0
55–64	−5.5	−4.5	−0.1	−1.3
65+	+0.3	+5.1		−0.9

[a]Annual rate per 1,000 expected population without migration
at end of census period.

population before the 1960s. Again, it must be remembered that the
figures are estimates, and to be precise they refer to the net loss
through both emigration and immigration. In this earlier period,
the corrosive effect of emigration cannot be underestimated.
Although less than 10 per cent emigrated in each decade, emigration
was significantly higher among young adults. There is no way of
telling whether it was the weak or the strong who were most
inclined to leave, but as the community aged it was inevitable that
its vitality should decline and its leadership become more cautious,
more backward-looking, and more conservative. Even for those
with energy and innovative ideas, the steady drain of emigration
usually forced them to think in terms of retrenchment and of
regrouping in ever smaller circles, rather than of growing and
striking out in new directions. Some of these difficulties also plagued
the Catholic community, but table 4 indicates that their emigration
experience was markedly different from that of Irish Anglicans.
Before World War II, it is not surprising to find that they emigrated
more frequently than did Catholics, although this situation was
reversed in the postwar years. The divergent trends of the two
communities can also be seen in their differing rates of decline
within rural and urban areas. Table 3 does not measure emigration,
but it suggests that Catholic migration was typical of an international movement to the cities and industrial areas. Although
Irish migrants were often compelled by depressed economic conditions to turn to the cities of Britain, the number of urban Catholics
in Ireland did grow as their rural population declined. For Irish
Anglicans, however, the notion of their rural-urban transition was

less applicable. Before 1946 there was hardly any difference in their rural and urban rates of decline, and afterwards their numbers continued to fall in urban areas. Despite some recent signs of convergence in the emigration trends of the two communities, these earlier differences indicate that Irish Anglicans were initially subject to a quite distinctive set of emigration pressures.

Referring primarily to these early years, R.E. Kennedy has argued that Protestant emigration was but one example of "the migration in recent decades of hundreds of thousands of persons of European stock to their home countries following the breakdown of European colonialism."[32] The analogy is very apt, although it must be borne in mind that Protestants had been resident in Ireland for many generations. They were deeply indignant at any suggestion that they were not really Irish, but at the same time it was an Irish identity with a twist. To use the terminology of the *Irish Times*, they tended to see themselves as "Imperial Irishmen."[33] Abroad, they felt unmistakably and unabashedly Irish, but at home they saw themselves as the representatives of British civilization, manning an outpost of the empire in an alien, inferior, and at times hostile sea of native culture. "This gave a certain solidarity to our community," claimed the *Gazette*. "Their outlook not only in the next world but on the affairs of this world was different from the majority around them. Now the ground has been completely cut from under their feet."[34]

Despite the shock of independence, the whole fabric of their world continued to be orientated to Britain and the empire for many years. Their confidence broken, many Protestants retreated and insulated themselves in an imaginary world of empire. Behind their lace curtains, they still referred to Dun Laoghaire as Kingstown, and when the British team won the Aga Khan Cup at the Royal Dublin show a few courageous souls would cheer lustily.[35] The Free State had to be accepted since there was no alternative. Yet in their defeat many contemptuously regarded it as no more than "a system to which one must now pay one's income tax, but they would never until the end of their lives speak of its government as 'our' government."[36] As the *Gazette* explained, "it is all very well to say that this loyalty can be transferred. Loyalty is an affair of the heart and it is not possible to force the heart to follow the hand."[37] Although both the *Gazette* and the *Irish Times* manfully attempted to redirect their readers' loyalties, they could not help but faithfully record the activities and health of the British monarchy until Ireland left the Commonwealth in 1949. Their pride and justification lay in their part "in the building and fashioning of the Empire."[38]

Like Archbishop Gregg, there were many who felt that they "had been banished from the Garden of Eden."[39] But for a time the British Empire survived, and the option was available to continue in this imperial role, though of necessity it meant emigration from Ireland.

Accompanying this cultural "pull" of British allegiance was the "push" of Gaelic, Republican, and Catholic exclusivism. The various ways in which the newly dominant culture of the majority created a sense of unease and marginality among Irish Anglicans must be left for later chapters. For the moment, what I wish to stress is that their departure after the Civil War did not stem from a concerted campaign of overt discrimination and physical intimidation. In this sense, their leaving was largely voluntary, although scattered events undoubtedly encouraged many more to emigrate than were directly affected. As ex-unionists and as symbols of what was seen as continuing British imperialism, a very small number of the minority did suffer. One example that reached the courts during the late 1920s involved the intimidation of Mrs Trench, the wife of a former justice of the peace in County Limerick. Patrick Keane, the local man involved, informed Mr Trench that Mrs Trench must either leave or risk being shot. Keane gave no reason for his demand, although he "opened his coat and showed a badge"[40] in order to demonstrate his authority. Apparently Mrs Trench took his threat seriously, for she left the area. A month later, she returned and the state prosecuted and convicted Keane, although he was given a suspended sentence because Mrs Trench requested that the matter not be pursued any further. Disturbing as this incident must have been both for the Trenchs and for all local Protestants, what makes it particularly noteworthy is the typical unwillingness of Mrs Trench to draw attention to herself and her community.

There seemed to be good reason for adopting this policy of "Lie low, say nothing, wait and see."[41] In fact, one of the minority died when he became involved in the intermittent conflict that flared during the 1920s between the factions created by the Civil War. Albert Henry Armstrong, an official of the Royal Assurance Company, had given evidence at the trial of four men who had been charged with the theft of a Union Jack which had been flying in front of the company building. The four men were convicted and then immediately released. But Armstrong's interference was not forgotten, for six months later he was shot dead outside his home, and the killers were never apprehended.[42] A few other instances of violence seemingly directed against Protestants could be cited, but by all accounts they were extremely infrequent. Contemporary Protestant commentators often railed at the people and government of Ireland for their economic policies, their anti-British outlook, their subservience to Catholic moral teaching, their insularity, and their general insensitivity to the cultural aspirations of the minority. Nevertheless, the same commentators were all agreed that the life and property of the minority were rarely threatened.[43]

It would be equally difficult to argue that Irish Anglicans were subject to widespread discrimination on the part of Catholics. In the private sector of the work world, where the great majority of Irish Anglicans were employed, the presence of so many Protestant employers afforded the minority advantages that were the envy of most Catholics. Given the opportunity, some Catholics might well have discriminated against Protestants, but under the circumstances few Protestants had any reason to turn to Catholic employers. However, one of the few contexts in which Protestants occasionally encountered open discrimination was in the treatment they received from local governments in rural and remote areas. The most celebrated example was the Dunbar-Harrison case. In 1930 Miss Letitia Dunbar-Harrison, a Protestant graduate of Trinity, was appointed county librarian for Mayo by a newly established central committee set up to reform local government. The Mayo Library Committee rejected her nomination on the grounds that she lacked the appropriate qualifications in Gaelic, although it soon became apparent that they were primarily motivated by the belief that a Protestant would be an unacceptable supervisor of reading material for a largely Catholic clientele. When the Mayo County Council decided to support its library committee, the Cumann na nGaedheal government stepped in and dissolved the council for its behaviour. The resulting uproar was then fuelled when a number of prominent Fianna Fail politicians, including Eamon de Valera, publicly expressed their support for the notion that Catholics should be favoured over Protestants in government positions which dealt with Catholic moral sensibilities. The government refused to change its decision, but in the face of a local boycott of Mayo's library services, it defused the situation by transferring Miss Dunbar-Harrison to Dublin. Since this kind of reasoning could be extended to virtually all areas of government activity, it would be difficult to find a more striking example of religiously sanctioned discrimination. However, it appears to have been a relatively rare occurrence. As we shall see, both political parties were conspicuously equitable in their treatment of the minority. For J.H. Whyte, the significance of the incident lay "not in what was done but in what was said."[44] And just four years later the *Gazette* publicly acknowledged that "In public appointments, it is generally recognised that there are no religious tests."[45]

It is possible that violent and discriminatory incidents occurred more frequently than has been suggested. The economically privileged position of Irish Anglicans meant that they were averse to drawing attention to themselves by making vociferous complaints about the treatment they were receiving. Catholics were equally loath to accentuate events that might strengthen the resistance of Northern Protestants to the much cherished goal of a united Ireland. This unwillingness of both parties to publicize untoward occurrences in their relations makes it impossible to assess the situation with complete certainty. On the other hand, there is a danger in exaggerating the frequency and significance of events like those just mentioned. The consistent claims of Protestants that overt violence and discrimination were rare cannot be ignored. Nor should it be forgotten that the government was generally quick to curb and redress excesses directed against Protestants. The most compelling support for the latter interpretation is to be found in the emigration estimates of table 5. In the prewar years when tensions of this sort were most acute, the emigration of a few young children and a slightly greater number of people in middle age suggests that some families felt compelled to bear the considerable costs and disruptions of a move in mid-life. But their numbers do not merit any suggestion of a community in flight from extensive persecution. In the main, emigration occurred among young adults who were probably influenced by the attitudes of their parents, but who could not have experienced much personal contact with Catholics. Without discounting the importance of the odd oppressive incident and without ignoring the pressures of Catholic and Gaelic exclusivism, it would seem best to leave the last word to one of the many who stayed: "The tumult passed and left us, who were once Lords of Creation, a shrunken timorous handful – professional men and traders for the most part. The role of underdog irked us. Again and again on the flimsiest of pretexts, numbers of my fellow Protestants pelted away to their spiritual home beyond the waters."[46]

As always, economic considerations also lay behind Church of Ireland emigration. Discontent with the social and cultural ethos of independent Ireland may have made Irish Anglicans particularly prone to emigrate, but their final decision was often based on rather more pragmatic considerations which affected all Irishmen. These economic pressures were of two types. In the once dominant agricultural sector, growing numbers of small farmers and labourers were displaced by the slow introduction of mechanization and by the consolidation of small holdings in order to increase farm incomes. These developments were the main causes of the large-scale rural exodus of Catholics that became especially marked after

1945.[47] According to the census, a similar though even more extreme trend occurred among Irish Anglicans, with their rates of decline on small farms exceeding by a large margin their losses on large farms. However, these economic pressures do not fully explain the minority's behaviour. Since Irish Anglicans were much less likely than Catholics to be small farmers and labourers, the existence of economic pressures alone would lead one to expect greater rates of decline within the Catholic farming community. The census bears out this expectation for the period after 1945, but quite the opposite was true prior to this date. In addition, if Irish Anglicans were simply more highly motivated than Catholics to consolidate their farms and increase their farm incomes, one would expect their numbers to grow on larger farms. Again, this did not occur to any appreciable extent. In fact, the number of Irish Anglicans on most medium and large farms usually fell, whereas Catholic numbers predictably rose. On both these counts, then, emigration within the Church of Ireland farming community was due to more than economic factors.

The other major economic stimulus was the stagnant character of the Irish economy before the 1960s and the consequent appeal of more numerous, more rewarding, and more promising careers abroad. Although real incomes in Ireland were slowly improving between the two world wars, British incomes were rising at an even faster rate. This disparity persisted until at least the beginning of the 1960s.[48] According to the working-class members of the minority, it was primarily the greater monetary rewards and career opportunities in England which lay behind the heavy rates of emigration. In the working-class parish of Drumcondra and North Strand, for instance, the parish roll fell from 3,000 in 1946 to 1,396 in 1959, and the census revealed equally high rates of decline in most working-class occupations. However, emigration was not confined exclusively to the less advantaged. For many years Ireland produced many more qualified professionals than it could absorb.[49] As Irish Anglicans were heavily involved in these occupations, they were especially prone to this brain-drain form of emigration. Indeed, throughout the more privileged sectors of the Church of Ireland community, there was "an understandable inclination to look abroad to the careers available in the United Kingdom and in the British colonies."[50]

But once again, the significance of depressed economic conditions in explaining minority emigration must not be overstated. A low rate of economic growth creates scarcity and competition for jobs only when the labour force is expanding. This certainly applied to the Catholic community, but Irish Anglicans were experiencing a process of natural decrease. This means that they encountered problems in obtaining employment only when they were in open competition with Catholics. This did occur in some situations, but in most cases Irish Anglicans were segregated within their own firms where they were protected from much Catholic competition.[51] In short, while the economic appeal of better-paid careers abroad cannot be discounted, the pressure to emigrate because of scarcity of jobs and the wish to escape from declining occupations weighed much less heavily on the minority than on Catholics. It follows that higher Church of Ireland emigration before 1946 was at least in part due to the cultural and social tensions to which I have already alluded.

The continuing sorry state of the Irish economy after 1945 gave many Irishmen ample reason to emigrate. With the growth of peace and prosperity in the western world, there were also more opportunities to seek a better livelihood abroad than at any time since the beginning of the depression. In this new climate, Catholics responded by emigrating at almost twice the rate of the prewar years, but there was no major change in the level of Church of Ireland emigration. The very fact that they did not emigrate more frequently than previously would seem to indicate that the cultural tensions which had once contributed to their emigration were on the decline. In other words, economic forces affecting all Irishmen were becoming the major cause of Church of Ireland emigration. And as expected, the confinement of emigration pressures largely to matters of economics created a situation in which the emigration of Irish Anglicans was now substantially lower than the rate for Catholics.

In the 1960s emigration throughout the country declined as a result of new government policies which stimulated the rate of economic growth and created a marked rise in the standard of living. According to tables 4 and 5, Church of Ireland losses through migration remained lower than the rate for Catholics, although their rates of emigration were probably somewhat closer than indicated, taking into account the growing number of Anglican immigrants whose entry during the 1960s can be discerned in the 0–14 and 35–44 age categories. There is every reason to believe that this Anglican and probably English immigration persisted during the 1970s, since economic expansion continued and Ireland actually became a net receiver of immigrants for the first time since the famine.[52] However, we will never know how many of the new immigrants listed themselves as Church of Ireland. Those who did so were probably drawn to the more secular and liberal ethos of the Protestant school system, and some became active churchmen. On the other hand, the typically secular outlook and nominal church allegiance of most English Anglicans did not incline them to active parish involvement, and they were much less likely to be imbued with the insular attitudes which had once been so characteristic of Irish Anglicans. For both these reasons, it cannot be assumed that they will revive the Church of Ireland community in its traditional form. Despite this uncertainty, it is highly probable that the general improvement in economic conditions during the 1970s led, at a minimum, to the virtual cessation of emigration among Irish Anglicans. And this alone was a very significant development.

MIXED MARRIAGES

As emigration declined, Irish Anglicans might have been expected to develop renewed confidence in the future of their community. Instead, many of their previous anxieties came to be focused on the issue of mixed marriages. As late as the mid-1940s, these were still a relatively rare phenomenon. Since then a growing rate of mixed marriages has probably become the major cause of the community's low and inadequate birth rate. The depressing effect of mixed marriages, of course, stems from the tendency for the children of such marriages to be raised as Catholics. In a strictly statistical sense, it is impossible to tell how much of the natural decrease was due to mixed marriages. However, there was a widespread and deeply felt conviction among older Irish Anglicans that the rate of mixed marriages threatened their very existence as a distinguishable community. This gloomy prognosis may yet prove to be false, but as long as mixed marriages continue any sign of numerical revival would still mean the resurgence of a vastly different community.

To the vast majority of Irish Anglicans, only marriages to Catholics were regarded as really mixed. In order to reflect this public perception as closely as possible, my estimates for 1946 and 1961 included Presbyterians as well as Irish Anglicans, while the other smaller Protestant denominations had to be excluded because vital information on their marriages was missing. For both these earlier years, the estimates followed a procedure developed by B.M. Walsh.[53] Bearing in mind that there is room for error in this very indirect method of estimation, we find that according to table 6 the mixed marriage rate among both Presbyterians and Irish Anglicans rose from a virtually nonexistent level in 1946 to roughly 16 per cent

TABLE 6
Protestant Mixed Marriage Rates
(percentages), 1946–1973

	Male	Female	Combined
1946[a]	0	3	1.6
1961[a]	19.8	12.5	15.8
1971–73[b]	39.1	31.2	34.4

[a]Church of Ireland and Presbyterian.
[b]Church of Ireland.

in 1961. To some extent this combined figure for 1961 is misleading. According to Walsh's technique, mixed marriages by Presbyterians were still so infrequent as to be unmeasurable as late as 1961, whereas the rate for the Anglican minority was 22 per cent. The low Presbyterian rate was probably due to their largely rural and conservative background, their concentration in the border counties, and their strong links with northern Protestants who shared an equal aversion to mixed marriages. These differences indicate more clearly than anything else that Irish Anglicans responded in their own distinctive way to their circumstances in the South. However, the 22 per cent figure for Irish Anglicans gives an exaggerated impression of their true mixed marriage rate, since it treats their marriages to all other Protestants as mixed marriages. Allowing for this overly stringent definition, it would appear that somewhere between 16 and 22 per cent of Irish Anglicans were marrying Catholics in the early 1960s.

For various technical reasons, Walsh's methodology cannot be usefully applied to the 1971 census. Instead, I gathered information for the years 1971 to 1973 on the denominational backgrounds of the spouses of Church of Ireland brides and grooms within the six parishes where interviews were conducted. Out of this sample of 164 Irish Anglicans, 39 per cent of the grooms and 34 per cent of the brides married Catholics. Because most of these individuals came from urban parishes where mixed marriages were more common, the combined national figure is somewhat overstated. On the other hand, the greater conservatism of rural areas and the tendency of rural young people to seek employment in the cities make it likely that the parish figures underestimate the real mixed marriage rate for those from rural areas. Taking account of this urban bias, we find that mixed marriages had risen to approximately 30 per cent by the early 1970s.

Since the 37 per cent rate in the three urban parishes was based on a sample of 142, we can place some confidence in it. But this is much less true of the 25 per cent rate for the twenty-four who married in the three small rural parishes. Fifteen were members of a parish in Ulster and three had married Catholics. For the rest of the countryside, the remaining sample of nine is clearly inadequate. Fortunately, more substantial information was available for two other rural areas. In the remote, southern, and sparsely populated diocese of Ardfert, a mixed marriage rate of roughly 18 per cent can be derived from a survey of all parishes for the years 1967 to 1971.[54] Later, between 1971 and 1973, a similar survey was conducted by the same author in County Wexford, where it was still possible to find a quite sizeable Church of Ireland community. Here the figures suggest that only 16 per cent were marrying Catholics. However, this is an extremely conservative estimate which should be raised to 24 per cent for the first nine months of 1973.[55] A year later, another survey by diocesan authorities found that mixed marriages had risen from eight to seventeen in twelve months. Such a rapid increase seems improbable, but the later figure may not be unreliable, since it covered a full year and H.W. Robinson's earlier survey failed to collect information on mixed marriages in some parishes. The total number of Church of Ireland marriages to fellow Protestants was not given for 1974; but if it is assumed that they increased by as much as a third, then the mixed marriage rate amounted to 30 per cent in 1974.[56] In the light of this apparent increase in rural areas, there is every reason to believe that a similar trend was occurring in the larger cities. Although no further surveys have been published, the "conservative estimate" of church leaders involved in collecting information on mixed marriages was that 40 per cent of their laity in the country as a whole were marrying Catholics in 1979.[57]

To anyone other than an Irishman it may not be readily apparent why mixed marriages should contribute to the minority's decline. In the face of emigration, there would seem to be good reason for thinking that Irish Anglicans might have been inclined to use mixed marriages as a means of selectively recruiting new blood. For economic reasons alone, one might expect that a good number of Catholics might have welcomed the opportunity to marry into the privileged Church of Ireland community. Irish Anglicans, of course, had their own prejudices against Catholics, but their segregated social and educational institutions were there to transform the children of such marriages into "decent Protestants." However, other more powerful forces were at work which largely held these temptations in check. In the aftermath of colonialism, it is perhaps understandable that Catholics were reluctant to join the ranks of their former masters or to permit their children to do so. But for the most part, the absorption of mixed marriage children into the Catholic world must be attributed to the vigorous demands of the Catholic church and the willing compliance of its laity. In accordance with canon law, the church discouraged mixed marriages as much as possible. If they did occur, the Ne Temere decree of 1908 stipulated that they would be recognized as valid only when official dispensation was granted. This required signed and witnessed promises from both parties that all children be baptized, educated, and raised as Catholics. In view of the educational segregation that prevailed in the country, conforming to these rules ensured that the children of mixed marriages were effectively cut off from the Protestant community. And Protestants, for their part, then sealed their fate by refusing to have anything to do with any member of their own community who married a Catholic.

The obligatory nature of these promises was greatly strengthened by a court decision of 1950 that the promises were legally binding. In the "Tilson case," as it was called, the Protestant father of a broken mixed marriage placed his children in a Protestant children's home, so that they might be raised as Protestants. The Catholic mother took her plea to the courts that the children be returned to her. Gavan Duffy, the president of the High Court, ruled in favour of Mrs Tilson on the basis of the written promises which Mr Tilson had made under the Ne Temere decree. This set a new precedent in Irish law, for previously the common law inherited from the British had recognized the absolute right of the father to choose the religious upbringing of his children – no matter what premarital agreements had been reached. What made this decision doubly disturbing to Protestants was that Gavan Duffy justified his new interpretation of the law by referring to the constitution of 1937 which accorded a "special position" to the Catholic church. The case was then appealed to the Supreme Court which also ruled in support of Mrs Tilson, although it did not make reference to the religious articles in the constitution. Instead, it argued that the constitutional provisions regarding the right of the parents to make decisions concerning the education of their children prevented either parent from breaking an established agreement. The one dissident vote was that of Judge Black, a Protestant, who questioned whether the court would have ruled the same way had the mixed marriage promises favoured the Protestant party.[58]

After the Second Vatican Council, the Catholic church began to develop a rather more tolerant attitude towards other Christian denominations, but it was not until 1970 that any changes were introduced in the church's mixed marriage laws. The Motu Proprio, or edict from Rome, tended to be much more conciliatory in its general tenor, in that it no longer made written promises from the Catholic partner mandatory, and it acknowledged that under certain circumstances marriages could be conducted in non-Catholic churches. Much of the old rigour still remained, but a new element of flexibility was introduced by permitting national churches and dioceses to place their own interpretations on the precise requirements. In Ireland, the interpretation was predictably conservative. In fact, the Catholic bishop of Cork, Dr Lucey, continued to require written promises from the Protestant partner throughout the 1970s,[59] although this was usually not asked for in the other dioceses. In all dioceses written promises were still demanded of the Catholic party, and the consulting priest was expected to advise the non-Catholic partner of the binding promises imposed on his spouse. The priest was then required to inform his bishop of the reaction of the non-Catholic on being informed of the promises and of the likelihood that the non-Catholic would abide by them. On this basis, the bishop alone decided whether a dispensation could be granted.[60]

In reality, Irish Anglicans who wished to marry Catholics found that the actual treatment they received was heavily dependent on the attitudes of the particular priest with whom they dealt. Among Catholic clergy in the Dublin diocese during the first half of the 1970s, J. Fulton found that the previous policies of either conversion or prevention were no longer as widely pursued. The majority now saw mixed marriages "as a fact that had to be accepted and coped with."[61] "Over half" continued to see the promises of the Catholic party as a matter of great importance, but "some found it hard to make such a demand on an intermarrying couple when it came to confronting them."[62] Within this smaller liberal group, many were concerned about the rights of the Protestant partner. Indeed, some acknowledged that where the commitment of the Catholic partner was weak they would prefer to see the children brought up in another faith, provided it was a Christian upbringing. However, a much larger number feared that mixed marriages would lead to indifference on the part of both parties, and they were uncertain whether to take a stricter or a more lenient approach. Thus a majority of the clergy remained suspicious of mixed marriages, but the extent of their opposition, the reasons for it, and their actual treatment of the couples involved varied enormously. Like Catholics in search of contraceptives, prospective partners in a mixed marriage were sometimes able to find a sympathetic priest who was prepared to give a liberal interpretation to his church's teaching, while many others were less fortunate. Although Fulton's study does not provide information on the statistical distribution of clerical attitudes, the general impression he conveys is of a conservative clergy who were being forced to change their thinking by their personal encounters with a growing number of mixed marriages which they could not prevent. In the latter part of 1979, it was rumoured that parish priests might be granted the power to grant dispensations without turning to their bishops.[63] If this occurs, diligent Protestants may well find it much easier to escape the officially rigorous demands of the Catholic church.

For the great majority of Irish Anglicans, these changes were simply unsatisfactory. What they believed was their just due and what they felt they needed for their survival was recognition of the equal rights of both parents in determining the religious upbringing of the children of mixed marriages. In the end, the final decision has always been in the hands of the laity, and here there seemed to be signs of greater change. It must be remembered, however, that the small size of the Church of Ireland community ensured that mixed marriages involved only a tiny proportion of Catholics. One crude index of this select group's willingness to move some way to accommodate Protestant sensibilities is the extent to which its members were prepared to marry in Protestant rather than Catholic churches. According to official statistics, this was true of only 15 per cent of the mixed marriages condoned by the Catholic diocese of Dublin during 1978 and 1979.[64] It is only in comparison with previous decades that this could be considered a significant development, but it probably underestimates the real extent of the change. In the Church of Ireland diocese of Ferns, for instance, twelve of the seventeen mixed marriages among Irish Anglicans during 1974 were solemnized in their own churches.[65] In other parts of the country, clergy claimed that they were encountering a small but growing proportion of young couples seeking mixed marriages who wished to avoid having any contact with the Catholic church and its requirements. In other cases, the ritual of promises and official Catholic sanction were endured in order to placate parents, but many of these couples were far from certain in their own minds. In most parishes, clergy proudly pointed to a few mixed marriages where the children were being raised as Protestants, and they anticipated a growing number of the offspring of such marriages in their own schools, whether the children were nominally Protestant or Catholic. Their emerging sense of hope, however, was now being tarnished by an awareness that the conflicting pressures of the two communities were sometimes being resolved by dissociation from both churches. Although statistical information is lacking, it is likely that Irish Anglicans were still losing more than they gained from mixed marriages. Nevertheless, the assumption that mixed marriages inevitably entailed the loss of the next generation was no longer as valid as it had once been, and it is possible that the day may come when the Church of Ireland may actually benefit from the mixed marriage market. Numerical revival was still far from certain, but with the general fall in emigration during the 1970s the prospect of achieving a stable Anglican population would seem all the greater.

This survey of demographic trends still leaves open the fundamental question of what caused the growing rate of mixed marriages. At the moment, all that can be said is that the minority's small, scattered, and diminishing population was not the principal cause. It is self-evident that the increasing shortage of Protestant marriage partners through emigration and natural decrease increased the likelihood of mixed marriages, but this line of reasoning should not be extended too far. If population decline was the only or even the major cause, it would be difficult to explain why the heavy losses prior to 1946 failed to create a substantial growth of mixed marriages. It may be contended that the minimal size necessary for communal life was passed after 1946. But this argument also poses problems because Irish Anglicans were least prone to marry Catholics in rural areas where their parishes were smaller than anywhere else and where their population was most widely dispersed. In other words, the causes of communal segregation and its recent decline were both essentially social rather than demographic in nature.

CHAPTER THREE

Ethnic Allegiance
and Political Life

By the time the treaty with Britain was signed in late 1921, the predominant feeling among Protestants was one of relief that the chaos and violence of the previous years appeared to be over. Their hopes were soon shattered by the ensuing Civil War, but within a few days of the signing of the treaty the *Gazette*, the *Irish Times*, the Board of Trinity, and Archbishop Gregg all publicly proclaimed their intention of giving their full allegiance to the new state. Much importance was attached to the clauses in the treaty safeguarding religious and civil freedoms, and the two newspapers went out of their way to urge that their readers should take part in the running of the new country.[1] However, these official statements were little more than the pragmatic advice of communal spokesmen faced with an irreversible decision. In much of the country the treaty was being hailed as the termination of 800 years of British rule, and in the rest it was being condemned as a betrayal of full Republican aspirations. Yet the *Irish Times* could still petulantly assert that "If Ireland accepts the Empire with her heart, and not merely in the cautious wording of an oath, and if she accepts themselves as Imperial Irishmen, they will come joyfully to her aid."[2] After the violence of the preceding years, it is doubtful whether many Protestants seriously believed that reconciliation on these terms was really possible, but in the circumstances it is hardly surprising that few Protestants could reject totally their ingrained, centuries-old British loyalties. As the *Gazette* acknowledged, their conciliatory attitude to the new government had been privately condemned as "a nefarious selling of the pass," and it readily admitted that most of its readers were bewildered and frightened at this final "break with all the traditions that were dear to them."[3]

POLITICAL REPRESENTATION:
EXTINCTION AND INCORPORATION

Despite the heartfelt aversion of most Protestants to the very idea of an independent Irish nation, fourteen were elected to the Dail or lower house of the legislature at the 1923 election which followed the end of the Civil War. In all, 153 deputies or TDs were elected, which meant that Protestant representation (9 per cent) was actually a little higher than the Protestant proportion of the total population. This rather surprising result was in part made possible by the introduction of proportional representation in the new state's elections. Its most important characteristic was that its multi-member constituencies facilitated the election of minority candidates who would have been excluded under the straight-vote system.[4] Predictably enough, most Protestant TDs were elected in the constituencies where the Protestant vote was strongest, and in a few constituencies around Dublin and in Ulster the Protestant vote was sufficient to elect a candidate on its own. Since eleven of the fourteen Protestant TDs in 1927 were not affiliated to any political party, it seemed that a strong and independent Protestant voice was about to emerge in politics. But in fact the number and independence of the Protestant TDs soon declined. By the 1940s only four Protestants were being elected to the Dail, and by the 1960s all four were members of the major political parties. And after the election in 1977, when two long-standing Protestant TDs were defeated, Protestant representation was reduced to only one seat in the Dail. It is only by reference to the changing political attitudes of Protestants and Catholics that these electoral changes can be understood. But before turning to these broader and more important issues, I shall briefly analyse Protestant political representation and the immediate reasons for its decline.

In the 1920s five types of Protestant representatives may be discerned.[5] The first and most short-lived was a collection of TDs whose distinctive mark in the Dail was their continuity with the minority's ascendancy leadership of the past, although in some cases it is an exaggeration to describe their background as ascendancy. All had been established figures prior to 1922 who had come to accept and occasionally to embrace the nationalist aspirations of the Catholic majority. They tended to be returned in constituencies where the Protestant vote was moderately strong but still insufficient to elect a candidate entirely of its own choosing. Jasper Wolfe from West Cork had been a crown solicitor and a member of the first governing body of University College Cork. He had been a nationalist for many years, but he had not been actively involved in politics in the years immediately prior to 1922. Fitting somewhat closer to the ascendancy mould was George Wolfe from Kildare, a former high sheriff with a Sandhurst background who was distinguished by his strong commitment to the Irish language. In a similar vein, Dermot Gun O'Mahony had been a deputy lieutenant in his home constituency of Wicklow; and Bryon Cooper, who represented County Dublin, had served as a Unionist MP at Westminster before his conversion to constitutional nationalism. Cooper owned extensive lands in County Sligo, and in his election address he asked for support so that he might serve his country as his "ancestors had served Ireland in Grattan's Parliament."[6] With the exception of Jasper Wolfe, the others eventually joined Cumann na nGaedheal, the pro-treaty party. As they retired, died, or were defeated, there were no successors to take their place. They themselves had survived the transition because of their nationalist sympathies and well-established place in public life, but in the new climate that was emerging there was little place in electoral politics for those with ascendancy backgrounds.

The exception that almost proves this rule was the up-and-down career of Douglas Hyde, who achieved the highest office of them all. As a scholar and a popular exponent of the Irish language, Hyde came into national prominence with his famous lecture on "The Necessity for De-Anglicising Ireland." In it he argued that a full and creative Irish nationalism was only possible when all manifestations of the pervasive English influence were replaced by a living Irish language and cultural tradition. In 1893 he helped to found the Gaelic League, which was to prove so influential in the nationalist movement, and he became its first president. But as the league grew ever more closely associated with political nationalism, Hyde became increasingly uncomfortable, for the nationalism he espoused was more cultural than political in orientation. In fact, he resigned from the Gaelic League, and for the next twenty years he was absent from public life. Then in 1938, near the end of his life, he was elected as the first president of Ireland under the new constitution of 1937. The *Irish Times* had initially put Hyde's name forward, and it is likely that many Protestants agreed with the guarded praise of the *Gazette* for this "unexpected"[7] gesture by the Catholic majority. But as we shall see, Hyde's devotion to the Irish language – no matter how apolitical it may have been – set him sharply apart from the vast majority of Protestants in the South.

The second and even more disparate collection of Protestant TDS possessed the most visibly nationalist backgrounds. The most colourful was Constance Markievicz, who was returned as a Republican for South Dublin between 1918 and 1927. Although she had been raised in the Church of Ireland and was a member of the old ascendancy Gore-Booth family, she became a champion of the poor in the Dublin labour troubles of 1911 to 1913, and she took an active part in the 1916 uprising. In this same loose category may also be placed Ernest Blythe and Thomas Johnson, an Englishman by birth, who served for a short time as the leader of the small Labour Party. Blythe was a Presbyterian from Northern Ireland, but his nationalist credentials were impeccable for he had been a member of the Irish Republican Brotherhood and the Gaelic League and had spent considerable time in jail between 1916 and 1919. He later served as minister of finance and vice-president of the Executive Council in the Cumann na nGaedheal government of the 1920s and early 1930s. All three were elected in strongly Protestant constituencies, but it is unlikely that they received many first preference votes from Protestants since they were in competition with other successful Protestant TDS. They were not seen by the minority as "one of our own"; indeed, neither Johnson and Blythe were southern Protestants. As might be expected, none defended specifically Protestant interests. Their one successor was Erskine Childers whose father had been executed during the Civil War because of his Republican activities. Childers was educated in England, but he subsequently returned to Ireland and was elected as a Fianna Fail TD in the late 1930s. He later occupied many government ministries, and his exceptional career culminated in 1973 when he was elected as the second Protestant president of the Republic. Once again, Protestants were gratified by the gesture, but to an even greater extent than in the case of Hyde they were deeply conscious that "Mr. Childers is neither by social background nor by education calculated to express the mind of Southern Protestantism."[8]

In the third category of Protestant representatives may be placed the three TDS for Trinity College Dublin and about a third of the members of the 60-seat Senate. In the treaty, both the disposition of the Trinity seats and the general structure of the Senate had served as guarantees to the Protestant and Unionist representatives that their interests would be represented politically. For obvious reasons, Protestants made no protest when the university seats were transferred to the Dail. Initially, both the *Gazette* and the *Irish Times* hoped that the members of this group would serve as the major spokesmen for the Protestant community, but the editorials of both papers later expressed dissatisfaction with their leadership. Nevertheless, they did represent the Protestant viewpoint more consistently than any other group. The Trinity TDs were especially well qualified for this role, since their electorate consisted of the predominantly Protestant graduates of their university. Most of the Protestant senators had been nominated by the government when the Senate was first established. Although some played virtually no part in the Senate's proceedings, another group under the leadership of Andrew Jameson were active and often quite effective critics of government policy. By 1936 the number of Protestant senators had been roughly halved by the growing influence of the Dail in later Senate elections. Until the very end, they continued to represent the landholding, business, and professional interests of the minority. Inevitably, their elitist outlook, British sympathies, and Protestant values put them in conflict with both Cumann na nGaedheal and the ardent republicanism of Fianna Fail. To Fianna Fail in particular, the Senate was a "bulwark of imperialism" that "was always hostile to the interests of Irish nationalism" and that gave "political power to a certain class that could not get that power if they had to go before the people."[9] Thus when de Valera and Fianna Fail came to power in 1932, bills were passed within a few years which abolished the Senate and removed university representation from the Dail.

In the new and constitutionally weaker Senate that was created not long after, the number of Protestant senators continued to fall. This occurred despite the addition of the three Trinity seats to the new Senate. Throughout the 1960s five Protestants were normally returned, although their number increased to six in the 1977 election. At that time three of the Protestants still fitted quite closely to the traditional Protestant mould in that they represented business and a concern for the handicapped, but much had changed for two had previously contested Dail elections on behalf of the major parties. Moreover, and much more importantly, only one of the three representatives for Trinity was now a Protestant. The first Catholic to be elected was Mary Robinson in 1969, who proved to be more active than her predecessors in pressing the traditional Protestant complaints over such matters as the legal ban on contraception. Noel Browne, who became the second Catholic senator for Trinity in 1973, was an even more outspoken critic of the political power of the Catholic church; and in 1977 his place was taken by Conor Cruise O'Brien, who was widely known for his critical view of the IRA and extreme republicanism. In the face of this threat to the last of the independent bases for Protestant representation, Catherine McGuinness stood as a specifically Protestant candidate in 1977, but she failed to secure election. It would obviously be erroneous to view these new representatives as defenders of traditional Catholic interests. Indeed, it is primarily in the sociological sense of the term that we may describe them as Catholics. Nevertheless, Trinity's still largely Protestant electorate[10] was now choosing representatives from outside of their own community, and their voluntary decision to make this break with the past would seem to indicate that the very existence of a separate Protestant viewpoint was starting to crumble.

The border counties of Cavan, Donegal, and Monaghan provided the electoral base for the fourth group of Protestant politicians. In each of these three Ulster constituencies, independent Protestant TDS were returned throughout most of the 1920s and 1930s. Due to the greater size of their communities and their close links with the North, they were much more willing than their counterparts further south of the border to present themselves as exclusively Protestant candidates. In the Monaghan election of 1927, the efforts of Ernest Blythe to secure the blessing of the local Catholic clergy stood in marked contrast to the backing the Protestant candidate, Alexander Haslett, received from the Orange Lodge. In supporting Haslett, the Grand Master of the Orange Lodge claimed that "the Protestants of Monaghan had every right to one of the three county seats," and he stressed that they "wanted a representative to voice their grievances." At the same meeting, J.J. Cole, the Protestant TD from Cavan, added his own support, and he commended Monaghan's Protestants for facing "the issue even now though Donegal and Monaghan thought they should have come in sooner."[11] I have no evidence of Major Myles making such direct denominational appeals, but his past election to Westminster as a Unionist MP and his use of Protestant churches as a political platform left no doubt as to his political and religious affiliations. Like most other independents in the Dail, the three Protestant TDS from Ulster served primarily as "contact men for their constituents in political and administrative circles."[12] They did not play a major part in Dail debates, and when they did involve themselves they tended to be concerned with agricultural matters and other issues of local concern.

Independent Protestant TDS continued to contest all three border constituencies during the late 1940s and 1950s, but only Major Myles and his successor Willie Sheldon were successful in Donegal. Their failure to secure election was in part due to their diminishing percentage of the electorate as the Protestant population declined. However, it was compounded by a succession of electoral revisions after 1935 which reduced the number of large multi-member constituencies and thereby increased the proportion of the vote that a candidate needed to be elected. This may be most clearly demonstrated in Donegal. Its eight-member constituency consistently returned Major Miles until it was divided into two four-member constituencies in 1935. Although this meant that the theoretical quota necessary to elect an independent candidate increased from 11 to 21 per cent, Protestants in East Donegal retained both their theoretical quota and Willie Sheldon until 1961. Further revisions in that year split the Protestant vote between two constituencies and reduced the new Donegal North East to a three-member constituency. These changes undoubtedly explain Sheldon's decision to accept the offer of a seat in the Senate since "Protestant candidates, per se, could no longer be elected."[13]

Besides Erskine Childers, whose atypical background has already been mentioned, only one other Protestant, James White from Donegal, was returned for Ulster in the 1970s. This does not, however, convey the full scope of the change. In 1973 local Protestant candidates contested all of the then four Ulster constituencies, and Billy Fox, a local Protestant farmer, had been previously elected for Monaghan in 1969. All ran as candidates of the Fine Gael party, which is the present-day descendant of Cumann na nGaedheal. Their absorption into the political structures of the Republic represented a fundamental change from the past, but it did not bring about the disappearance of a distinctive Protestant vote. In Monaghan, a local Protestants' Association was still reckoned to be a powerful force in channelling the Protestant vote.[14] In Donegal, Sacks' detailed analysis of the 1969 election showed that Protestants gave their first preference votes to Boggs, the Protestant candidate. This occurred even outside his own part of the constituency where common practice dictated that his Fine Gael partner should have received the first preference votes of Fine Gael supporters.[15] And in Cavan, I found through my own enquiries that Protestants still strongly supported their "own man," although they were now prepared to use their second and third preferences for Catholic candidates. Obviously much has changed, but the present situation may be best described as one of political incorporation rather than of either full assimilation or total integration.

The final category of Protestant TDs consisted primarily of businessmen from Dublin constituencies who initially showed little sympathy for the ideal of an independent Ireland. In 1923 they formed a businessman's party of six candidates, but only two Protestants, Good and Hewat, were elected. Since Hewat never secured reelection, they cannot be considered even a minor party. In their manifesto of 1923, they claimed that they had "no political fads to foist on the country" and that they did "not seek office." They offered "common sense and practical business experience," and stated that they ran only to insure that "commerce, industry and agriculture ... may not be neglected while political matters absorb the attention of the Nationalist assembly."[16] Although it was rumoured that Good would join Cumann na nGaedheal in 1927, he retained his independent status and persisted in his emphasis that he was "going forward as a businessman and not in any sense as a politician."[17]

After the 1920s there were a small number of additional Protestant TDS from the Dublin area who also tended to come from business backgrounds, although all but one became members of Cumann na nGaedheal / Fine Gael. The best-known and most enduring were the three members of the Dockrell family. Two of them continued to be elected for Dublin constituencies until 1977 when they and their party were defeated. None were prominent within either their parties or the legislature. It is likely that they collected most of the Protestant vote in their constituencies for many years, but from the crude evidence available it would appear that they could not muster a theoretical Protestant quota after the constituency revisions of 1935. Their early decision to join Fine Gael was partly a matter of political necessity, but this alliance was also facilitated by the predictable sympathy they felt for its economically conservative and pro-Commonwealth stance. In effect, Fine Gael served as a convenient halfway house for the incorporation of Dublin Protestant TDS between the two world wars.

With the loss of their independence, the Protestant TDS from Dublin grew less willing and less able to serve as spokesmen for the Protestant community. Although there were a number of legislative developments that deeply disturbed many Protestants, protest increasingly came from outside the Dail. By the early 1970s Maurice Dockrell readily admitted in a mild speech favouring contraceptive legislation that he had "no authority to speak as a Protestant."[18] Indeed, he was quite correct, for by this time his city-centre constituency could not have contained a very large Protestant vote. It would appear from the census that his brother's constituency in the Dun Laoghaire area had a much larger, though still not autonomous, Protestant vote. But any claim that Percy Dockrell might have cared to make that he represented the Protestants of Dun Laoghaire had already been undermined by the 1957 election of Lionel Booth, another Protestant, who ran as a Fianna Fail candidate. Since both men contested the constituency during the next twelve years, there is every reason to believe that the

Protestant vote was now split. When Booth retired in 1969, after having held his seat for the full twelve years, Fianna Fail nominated another Protestant, Neville Kerry, who was unsuccessful in two attempts. Clearly both parties remained aware of a potential Protestant vote. However, the relatively early incorporation and recent diffusion of Protestant TDS from Dublin within both parties suggest that the old divisions had crumbled in Dublin to a greater extent than anywhere else.

Overall, there can be little doubt that the most striking trend was the radical decline in the number of Protestant TDS. Its immediate causes were the abolition of university representation in the Dail and the various constituency revisions which intensified the already declining electoral power of the shrinking Protestant community. More generally, it stemmed from the tendency for TDS to be nominated on the basis of a good "National record" in the independence movement, or on the basis of local prestige and service within the community.[19] With a few conspicuous exceptions (e.g., Hyde and Childers), a good "National record" was predictably scarce among Protestants. Similarly, the high degree of social segregation of the minority often ensured that service within their own community did not create the wider prestige necessary for public office. Moreover, the strong Gaelic, Catholic, and Republican values of the state did little to attract Protestants to a political career. The emergence of a number of new Protestant candidates in the Ulster constituencies, and the equally recent candidacies of men like Neville Kerry in Dun Laoghaire, Gerard Buchanan in Dublin South Central, and John Blennerhasset in North Kerry may indicate a weakening of the old deterrents and the possibility of future growth in the number of Protestant politicians. But the fact remains that the once largely independent body of Protestant TDS had all been absorbed into the major parties by 1961. In the process, a distinctive Protestant voice virtually disappeared from the legislature.

POLITICAL ATTITUDES AND
ELECTORAL ALLEGIANCES

From indignant to indifferent marginality, 1922–1951. During the 1920s there were three closely related strands in the political thinking of the minority. As might be expected from the early election of a large number of independent Protestant TDS, the *Irish Times* and the *Gazette* initially took a rather independent and activist approach. Now that the Union was gone, they felt that they could no longer be legitimately reviled as "the garrison," and they argued that they had a duty to contribute their many "gifts of education, character and experience ... to the building of a new nationhood."[20] In many parts of the country, they advised that the only sensible course was to vote for the candidates of Cosgrave's pro-treaty party. But wherever possible, they repeatedly emphasized that votes would be most profitably cast for business party candidates and certain independents, and they specifically recommended men like Good, Hewat, Cooper, and Myles. Such men, they believed, would provide the intelligent criticism necessary for the country to prosper, and they hoped that Cooper and the others would "act as a corrective to any attempt on the part of certain groups to hasten too quickly with the Gaelicisation of the country."[21] Similar arguments were also put forward in the first election of 1927, but after that date they paid little attention to Protestant independents. And, as we have seen, few were forthcoming.

Increasingly, the primary and most pressing need was felt to be the election of a Cumann na nGaedheal government. In fact, there had been a certain air of unreality to the years between 1922 and 1927. Successful Sinn Fein candidates had refused to take their seats in the Dail because they were not prepared to sign the oath of allegiance to the Crown required by the treaty of 1921. In this situation, Protestant support for independents had not seriously jeopardized the position of the Cumann na nGaedheal government. Then de Valera broke away from Sinn Fein to form Fianna Fail in 1926, and he and his new party entered the Dail in 1927 after agreeing to accept the oath as an empty formality. With this decision, Cumann na nGaedheal became a minority government, and there was now the much more frightening prospect of Fianna Fail becoming the legitimate government of the state. From this point on, both the *Gazette* and the *Irish Times* were shrill in their repeated warnings of the many dangers that lay ahead. To the *Gazette*, the issue was dramatically clear: "It is Fianna Fail versus Christendom."[22] Thus it recommended that independents and the smaller parties "ought to disappear out of the minds of the electors,"[23] and in the interest of "self preservation"[24] the *Irish Times* urged support for Cumann na nGaedheal.

There were numerous reasons for Protestants to fear and to hate Fianna Fail. To begin with, they felt that disorder and lawlessness would follow if Fianna Fail came to power. In their eyes, de Valera and his followers had been responsible for the Civil War and its attendant destruction, and they believed that his republican sympathies were indirectly responsible for the occasional acts of intimidation and violence which they and others had suffered

through the 1920s. Secondly, they were convinced that the economic policies of Fianna Fail were untried and unsound. "If Fianna
Fail takes office," warned the *Irish Times*, "the wealth and security
of every citizen, including the ex-unionists, will be impaired and
gravely imperilled."[25] De Valera's protectionist policies, in particular, had little appeal for the many large farmers and merchants
among the minority whose economic interests lay in the perpetua-
tion of free trade with Britain. As a relatively privileged group, they
were also worried that Fianna Fail would "impoverish the middle
classes in an effort to placate the claimant elements among their
supporters."[26] Moreover, they sensed what Archbishops Gregg and
D'Arcy described as a "jealous hostility" directed specifically
against themselves because of their colonial past. So strong were
their feelings that the Standing Committee of the Church of
Ireland's General Synod sent a deputation to the government's
Executive Council. When they failed to gain sufficient reassurance,
the two archbishops made one of their few public appeals in the
latter part of 1930. The immediate issue was their fear that the
government was planning to remove the existing right of appeal to
the British Privy Council on all decisions of the Irish Supreme Court.
Protestants saw this constitutional measure as a safeguard against
any form of discriminatory legislation. Cumann na nGaedheal had
previously introduced ad hoc legislation that severely limited such
appeals, but protest at that time had been remarkably mild. In their
letter, Gregg and D'Arcy made it clear that they did "not impute to
the Government ... any desire to invade our rights either of property
or of religion," but they pointedly observed that "the present
Government will not always be in office."[27] Clearly, their concern
was with Fianna Fail which took office a little over a year later.

The third and most deeply felt objection to Fianna Fail stemmed
from its strong commitment to republicanism. Protestants correctly
saw de Valera as the major threat to the remaining constitutional,
symbolic, and economic ties upon which their British ethnic
allegiance was based. Nor could they fail to notice that the
tendency of many Protestant TDs to side with Cumann na nGaedheal
had led Fianna Fail to taunt the government for relying on "the
freemason vote."[28] When Bryon Cooper joined Cumann na nGaedheal in 1927, Cosgrave was castigated by Sean Lemass as a puppet of
"the leaders of England's faithful garrison in the past," and for this
reason, Lemass claimed, "every man and woman who was proud of
Irish nationality had deserted him."[29] In 1931 the *Irish Press*, de
Valera's newspaper, published a confidential circular soliciting
financial support for Cumann na nGaedheal during the coming

election. The organizing committee consisted primarily of senators with unionist backgrounds, and many were Protestant. On the next day the editorial comment of the *Irish Press* returned to Lemass's theme of "Who Rules" by arguing that the circular demonstrated the still active influence of English imperialism and the unfitness of such a government to lead an independent Ireland.[30] This exclusive conception of Irish nationalism, with its implication that those who had once been unionist could never be trusted to be true Irishmen, could only have strengthened the already strong antipathy of the minority towards Fianna Fail.

However, hatred for Fianna Fail did not convert all Protestants into enthusiastic supporters of Cumann na nGaedheal. There was a solid core who refused to give electoral support to any party or politician. The "Non-Voter" who wrote to the *Irish Times* in 1923 claimed that, since he would not take the new oath of allegiance (with its requirement of loyalty to the constitution of the Irish Free State), he would "not sanction the taking of it by any other man."[31] While sympathizing with this viewpoint and acknowledging that it was far from unique, the *Irish Times* deplored its lack of realism and emphasized its perilous consequences. After the by-elections of 1924, the *Gazette* attributed the Republican victory in South Dublin to the fact that "the ex-unionists, or if you will the Protestants, are not voting for Government candidates."[32] The root cause for their feeling so "grievously disappointed" was that the Cumann na nGaedheal government "went out of its way to make little of the British Empire."[33] "The place of the King in the Irish constitution is concealed rather than avowed," claimed another ex-unionist, "and this has discouraged a more general support of the Free State Government than it has already received."[34] Nevertheless, the *Irish Times* and the *Gazette* increasingly threw their weight behind Cumann na nGaedheal in the build up to the Fianna Fail victory in 1932. Although few editorials failed to mention the many dangers of Fianna Fail, the *Irish Times*, in particular, went out of its way to stress that Cumann na nGaedheal deserved Protestant support because of its fair treatment of minorities, its law and order platform, its pro-Commonwealth stance, and its conservative economic policies. And both papers continued to berate the abstentionist voting tendencies of their readers, which were imputed to the minority's faithfulness to "ancient loyalties."[35]

In short, the early political outlook of Protestants consisted of a complex mixture of independent activism, fear, and aloofness. However, this initial stance of indignant marginality rapidly evolved into one of indifference, estrangement, and apathy. In order to understand the causes of this transition, as well as the minority's persisting sense of alienation, we must examine the emerging Gaelic, Catholic, and Republican values of the new state.

In secular terms, the distinctive source of Irish nationalism was thought to lie in its Gaelic tradition. Under the stimulus of men like Douglas Hyde, the emerging nationalist leadership was convinced that the pursuit of independence was as much a cultural as a political movement. Their aspirations are best conveyed by the stirring claim of Patrick Pearse that he sought an Ireland "not free merely, but Gaelic as well; not Gaelic merely but free as well."[36] Pearse's vision of a Gaelic Ireland was readily embraced by de Valera and Fianna Fail, and even Cosgrave's Cumann na nGaedheal showed itself to be strongly committed to the principle of Gaelic revival. Revival it would have to be, for less than 20 per cent of the population was able to speak Irish in 1911. Hyde and others had taught that the English language policy of the national school system under British rule was the main reason for the decline in Irish usage. We now know that this was an overly simplistic explanation, since English had already become the major Irish language before the spread of the national school system. But reasoning of this sort led the major parties to believe that revival could be achieved if sufficient stress was placed upon Irish in the school system. Thus one of the first decisions of the government in February 1922 was that it should be taught for a minimum of one hour a day, and much more rigorous regulations were later added.[37]

As it turned out, the efforts of the language enthusiasts to convert Ireland into an Irish-speaking country were a conspicuous failure, and the dominant place of English in Protestant schools was never threatened. Nonetheless, Protestants remained intensely opposed to the government's language policy. Both the *Gazette* and the *Irish Times* repeatedly condemned its compulsory nature, and in 1926 the *Irish Times* suggested that support be withdrawn from any politician who condoned compulsion.[38] Dr A.A. Luce, a prominent fellow of Trinity, denounced Irish as "eye wash, political window dressing, dope for Republicans, anything but a genuine educational experiment." He argued that it was a "wrong to the religion of Protestants" because "all the associations of compulsory Irish are Catholic;" because school texts in Irish Catholic contained religious teaching; and because "there is little or no Protestant literature in the language."[39] Others also argued that the "wave of nationalism," of which Irish was but a symbol, was "attempting to prescribe our thought and hinder our access to ... our birthright and heritage of British tradition and culture which I am not ashamed to regard as the finest in the world."[40] To most Protestants, the whole Gaelic tradition was not only alien but primitive and inferior to their own British heritage, and they deeply resented being forced to study what they contemptuously regarded as "back country gab."

However, these views were rarely expressed in public because it was feared that any form of protest would be interpreted "as hatred against the language itself, as contempt for national ideals, or as a form of sectarian prejudice."[41] These fears were not unfounded, for even the more moderate stance of the *Irish Times* was condemned by the *Catholic Bulletin* as being "against the very idea of the Irish Nation as it really is."[42] Similarly, the secretary of one of the major Irish language associations wrote a public letter to the *Gazette*, demanding to know whether "you desire that your Church should stand in definite opposition to the national will." "It must be settled," claimed Mr Fahy, "whether Ireland is to become a feeble imitation of England, a West Britain, or preserve her national and historical continuity by becoming definitely Gaelic."[43] Under these conditions, the public statements of Protestants usually emphasized that their motives were not unpatriotic but rather were based on their concern that the heavy emphasis on Irish was educationally unsound.

Because of the widespread unanimity on the matter, there was little opportunity within the Dail to debate the principle of compulsory Irish. One of the few exceptions occurred in 1928 when a private member's bill was introduced to require that an Irish examination be made mandatory for all those who in future sought to qualify as lawyers. The bill elicited lengthy protestations from many of the Protestant TDS. Most said that they were opposed to the compulsory aspect of the bill and they usually emphasized that they were "not hostile to the Irish language," although the general tone of their speeches often indicated otherwise. Sir James Craig, one of the Trinity TDS, described the bill as "a waste of money" and as "tyrannical," and he claimed that the whole thrust of the language movement was "driving people out of the country."[44] John Good argued that it was a "hardship"[45] for those from the middle class educated in the North and in England, while Bryon Cooper pointed out that the bill would probably lead to a breakdown in the reciprocal recognition that prevailed between the English and Irish Inns of Court.[46] Such appeals on the basis of tolerance, the pragmatic value of cultural uniformity with Britain, and the possibility of discrimination against the already privileged fell on deaf ears. The response of T. Mullins, a Fianna Fail TD, well expresses the majority sentiment: "The garrison must give place to the nation."[47] In the division that followed, the bill was passed by 110 to 15. Faced with this intransigence, the Protestant sense of marginality grew all the stronger. At the same time, there seemed to be little point in pressing their opposition. For the other cultural tradition that they wished to preserve was British, and this was patently unacceptable to the Catholic majority. In consequence, protest was not only futile but positively harmful, for it could be easily interpreted as evidence of their unfitness to participate in the public life of independent Ireland.

The religious parallel to this ethnic alienation derived from the growing tendency of both parties to assume the Catholic allegiance of the nation and to incorporate Catholic moral precepts into the laws of the state. The protestations of the minority in this area were much less vehement because the issues did not impinge so directly on everyday life. Nor was the infringement of the minority's religious values always clear. What was felt to be at stake was the matter of civil liberties and the right, as W. Thrift put it, of "liberty of thought and independence of conscience."[48] Three pieces of legislation especially aroused Protestant concern that their rights were being curtailed. The first involved an effort to prohibit divorce. Although Ireland did not have divorce courts, it was technically possible to obtain a divorce by means of a private member's bill in the Dail. In 1925 Cosgrave and O'Higgins attempted to close this loophole by introducing an amendment to standing order designed to prevent divorce bills being considered. The *Irish Times* condemned their effort as a "national injustice" because it violated "the right of 'freedom of conscience' which is guaranteed to every citizen of the Free State by article 8 of the constitution."[49] However, the *Gazette* was much more diffident in its appeal to civil rights because the Church of Ireland did not condone the remarriage of divorced persons, and it felt that very few Protestants personally approved of divorce.[50] In the Dail, Thrift, who had been nominated to speak on behalf of "some Independent Members," emphasized that he had "just as strong views as the President on the sanctity of marriage," but he argued against the amendment because "it will have the effect of imposing on the whole population the religious views ... of the majority."[51] In reply, O'Higgins declared that the will of the majority must prevail, and the amendment was passed.

The second piece of legislation, the censorship of publications bill in 1929, was designed to prohibit the sale and distribution of obscene literature. Protestants both inside and outside the Dail readily admitted that there was a need for such legislation, but at the same time they were worried that the rather broad terms of the legislation might lead to a general form of censorship over literature and other political and economic writings contrary to the views of the majority. As usual, the most extreme criticism came from the *Irish Times*, which charged that the bill was a Catholic attack on Protestant freedom of thought. In its letter columns, it was also claimed that the real object of attack was English rather than indecent literature. Once the bill was implemented, it became evident that the Censorship Board was prepared to stick to the narrower grounds of obscenity, although there can be little doubt that it was extremely zealous in its pursuit of obscenity. In fact, many well-known works of literature by both English and Irish writers were eventually banned, and even the Irish classic, *The Midnight Court*, was banned when it was translated into English.[52]

The third and least divisive development was linked to the censorship bill, which also prohibited the selling and distribution of any literature or advertising on behalf of contraceptives. Later in 1935 this restriction was extended to include a complete ban on the sale and importation of contraceptives under section 17 of the Criminal Law Amendment Act. In the earlier debate of 1929, all three of the Trinity TDS stated that they did not condone the use of contraceptives or any propaganda on their behalf, although Thrift did add that he was reluctant to ban literature discussing their medical and sociological implications.[53] Similarly, in the brief 1935 debate, only one Protestant TD, R. Rowlette from Trinity, spoke in opposition to the government's bill, which was the work of an all-party committee.[54] He too stressed that he was personally opposed to the use of contraceptives by both married and unmarried people. In taking this stand, he was undoubtedly reflecting the view of the great majority of Protestants, for not until 1930 had the Lambeth conference of Anglican churches given guarded approval to the principle of contraceptive use.[55] However, Rowlette felt compelled to voice his objection on the by now familiar grounds that he was reluctant to impose his views on others who might differ with him as a matter of private conscience.

On a more general level, there was a recurrent tendency for de Valera in particular to equate Irish nationalism with Catholicism. When Fianna Fail took office in 1932, the government sent a message to the pope, stressing its resolve "to maintain with the Holy See that intimate and cordial relationship which has become the tradition of the Irish People."[56] This style of thinking was most clearly reflected in the new constitution of 1937, which was largely the creation of de Valera. Divorce was prohibited, and many of the articles dealing with the family, education, and private property closely followed

the phraseology and principles of Catholic teaching. More importantly, the articles on religion explicitly affirmed "the special
position" of the Catholic Church "as the guardians of the Faith
professed by the great majority of the citizens." In contrast, the
Church of Ireland and other denominations were accorded the
somewhat more dubious status of simply being "recognized." In a
similar vein, the preamble to the constitution acknowledged "all
our obligations to our Divine Lord, Jesus Christ, who sustained our
fathers through centuries of trial." As others later pointed out, one
might legitimately ask whether Protestants were considered to be
descendants of those who had suffered these centuries of trial. On
the other hand, the religious articles guaranteed that no religion
would be endowed; there were subsections affirming the right of
religious liberty and freedom from any form of discrimination on the
basis of religion; and the legal implications of the Catholic church's
"special position" were by no means clear.[57] The *Gazette* voiced its
strong dissatisfaction, but no demands were made for the Protestant
TDS to assert their opposition, as had been done ten years earlier on
the issue of the Irish language.[58] In part, this was because Protestant
TDS were less numerous and less independent, but it also stemmed
from the fact that no real disability was involved. Nevertheless, the
Catholic character of the state was now fully manifest, and it was
one with which Protestants could not be expected to identify.

Cumann na nGaedheal's willingness to enshrine these Catholic
and Gaelic values in the laws of the state further explains the
limited support it received from the minority. What is perhaps more
surprising is that the 1932 election, which marked the establishment
of almost continuous Fianna Fail rule thereafter, also led to growing
political apathy and indifference. There were two major reasons.
First, de Valera enacted legislation that effectively removed all the
remaining symbols of the British crown from the internal workings
of the Free State. The hated oath of allegiance was the first to go.
Opposition was expressed both outside the Dail and within it by
speeches and by the votes of the Protestant TDS. Thrift, who gave one
of the major Protestant speeches, argued that the bill would add to
the growing rift with the North. He also asked that "attention and
consideration" be given to the minority who had already lost so
much, but there was a strongly pessimistic tone to his ready
admission that "I am speaking very uselessly about it."[59] Although
Cosgrave's party resisted the bill because it tampered with the treaty
of 1921, the comments of the *Irish Times* were tinged with the same
sense of futility for it was well aware that Cumann na nGaedheal
had "no desire for the role of an uncompromising champion of the

Oath."[60] Shortly afterwards, the right of appeal to the Privy Council was abolished, and this was followed by three bills which resulted in the abolition of the governor general's office. With de Valera's new constitution in 1937, Ireland became a republic in all but name, although it did retain its membership in the Commonwealth through de Valera's complex formula of external association.[61] These measures were equally offensive to Protestants, but once again their protest seemed even less strident and voluble than it had been previously. Opposition was clearly pointless, and besides it did not make "the slightest difference to our affairs."[62] However, underlying this pragmatic withdrawal from public affairs was the awareness that too ardent an opposition still tended to be seen as evidence of a lack of nationalism and a continuance of the hated ascendancy mentality.

The second factor that contributed to the minority's waning political interest was that de Valera did not prove to be the oppressive ogre that many thought he would be. When several Church of Ireland churches were burned in 1935 as a reprisal for attacks on Catholics in Belfast, de Valera saw to it that government reparations were made and he publicly expressed his regret.[63] He showed no interest in publicizing or restricting their economic privileges, and it was acknowledged that their fears of discrimination had proved false.[64] In fact, it soon became apparent that "de Valera was by no means a revolutionary, but rather a pious bourgeois conservative."[65] Nevertheless, neither the *Irish Times* nor the *Gazette* would countenance electoral support for Fianna Fail. They were still not prepared to forget either de Valera's economic war with England or his constitutional reforms. But above all else, Ireland was still a part of the Commonwealth, due to the External Relations Act of 1936, and for this reason they continued to give rather lukewarm support to the pro-Commonwealth Fine Gael party.[66] All that remained of the earlier Protestant political orientation was their tendency "to act and to think as if the nation's political fate were something outside their own sphere of interest."[67] "Nothing could be more reprehensible or more stupid," claimed the *Irish Times*, than to "dream mournfully of 'the good old days'," but it admitted that there were a large number of voters who "give the impression that they are entirely indifferent to the outcome of tomorrow's election."[68]

This residual attachment of Protestants to Fine Gael was further weakened – and for many it was permanently shattered – by two developments during the short reign of the Coalition government (1948–51), of which Fine Gael was the largest party. One of these was the collapse of the Mother and Child scheme in 1951, which is still regarded as the prime example of intervention by the Catholic church in the decisions of the legislature. The minister of health, Dr Noel Browne, developed a scheme to provide free medical care for mothers and their children. At first, Dr Browne spent much of his time negotiating with the Irish Medical Association, which feared that this was the beginning of socialized medicine. He also had less than full support within his own cabinet due to internal political conflicts and sympathy for the IMA's stand, but it was opposition from the Catholic hierarchy that killed his scheme. Although some private negotiations were conducted with the hierarchy, they refused to accept his scheme because they felt it was contrary to Catholic principles. In brief, they argued that it was an unwarranted intrusion by the state into matters that should properly be the responsibility of the family, and they expressed fear that the services provided might foster such taboo practices as contraception and abortion. When it became clear that the hierarchy would not budge, the cabinet withdrew Dr Browne's proposals. Dr Browne resigned, and then fuelled the ensuing controversy by making public his private correspondence with the hierarchy and the Taoiseach, or prime minister.[69] The *Irish Times* immediately proclaimed that the "Roman Catholic Church would seem to be the effective Government of the country."[70] In reply, John Costello, the Taoiseach, asserted that "I, as a good Catholic, obey my Church authorities and will continue to do so in spite of the *Irish Times* or anything else."[71] The *Gazette* was rather more conciliatory, expressing sympathy with any objection to the growth of government bureaucracy and arguing that the Catholic hierarchy had as much right as the Church of Ireland bishops to make their views known.[72] However, I suspect that the *Irish Times* was closer to the thinking of most Protestants. In fact, a week later a leading columnist for the *Gazette* stressed that the secrecy of the negotiations with the hierarchy was proof to him that "there does seem to be some point after all in asking who are the effective rulers of the state."[73]

The other development was the unexpected decision of Costello in 1948 to declare Ireland a Republic and to remove it from the Commonwealth. The *Irish Times* was enraged, claiming that the Coalition had no mandate, that for Fine Gael it was a flagrant breach of its election promise and that "those who believed and still believe that the link with the Crown ought to be kept voted to a man and to a woman for Fine Gael."[74] In the Dail, Sheldon made an impassioned speech, arguing that it was "an insult to the intelligence" of those who had been deceived into supporting Fine Gael to be now told "that by going further apart we are getting nearer together."[75] Not long after, he announced he was withdrawing his support for the government.[76] For Dockrell, it was "the most important debate in which I have had the privilege to take part." He did not leave Fine Gael, but on this occasion he felt obliged to go against his party by pleading to retain the link with the Commonwealth, "that great body, speaking the same language, having Christian Faith ... and having largely the same ideals."[77] After the implementation of the Republic of Ireland Act in 1949, the *Irish Times* felt certain that those who had previously supported Fine Gael for its commonwealth stance were now "disgusted and disillusioned," and it predicted that "many of them will be inclined to stay home"[78] at the forthcoming election. In short, by the end of the Coalition's short reign, there was little left in Irish politics to interest Protestants. Their divergent religious interests were clearly of no account to either party, and there were now no public issues or symbols around which they could focus their fading British allegiance. As one of my respondents recalled, he and his fellow Protestants "didn't have strong views after 1949 – one way or the other."

The decline of political marginality, 1951 to 1970s. The political apathy and disaffection of Protestants persisted throughout the 1950s. Occasionally an individual would write to the letter columns of the *Irish Times*, claiming that he was not prepared to vote because "of the two parties one gave us the Civil War," and "the other ratted on its promise not to disturb the External Relations Act."[79] In a similar vein, the pre-election editorials of the *Irish Times* continued to acknowledge that there was "much temptation to abstain in the absence of any solid reason for approving of either of the major parties." But if Fine Gael was now no better than Fianna Fail because of the Republic of Ireland Act, then at least Fianna Fail had never demonstrated such a ready willingness to bow to the political pressure of the Catholic church. Thus at the 1954 election the *Irish Times* advised its readers for the first time to vote for Fianna Fail because "the voter knows approximately where he stands." Fine Gael, on the other hand, no longer merited "trust" as it had "sacrificed principle under pressure during the Inter-Party experiment of 1948 to 1951."[80]

Increasingly, the major thrust to the Protestant complaint was that "once again, old, and for the under forties, meaningless bitterness will be flogged in an endeavour to show that there is some difference between Fine Gael and Fianna Fail."[81] What was new, in emphasis if not entirely in expression, was that Protestants wished to bury the uncomfortably tendentious past. By the middle of the 1950s they believed that the major issues that should now concern the country were those of economic and national development, unemployment, and emigration. This transition was especially evident in the *Irish Times*, although here too the beginnings of the change may be traced back to the 1930s. To this day it has remained under Protestant ownership, but by the 1960s it had become "an outspoken, liberal, middle class newspaper" which tended to give critical support to Fianna Fail throughout most of this decade.[82] At the 1973 election both the *Irish Times* and the *Gazette* supported the successful coalition of Fine Gael and Labour; and in 1977 the *Irish Times* returned to a very guarded support for the defeated Coalition. During these elections the predominant element in the thinking of both papers was their concern with pragmatic questions of social and economic policy, and the leadership qualities of individuals and their parties. Furthermore, there was no sign in their editorials of a conscious effort to bemoan or deride political apathy among Protestants, as had occurred so often in the past.

By 1973–74 there had also been a marked decline in the previous disenchantment and marginality of Protestants within my six sample parishes. Only four of eighty-three respondents claimed they would not vote, although most admitted that "we do not have a strong involvement" and that "we often swing our vote around." In the two rural parishes where Protestants were unsuccessful Fine Gael candidates, the great majority of respondents gave their first preference vote in the 1973 election to their "own man." Elsewhere there was less interest in the election, but in all six parishes they had willingly cast their transferable vote in recent years to Catholic candidates from the major parties. This apparent disregard for the political divisions of the past was also evident in M. MacGreil's large survey of Dublin Catholics in 1972 and 1973, in which he included 132 Protestants in his sample. On a series of questions concerning the goals, benefits, peace-keeping capacity, and leadership of the government, MacGreil found that Protestants did not differ significantly from Catholics in their overall pro-establishment scores.[83] However, in the 1973 election, only 16 per cent of my own small sample voted for Fianna Fail; whereas in the country as a whole, Fianna Fail was the single most successful party with 46 per cent of first preference votes. The national vote was distributed in much the same way in 1969, and in that year 43 per cent of my respondents voted for Fianna Fail. In other words, this small and statistically unreliable sample suggests that the Protestant vote was largely dispersed and similar to the national vote in 1969 – but not in 1973.

Renewed Protestant support for Fine Gael was largely due to the eruption of violence in Northern Ireland after 1969, which strengthened the minority's otherwise diminishing sense of marginality and insecurity. This was especially true of Protestants in the three border counties of Ulster. With their physical proximity to the North and their strong Presbyterian component, they were most inclined to sympathize with northern Protestants, and they felt particularly vulnerable to the dangers of the northern violence spilling over the border. P.M. Sacks has argued that Fianna Fail had managed to gain considerable support from Protestants in Donegal before "the troubles," but this trend was almost entirely reversed in the 1969 election. Fianna Fail, of course, was the most overtly republican of all the parties, and Neil Blaney from Donegal was one of the party's most outspoken nationalists. Inevitably, Donegal Protestants interpreted his public condemnations of the northern regime as a "coded threat" to themselves.[84] These fears were then further enhanced when Blaney, Charles Haughey, and two others were ejected from the Fianna Fail cabinet for their alleged misuse of government funds to smuggle guns to Catholics in the North. Although Haughey was later reinstated, Blaney was eventually expelled from Fianna Fail for his continuing criticism of his party's policy on the North.[85] However, the elevation of James White, the Protestant member of Fine Gael, to the top of the Donegal poll in 1977 would suggest that Protestants were continuing to throw their entire weight behind Fine Gael.

In the remainder of the country, Protestants felt far less sympathy or affinity with northern Protestants, but "this scandal of the guns" was largely responsible for their desertion of Fianna Fail after 1969. With their small and scattered numbers, they too were understandably fearful of being dragged into the northern conflict. During the particularly tense period in 1972 surrounding the "Bloody Sunday" incident in Northern Ireland, when the British embassy in Dublin was burned, southern Protestants did occasionally suffer as "a convenient and relatively helpless target" for republican violence. Although there was no concerted campaign of terror, "minor incidents have taken place here and there involving threatening letters or telephone calls, the daubing of church walls or business premises owned by Protestants." The *Gazette* went on to claim that "the Southern Protestant cannot be cast in any particular role ... apart from their being Irish," and it pointed out that Catholics were usually quick to make amends for any of these incidents of which they were aware.[86] Fianna Fail did not condone such violence, but its more open support for the goals of the men of violence undoubtedly lay behind the minority's suspicions of the party. The success of the coalition in 1973 and its less sympathetic treatment of the IRA would suggest that Protestants were not alone in their views. MacGreil's Dublin survey also found that just after "Bloody Sunday" the great majority of both Catholics and Protestants continued to believe that they had more in common with each other than did southern and northern Protestants.[87] Although one might think that attitudes differed in the rest of the country, Sacks demonstrates convincingly that even in Donegal the efforts of Fianna Fail extremists to portray Boggs, the Protestant and Fine Gael candidate, as anti-Catholic did not deter Catholics from voting for him.[88] Catholics, it would appear, were prepared to make a firm distinction between Protestants north and south of the border. But as long as the conflict persists in the North, southern Protestants are likely to remain rather wary.

In order to account for the still considerable erosion of political marginality among Protestants after 1951, we must look at the changes that have occurred in Irish political life as a whole. In the area of secular political issues, the Republic of Ireland Act of 1948 was a crucial turning point in the political outlook of Catholics as well as Protestants. Once the last of the constitutional issues of the nationalist movement within the South had been resolved, D. Thornley has argued, the political identity of both the major parties was undermined. From this point on, they were forced to reorientate themselves and their concerns to "the social and economic criteria of modern politics."[89] As in the Protestant experience, this change was slow to take effect, and throughout the 1950s the old issues of the Civil War, the oath of allegiance, and the Commonwealth continued to dominate elections. Then, in 1959, de Valera resigned from the Dail on his way to becoming president. In the following election of 1961, all three parties were led by new men. Sean Lemass, who became Taoiseach, had a political career that went back to the independence movement, but by the time of his retirement in 1966 the bulk of the old revolutionary elite were gone. This postrevolutionary elite, which encompassed government as well as politics, ushered in a new political era in which the predominant concerns were increasingly those of trade, production, consumerism, economic planning, and the extension of social services.[90] At the same time, this transformation did not lead to a polarization of political parties along class lines. Although Fine Gael and Labour drew their greatest support from the privileged and nonprivileged respectively, Fianna Fail's appeal now extended fairly evenly across all classes and in most cases it was greater than that of either Fine Gael or Labour.[91] Thus despite the relative privilege of Protestants, the lack of a class base in politics further assisted the diffusion of Protestant political allegiance.

Over the same years, the creation of a distinctively Gaelic and Irish culture began to receive less attention than such pragmatic concerns as industrial policy, emigration, and the European Economic Community. Indeed, even the efforts to provide an economic base for the shrinking Gaeltacht through tourism and industry strengthened the use of English.[92] As we shall see in chapter six, the use of Irish throughout the nation's schools and government regulations regarding teaching through the medium of Irish both began to decline after World War II. Then in 1973 the new Coalition government went a long way to meet the earlier objections of Protestants by no longer requiring that success in Irish language examinations be a prerequisite for obtaining secondary school diplomas. Recent surveys showed that the ideal of replacing English with Irish was rejected by at least 60 per cent of the population, although MacGreil's study found that the great majority still paid lip service to the notions of revival and preservation. What is more surprising is that Protestants and Catholics in Dublin did not differ in any significant way in their attitude towards Irish.[93] While Protestants showed no signs of the marked bitterness and animosity of the past, it is my own impression that their attitude towards Irish may best be described as one of indifference. Perhaps Protestants have simply learned to voice the appropriate nationalist sentiments on such matters, but one wonders if the same might now be said of the great majority of Catholics. However, the essential development here is the growing irrelevance – indeed the absence – of the constitutional and ethnic issues of the past in Irish political life. The result has been that Protestants and Catholics are able to share a wide range of secular political interests without regard for those differences that still remain.

In this new climate, the British ethnic allegiance of the minority finally seemed to die away. With the exception of a small proportion of upper-class "West Britons," all insisted that they regarded themselves as simply Irish Protestants. Among those over the age of sixty, this claim did not always reflect their innermost feelings. As one older accountant admitted, he still felt a sneaking loyalty to England when watching international horse-jumping competitions on television, although his children, he said, had no thought of cheering for any country other than Ireland. Even with this qualification, my observations do not appear to be fully confirmed by MacGreil's study, for he found that 74 per cent of Dublin Protestants described themselves as Irish; 9 per cent classified themselves as Anglo-Irish; 10 per cent considered themselves British; and 6 per cent claimed to have another ethnic origin.[94] However this discrepancy may have been due to his sampling method, which included all foreigners with six or more months of residence in the country. Since a substantial minority of foreigners were probably Protestant, there is every reason to believe that he underestimated the degree of Irish identity among Irish-born Protestants. No doubt there were still some older and more conservative Catholics who continued to regard Protestants as an alien remnant of the Ascendancy. But on the whole, MacGreil found that Dublin Catholics had come to view Protestants as occupying an "in-group standing" when compared to a wide range of other ethnic, political, religious, and social groups.[95] In fact, according to his complex measures of social distance, Catholics were as favourably disposed to Protestants as they were to members of Fianna Fail. When all this is added up, it is difficult to quarrel with his conclusion that by the 1970s Protestants had undergone "quite a degree of ethnic almagamation and assimilation."[96]

Protestants' new status as an "in-group" suggests that considerable change must also have occurred in the religious sphere. I shall touch here on only the more public and political aspects of this trend, since religious divisions will be examined in detail in chapter five. As with the ethnic dimension, the religious alienation of the minority reached its height between 1948 and 1951. The pervasive influence of the Catholic church was not seriously questioned until much later, but as early as the 1950s some Catholics were beginning to show signs of discomfort with certain of the institutional expressions of their faith. Two examples of this incipient transformation merit brief mention. The first was the restructuring of the Censorship Board in the mid-1950s. Public criticism of the board had been generally muted in the 1930s. Even in later years, only the better educated and more affluent of the Protestants I interviewed recalled censorship as an issue that really concerned them. Their discontent peaked in the later 1940s and early 1950s when the board's ever more avid pursuit of obscenity led it to ban an increasing number of internationally acclaimed works of literature. Faced with growing criticism from the *Irish Times* and elsewhere, the Coalition minister for justice took advantage of two resignations from the board to appoint two more liberal members. The ensuing row within the board led to the resignation of the three remaining conservatives. This time it was Fianna Fail which appointed three more liberals in their place. After this sudden change in the board's composition, there was little complaint about its later decisions. However, it was not until 1967 that the great majority of previously banned books were released by a decision to put a twelve-year limit on all bannings.[97]

In a rather paradoxical way, the other early sign of restlessness with traditional Catholic values came out of a mixed marriage dispute which involved the normal premarriage promise of both parties to raise their children as Catholics. The incident at Fethard-on-Sea arose in 1957 when the Protestant wife of a Catholic farmer took their children to Belfast. From there, she informed her husband that she would return only if he agreed to the chidren being raised as Protestants. Believing that the local Protestants had assisted the wife, Catholics responded by initiating a boycott of Protestant businesses. The organizers of the boycott were then given considerable moral support by the local Catholic clergy and by a few outspoken Catholic bishops. But this time de Valera – who had previously defended the boycott of the Mayo library services when a Protestant had been appointed chief librarian in 1930 – gave a strong speech in the Dail roundly condemning the Fethard-on-Sea boycott. However, de Valera did not go so far as to criticize the mixed marriage promises which were at the root of the whole incident.[98] And if exclusivist attitudes were beginning to thaw in the national political arena, it was equally clear that local divisions could still be far more intense and enduring.

During much of the 1960s the Catholic church was relatively quiet and the state was concerned with secular matters, but since then the strongly Catholic character of the Republic's laws have been subject to increasingly heavy criticism and resistance. The first of these developments emerged from an all-party committee set up to revise the constitution of 1937. It recommended in 1967 that the subsection referring to the "special position" of the Catholic church be removed from article 44 on the grounds that it would "dispel any doubts and suspicions which may linger in the minds of non-Catholics, North and South of the border."[99] In making this recommendation, the committee went out of its way to demonstrate that the amendment would not harm the Catholic church in any way and was compatible with the doctrines promulgated by the Second Vatican Council. Although other recommendations of the committee provoked severe criticism, the hierarchy was silent on article 44. In 1969, when the Taoiseach, Jack Lynch, indicated that he favoured the proposed amendment, the hierarchy then publicly stated that it had no objection. In 1972 the appropriate bill was passed by all parties, deleting the relevant subsections. As the measure entailed a change in the constitution, it was submitted for a referendum and was supported by 84 per cent of those who voted.[100] The quiescence and eventual agreement of the hierarchy indicates that the change in article 44 did not threaten the prominence of the Catholic church and its social values. Nevertheless, one of the old elements in the Protestant complaint had been removed at the behest of the great majority of the Catholic population.

The second issue, concerning the use of contraceptives, proved to be far more controversial. Both the sale and importation of contraceptives, it may be remembered, had already been prohibited by legislation enacted in 1935. The first salvo occurred in 1971, when three university senators introduced a bill in the Senate to remove the above restrictions. Mary Robinson, one of the proposers, argued that it was "necessary not to discriminate on the basis of religion or on the basis of a majority viewpoint," and she went on to ask, "how can one eliminate territorial partition if this religious and moral partition of the country is retained?"[101] The now aging Catholic archbishop of Dublin, Dr McQuaid, replied that, since contraception "is always wrong in itself," no individual or group could legitimately lay claim to "a right that cannot even exist."[102] The Fianna Fail government was at first unwilling to allow the senators to introduce their bill, and when it did accede the bill was refused a first reading in the Senate by a vote of twenty-seven to fourteen. The most significant aspect of this initial effort was that two of the three proposers were Catholic.

The Church of Ireland supported the defeated Senate bill with a unanimous motion in the General Synod,[103] but far greater pressure was placed upon the government in 1973. In the McGee case, as it became known, the Supreme Court ruled by a four to one majority that the law banning the importation of contraceptives was unconstitutional because it violated a married couple's right to privacy.[104] Faced with this contradiction between the law and the Supreme Court ruling, the new Coalition government brought in a cautious bill in 1974 to make contraceptives available to married couples from licensed suppliers. In the light of the Mother and Child controversy, there seemed to be good reason for this caution. However, the increasingly urban and industrialized Ireland of the 1970s was a very different place from the Ireland of twenty years earlier. By 1974 a national survey found that 34 per cent of Catholics were against any form of contraceptive legislation; 42 per cent felt they should be available to married couples only; and another 15 per cent believed there should be no restrictions on access.[105] In 1973 the Catholic hierarchy had already made public their opposition to any form of contraception, but here too there had been a change, for they stressed that "it is not a matter for the Bishops to decide whether the law should be changed."[106] In the Dail, the issue seemed far less certain. The government allowed a free vote, and Fianna Fail opposed the bill. When seven Fine Gael TDS, including the Taoiseach, voted against their own party's bill, it was defeated by seventy-five votes to sixty-one.[107]

This did not resolve the issue, for it became clear that there was now massive disregard for both the law and Catholic moral teaching. On the pretext that the pill was a cycle regulator, some 48,000 women were reported to be using it in 1978.[108] As early as 1973 there had been much more open defiance of the law, for the expanding number of family-planning clinics (the first opened in Dublin in 1969) were said to have fitted 2,700 inter-uterine devices over the preceding two years.[109] Then with the McGee case the legal situation became all the fuzzier. By 1979 there were ten clinics across the country which provided a wide range of contraceptives in addition to the pill and professional medical advice.[110] Technically, the clinics could not sell the contraceptives they imported, but again the law was circumvented by the common practice of accepting "donations" of a fixed amount for the various contraceptives they distributed. No doubt the government could have prosecuted the clinics, but it wisely decided to turn a blind eye, for by 1977 another survey showed that a full 77 per cent of the population now favoured some form of contraceptive legislation.[111]

After Fianna Fail returned to power in 1977, it was inevitable that it too would feel obliged to introduce some form of contraceptive legislation. When asked, the Church of Ireland publicly stated that it favoured legislative change, providing contraceptives were restricted to married couples.[112] The Catholic bishops again emphasized their doctrinal opposition, although they reiterated their earlier qualifications that "it does not follow from this that the state is bound to prohibit the sale and distribution of contraceptives."[113] Charles Haughey's bill, which was introduced in 1978, endeavoured to appease conservative Catholic thinking. Besides banning abortifacients and agreeing to promote natural methods of family planning, it stipulated that no doctor or chemist could be forced to participate against his or her will. Doctors were also to be responsible for prescribing all forms of contraceptives. They could do so only if they were "satisfied that the person is seeking the contraceptive, bona fide, for family planning purposes or for adequate medical reasons and in appropriate circumstances." In effect, this meant that contraceptives were to be restricted to married couples.[114] As Haughey aptly put it, the bill that was passed in 1979 was very much "an Irish solution to an Irish problem."[115] In many ways, the new act imposed more restrictions on the availability of contraceptives than had existed immediately prior to its enactment, and there were signs that there would be pressure for further change in the future.[116] But what was most important was that a majority of Protestants and Catholics had come to espouse and to share a common political interest in what had once been a forbidden and communally divisive issue.

The third and last major issue of this period concerned the constitutional prohibition on divorce. As early as 1967, the Dail committee on the constitution had recommended that it be rescinded because of its harmful effect on relations with the North and because "it takes no heed of the wishes of a certain minority of the population who would wish to have divorce facilities."[117] In its place, the committee recommended that the right of divorce be restricted to those whose religion specifically tolerated divorce. Since the Church of Ireland did not condone the remarriage of divorced persons at the end of the 1970s, the proposed change was more apparent than real. The fact still remains that an entirely Catholic body of TDs was prepared to suggest legislative change that provoked strong condemnation by the Catholic hierarchy. For once the members of the Dail seemed to be a little ahead of their electorate. But in the 1970s the thinking of the Irish population again underwent a major change. In 1971 only 22 per cent were in favour of divorce legislation; by 1974, 48 per cent were prepared to see divorce legalized in certain circumstances; and then in 1977 a solid 65 per cent indicated that they wished to have some form of divorce facilities.[118]

In the surveys where a breakdown of attitudes by religion was available, Protestant support for divorce legislation was consistently higher, but they were by no means united on the issue. The General Synod of the Church of Ireland has been considering whether to accept the remarriage of divorced persons since the early 1970s. Although the committee entrusted with this responsibility recommended that it be permitted, the proposal proved so divisive that no decision had been reached at the end of 1979.[119] Clergy were quick to deny that "the Church of Ireland is crusading for divorce," and they stressed that "marriage is intended by God to be monogamous and lifelong." On the other hand, they admitted that "real and irretrievable breakdowns in marriage do occur," which "require the Church's compassion."[120] They also vehemently condemned the short-lived proposal of the Coalition government that the grounds for annulment of marriage be extended to conform more closely with Catholic doctrine. Such a solution, they complained, was "unfair to children," capable of "being adjudged sectarian," and inadequate since "properly launched marriages also ... collapse."[121] Thus their conservatism was mixed with deep concern that the constitutional prohibition and the nullity scheme were solely a reflection of Catholic thinking and thereby raised "many unavoidable questions concerning the minority's religious and civil rights."[122] For these reasons, the General Synod's Role of the Church Committee had recommended as early as 1973 that the constitutional prohibition be removed.[123] As might be expected, the Catholic church was far less ambivalent in continuing to advise its laity that divorce legislation was unacceptable.[124] In view of the reluctance of the politicians to accede to the demand for contraceptive legislation, there is every reason to believe that they will avoid the divorce question for as long as they can. However, a majority of Irishmen of all creeds were again in agreement on the once improbable issue of a need for divorce legislation.

Faced with this marked change in Catholic thinking on such diverse topics as contraceptives, the Catholic church's "special position," and divorce, Protestants grew more outspoken in their demand that their divergent interests as a religious minority be recognized in the laws of the country. Their renewed self-assertiveness was especially evident in the vigorous demands of the Role of the Church Committee, which was formed after the outbreak of violence in the North. Its forthright style can be seen in the call to "rid ourselves of any commitment or desire for 'a Protestant state for a Protestant people' or 'a Catholic state for a Catholic people'."[125] Although the northern conflict undoubtedly sharpened southern Protestant awareness of minority rights, I believe it would be a mistake to dismiss these demands as simply a form of northern propaganda. In large measure, Protestants were more outspoken because they sensed a greater support and sympathy from Catholics. As one writer to the *Irish Times* put it, "we now know and trust each other well enough to speak out on matters that hurt us without incurring the charge of bigotry;"[126] while another Protestant layman at the General Synod claimed to see in Catholics a new "recognition that there was more than one form of Irishness."[127] This does not mean that relations between the two communities were now fully harmonious, for to the irritant of divorce must be added the more irksome matter of mixed marriages and certain educational issues which will be covered later. However, there was now an increasingly widespread debate among Catholics as well as Protestants over the propriety of imposing Catholic values on the state and its citizens. Protestants will continue to be vocal participants in this discussion, but the persistence of these religious issues no longer divides Protestants and Catholics in the same way as in the past.

CHAPTER FOUR

Class Differences
and Occupational
Segregation

The fears of the minority that independence would lead to the confiscation of their property and restrictions on their commercial interests proved to be groundless. After the land question had been largely defused by the various land acts of the British government, Irish nationalism became primarily concerned with political and cultural matters. Griffith and Connolly had been the major proponents of giving an economic thrust to the nationalist movement, but both were dead by the end of the Civil War. The deep divisions created by this tumultuous event ensured that the Cumann na nGaedheal government devoted most of its attention to political affairs during its ten-year period of office. Since it drew much of its support from large farmers and the more privileged sectors of urban society, the government was neither electorally nor ideologically inclined to alienate the Protestant vote. In fact, it proved to be "sound on the rights of property, austerely virtuous on financial matters and generally reassuring to the gentry and businessmen who were so prominent in the Church of Ireland community."[1] The more radical tenor of Fianna Fail during its rise to power again rekindled Protestant fears of economic discrimination. But in the event, these worries also proved to be unfounded. In general, little change of any significance occurred during these early years to alter either the general structure of the Irish economy or the relatively privileged and influential position of Irish Anglicans within it.

There were, however, sound reasons for their economic anxieties. Although their dominance of the major agricultural sector had been largely broken by 1922, the legacy of past privilege was still everywhere to be found. A good number were clerks, working men, and small farmers, but Catholics were much more likely to be found in lower-class occupations. At the other end of the social ladder – in the professions, at the highest levels of the commercial and industrial world, and on the largest farms – Irish Anglicans vastly exceeded their proportion of the total population. In each of these fields, many of the oldest and most prominent firms continued to be Protestant-owned and managed, and this visibility further strengthened their already strong sense of economic superiority. On the other hand, this top-heavy occupational distribution created an extensive set of bounds between the two communities, which ensured that the minority's economic power and privilege was tempered with a fair measure of vulnerability. In many parts of the economy, members of the Church of Ireland were dependent on Catholics, either as the greater part of their work force or as their customers and clients. Inevitably they feared that their readily apparent wealth would attract the attention and ire of the now politically dominant but still economically subordinate majority. Nor could they have felt especially secure in the knowledge that certain sectors of the Catholic community still saw them as alien and illegitimate usurpers whose inherited privileges were no longer acceptable in an independent Ireland. Under such conditions, it is not surprising that the minority regarded Catholics with a complex mixture of fear and snobbery. In return, envy and resentment pervaded the Catholic view of Protestants, although older Protestants recalled that these hostile sentiments were formerly combined with a certain deference and "respect for the quality." Especially during the early years of the new state, these economic divisions and the tensions which they created played a major role in putting the two communities at odds with one another. Without them, their ethnic and religious differences might have seemed much less important.

These economic differences were of two basic types. The first consisted of class differences, while the second involved the segregation of the minority into separate Protestant firms. This second theme, which will be dealt with later, is relatively straightforward. However, the issue of class differences requires elaboration, for there are two separate aspects of such differences which are revealed by the concepts of influence and privilege. *Influence* refers to the extent to which the minority controlled the higher levels of the occupational hierarchy. Irish Anglicans were in a position of influence whenever their proportion of an occupational group or stratum exceeded their percentage of the total labour force. *Privilege*, on the other hand, refers to the extent to which the minority was concentrated in higher status occupations. Strictly speaking, the minority was privileged whenever the proportion of

Irish Anglicans in a higher occupation was greater than the percentage of Catholics in the same occupation. In order to comprehend fully the changing significance of class differences between the two communities, we must examine the extent to which both the privileged and the influential positions of the minority within the Irish economy have altered since 1922. Both these crucial concepts are measured by occupational trends derived from the census.[2]

THE ENGULFMENT OF MINORITY PRIVILEGE

Our major concern is with the changing class position of the minority in the private sector, where the vast majority of Irish Anglicans were employed, but their reluctance to take up government employment deserves a few brief comments. By the time independence had been achieved, there had already been a marked reduction in the number of Irish Anglicans in the army, police, and civil service. In the reconstituted bureaucracies of the new state, this much smaller group of Irish Anglicans carried on, but their numbers continued to decline at every census after 1926. By 1971 they accounted for only 1.5 per cent of senior civil servants and less than 1 per cent of the police and military. These figures stand in sharp contrast to the much higher influence of the minority in the private sector. Their withdrawal was partly due to the government's much resented emphasis on the Irish language as a basis for admission to the public service. Although outright discrimination was rare, many were probably affected by such well-known incidents as the previously mentioned Dunbar-Harrison case, when the government was pressured into removing the Mayo County librarian because she was a Protestant supervising Catholic reading material. At the same time, the many opportunities available in the strong Protestant business community gave them little reason to consider government service. However, underlying these pragmatic considerations were also the fundamental differences in outlook and aspiration between the two communities. For much the same reason that led to the Protestant retreat from the legislature, the minority was, to say the least, reluctant to join Catholics in their endeavour to create a Republican, Gaelic, and Catholic state. Many of these old conflicts were on the decline by the 1960s, but in 1971 there was still no evidence of a significant return of Irish Anglicans to government service.

During the 1920s, when the government was relatively small, the failure of Irish Anglicans to penetrate its ranks did not appreciably affect their overall class standing. However, its implications grew rather more serious as government involvement in the economy began to grow after de Valera came to power. This interventionist policy was not pursued consistently, but in the 1930s, the late 1940s, and after the late 1950s, the level of government spending increased rapidly. Over the whole period, the public sector's proportion of the gross national product grew from 23 per cent in 1926 to 53 per cent in 1973.[3] This very striking growth in the economic power of government was accompanied by a marked expansion of its bureaucracy. It occurred in two major ways. The first and more predictable development involved the extension of the civil service as its regulatory responsibilities increased. We may also include in this category the recent expansion of educational and social welfare facilities as governments came to accept an ever wider definition of their responsibilities. The second part of government strategy can be traced as far back as the 1920s. It consisted of the formation of a host of state-sponsored bodies to perform tasks that private enterprise could not or would not perform adequately. By the early 1960s there were fifty-five of these bodies, employing over 50,000 people. Some were concerned with such matters as radio and television, cultural endowment, research and the like, while others were much more directly involved with the private sector of the economy. The latter included organizations as diverse as sugar, electricity, and peat companies, a country-wide transport system, a national airline, an industrial development agency, and even an insurance company.[4] What is important about all these increasingly powerful government bodies is that they provided a largely closed world where Catholics were able to rise on the social ladder without being hindered by the entrenched interests of Protestants. This largely parallel development did not directly alter the privileged and influential position of the minority within the private sector. But government bureaucratic expansion did help to create the growing body of educated, powerful, and affluent Catholics who have recently made the minority feel far less certain of their superior class standing.

Agriculture. Agriculture remained the most important sector of the Irish economy for many years after independence. In 1926 it accounted for over 75 per cent of exports and almost 60 per cent of all gainfully employed men. A slightly lower proportion of Irish Anglicans (45 per cent) were in farming, but it was still their major source of employment. Table 8 shows that Church of Ireland influence was most pronounced within the largest farm-size category of over 200 acres, where 24 per cent were owned by Irish Anglicans. Such a figure probably underestimates the real level of their economic power because they tended to be concentrated in the more productive midlands and eastern counties. In the relatively rich province of Leinster, they accounted for 35 per cent of farmers with over 200 acres, and fewer than 50 per cent of these large farmers were Catholics in the counties of Cavan, Carlow, Longford, Monaghan, and Wicklow. As these five counties do not contain the best agricultural land in Ireland, it would be best to describe the minority as occupying a highly influential but not exactly dominant position in farming during the 1920s. Compared to Catholics, the minority, as table 7 indicates, was much more likely to be found on larger farms, but this statistical measure of privilege should not be taken to mean that all or even most Irish Anglicans were large and prosperous farmers. In fact, only 10 per cent of Church of Ireland farmers owned more than 200 acres, and just over half of them worked farms of less than 50 acres.

By 1971 both communities had experienced almost identical 53 per cent declines in the total numbers of their agricultural workers. These losses did not appreciably alter Church of Ireland involvement in farming, since the total Anglican work force diminished by 45 per cent between 1926 and 1971. But for Catholics, their flight from agriculture represented a very significant shift to urban occupations, since their total work force fell by only 13 per cent. The net result was that the 39 per cent of the minority in farming in 1971 exceeded the Catholic rate of 32 per cent by a considerable margin, whereas the reverse had been true in 1926. However, the more vital question is how well Irish Anglicans fared in this shrinking agricultural sector. Although there had been especially rapid declines among small Catholic farmers, table 7 shows that the relatively privileged position of Irish Anglicans had not been reduced by 1971, and they were now more concentrated on medium and larger farms. Nevertheless, 36 per cent of Church of Ireland farmers still owned farms of less than 50 acres in 1971, and only 11 per cent occupied farms of more than 200 acres. With such marked internal class differences persisting into the 1970s, it would clearly be false to think of Church of Ireland farmers as sharing a common class identity.

Despite their continuing privilege, table 8 reveals that there was a small but consistent decline in the degree of their influence. On farms of over 100 acres, for instance, their diminishing influence was due to a small decrease in the number of Irish Anglicans (1 per cent) and a substantial increase of Catholics (19 per cent). Closer scrutiny

TABLE 7
Denomination by Farm Size, 1926–1971

Acres	1926			1971		
	R.C.[a]	C. of I.[a]	I.D.[b]	I.D.[b]	C. of I.[a]	R.C.[a]
1–14	27.5	11.1	−16.4	−7.4	4.2	11.6
15–29	29.0	20.7	−8.3	−11.0	11.8	22.8
30–49	19.5	19.6	+0.1	−6.3	20.5	26.8
50–99	15.1	22.2	+7.1	+4.4	30.5	26.1
100–199	5.8	13.9	+8.1	+11.7	21.6	9.9
200+	1.7	10.1	+8.4	+8.4	10.6	2.2
Not stated	1.4	2.4	+1.0	+0.2	0.8	0.6
Total	100	100	∓24.7	∓24.7	100	100

[a]This refers to the percentage of male Church of Ireland farmers and the percentage of male Catholic farmers who owned farms of different sizes.
[b]This measures by how much the percentage of Irish Anglicans on each farm size is greater (+) or less (−) than the percentage of Catholics on the same farm size.

of the same table might lead one to think that the resulting loss of Church of Ireland influence was not of a sufficient order to bring about any real change in their capacity and willingness to exclude Catholics. For even on farms of over 200 acres, where the fall in minority influence was most marked, the decline was only from 24 to 19 per cent. There is something to be said for such an argument, and there is little doubt that Irish Anglicans were much more successful in preserving their influence in farming than they were in the rapidly expanding urban environment. But even in rural areas, there were sound reasons for the widespread belief that they were not nearly as powerful as they had once been.

In part this conviction was due to a long historical memory which extended far beyond 1922. The era of the Protestant Ascendancy in rural areas was not fully broken until 1922, and it was still part of folk memory in the 1970s. For some years after 1922 small pockets of Protestant gentry continued to remind the rural minority of its once powerful heritage. These remnants of the Ascendancy and their remaining gentry ways then went into further decline after 1945, when they found it especially difficult to adjust to an Ireland dominated by their former subordinates.[5] Inevitably, the contrast between this not too distant past and the now often vacant or otherwise occupied 'big houses' of the Ascendancy strengthened perceptions within both communities of the minority's collective decline.

However, the demise of the Protestant Ascendancy and its

TABLE 8
Farm Size by Denomination, 1926–1971

| | % C. of I.[a] | | % Change 1926–71[b] | |
Acres	1926	1971	C. of I.	R.C.
1–14	2.3	1.7	−75.6	−68.6
15–29	3.9	2.5	−63.0	−41.9
30–49	5.4	3.6	−32.9	+1.8
50–99	7.6	5.4	−10.9	+27.5
100–199	11.8	9.6	+0.6	+26.8
200+	23.9	18.9	−31.4	−7.4
Not stated	8.3	5.7	−77.2	−65.4
Total	5.3	4.7	−35.2	−26.0

[a]This refers to the percentage of all male farmers of different farm sizes who were members of the Church of Ireland.
[b]This refers to the percentage change in the number of Church of Ireland male farmers and the number of male Catholic farmers between 1926 and 1971.

refracted glories were not the only factors at work. Table 8 shows that after 1926 the prevailing trend on farms of over 50 acres was one of Catholic ascent and Church of Ireland decline. What matters most of all is the clear and steady direction of this trend. In every parish, respondents could readily identify Protestant farms that had fallen into Catholic hands in living memory, but far fewer examples could be produced of the opposite trend. The impact of these and other forces is best illustrated by the experiences of a middle-aged farmer whom I interviewed. During his youth, his father had been known as "Mr Robert" by the neighbouring Catholics whose sons often provided day labour on the family farm. By the 1970s Mr Robert's farm of approximately 100 acres had not grown any smaller. But as the farm was now mechanized, there was little need to employ local Catholics, and this contributed to the diminished stature of his son in the local area. With farm subsidies, improved social services, and a growth in the average size of their holdings, local Catholics appeared to be much more prosperous than in the past. Although a number of smaller Protestant farms had also disappeared or amalgamated, table 8 shows that the overall growth of larger Catholic farms was greater. In addition, most Catholic children in the area were now attending secondary school, whereas in the previous generation Mr Robert's son had been one of the few to do so. None of these various improvements in the local Catholic community threatened the material well-being of Mr Robert's family. However, their net effect, especially in psychological terms, was to narrow the local status gap between the two communities. In these changing circumstances, Mr Robert's son still retained a strong sense of his religious identity, but to his Catholic neighbours he was now known simply as "Bob." And for the same reason, the still privileged Church of Ireland farming community was now less inclined to look down upon the rising Catholic community.

Professions. With the previously noted exceptions of the military, the police, and certain civil servants, the formal changes associated with independence did not directly affect Irish Anglicans. Yet it does seem likely that the violence, uncertainty, and anti-British sentiments of these transitional years affected their position in the Irish economy. The available evidence is slim because the censuses of 1911 and 1926 differ, but they do provide some limited information on certain professional occupations. They show that the number of Church of Ireland doctors and other professionals diminished by 39 and 36 per cent respectively, and their proportions of these occupations fell from 28 to 16 per cent and from 39 to 32 per cent. Such a steep decline serves as a reminder that the overall drop of a third of the Church of Ireland population between 1911 and 1926 inevitably weakened their influence. Nevertheless, minority involvement in the professions in 1926 was still quite substantial for a community that provided less than 6 per cent of the total labour force. When students, religious, and teachers are excluded from the census category, table 10 indicates that the minority accounted for 19 per cent of secular professionals whose services extended beyond their own community. And in certain occupations such as law, engineering, and chartered accountancy, Church of Ireland influence was at the even healthier levels of 30 to 35 per cent.

In the expanding urban economy, Irish Anglicans slightly increased their relative position of privilege within the professional world. But at the same time, their influence had fallen to below half its 1926 level by 1971. For the broad professional category, table 10 shows that this was due to an immense increase of 177 per cent in the number of Catholic professionals and a virtually static rate of change among the minority. To put the abstract trends of table 10 in a more concrete form, the minority's sense of economic superiority must have been weakened by the emergence of 29,998 Catholic professionals during a period when the number of Church of Ireland professionals actually diminished by 24. If we again exclude teachers and religious, the rate of growth among Catholic pro-

TABLE 9

Denomination by Professional Occupations, 1926–1971

	1926			1971		
	R.C.[a]	C. of I.[a]	I.D.[b]	I.D.[b]	C. of I.[a]	RC.[a]
Total	1.9	5.8	+3.9	+4.3	10.3	6.0
Total (minus religious)	1.3	3.9	+2.6	+3.2	8.7	5.0
Total (minus religious & teachers)	0.7	3.0	+2.3	+3.7	7.5	3.8

[a]This refers to the percentage of male Church of Ireland workers and the percentage of male Catholic workers who were members of the professions.
[b]This measures by how much the percentage of male Irish Anglicans in the professions is greater (+) or less (−) than the percentage of male Catholics in the professions.

fessionals rose further to 388 per cent, while the minority experienced a vastly lower increase of 38 per cent. Strictly speaking, some of this huge growth is misleading because it included the emergence of many technical occupations which did not exist in 1926 or were not sufficiently sophisticated at that time to merit a professional label. There is, however, a continuity in class terms, for even these new professionals were part of the expanding middle and professional class that was being created by urbanization and industrialization. Had it not been for the 45 per cent decline in the total Church of Ireland work force, Church of Ireland professionals would probably have increased much more rapidly. But the very fact that their secular professional category grew by 22 per cent at a time of general decline suggests that Irish Anglicans in the middle and upper-middle classes were not subject to any exceptional pressure from Catholics.

The one noteworthy exception to this general trend was in medicine, where the number of Church of Ireland doctors and dentists declined by 40 per cent between 1926 and 1961. Information of this sort is not available after 1961, but the development stood in marked contrast to the general pattern of stability or small growth among Irish Anglicans in other secular professions. It was partly due to the falling demand for their services as the Church of Ireland population declined, although this was initially offset by their tendency to rely on Catholic patients. Another part of the answer lay in the excessive number of doctors produced in Ireland and the consequent need to emigrate in order to find employment. But this explanation is also limited, because the 44 per cent growth of

TABLE 10

Professions by Denomination, 1926–1971

	% C. of I.[a]		% Change 1926–71[b]	
	1926	1971	C. of I.	R.C.
Total	14.5	5.7	−0.8	+177.4
Total (minus religious)	14.8	5.2	+22.4	+247.0
Total (minus religious & teachers)	19.4	6.8	+37.8	+387.9

[a]This refers to the percentage of all male professionals who were members of the Church of Ireland.
[b]This refers to the percentage change in the number of male Church of Ireland professionals and the number of male Catholic professionals between 1926 and 1971.

Catholic doctors indicates that many new positions were opening up. Of more relevance were the highly transferable skills which enabled medical practitioners to emigrate much more easily than other Irish Anglicans when they became dissatisfied with life in independent Ireland. However, there was one other particularly important pressure which stemmed from the public service nature of their profession.

This last pressure is best illustrated by the events surrounding the 1949 attempt by the Catholic Knights of St Columbanus to take control of the Meath hospital in Dublin, which was largely managed by Protestants. By suddenly taking up a large number of memberships in the loosely controlled governing body of the hospital, the Knights were able to elect their own Catholic candidates to a majority of positions on the central committee that ran the hospital. But the Knights' victory was short-lived. Not long after, a group of politicians from all parties secured the passage of a private members' bill in the Dail which effectively reinstated Protestant control of the Meath. Since the Catholic archbishop of Dublin also supported this reversion to the status quo, it would be unwise to view the incident as evidence of an officially sanctioned policy of discrimination against Protestants.[6] Yet it must also be remembered that this was the era of the Mother and Child bill, when it was widely assumed that social services and medical care in particular should reflect religious thinking and be under denominational control. From this perspective, equality meant the maintenance of separate Protestant and Catholic medical preserves. Such thinking may have been technically equitable, but it cannot have been very reassuring for Church of Ireland doctors, whose practices included Catholic patients as well as their own shrinking community. These views could not have been shared by all Catholics for the 8 per cent of doctors and dentists who were Church of Ireland in 1961 were still too numerous to rely exclusively on their own community. Nevertheless, their atypical decline in the field of medicine does suggest that Irish Anglicans partly maintained their privilege by shifting from the public sphere to the more protected and insulated areas of private enterprise.

Commerce. Next to farming, the commercial and financial worlds attracted the greatest number of Irish Anglicans during the 1920s. Any notion that they were all members of the bourgeoisie must be discarded, for they were more likely to be shop-assistants and clerks than owners and managers. Yet their influence at this time was still very striking. This was especially true of the major financial institutions where 32 per cent of those in banking and 26 per cent of insurance workers in central offices were members of the Church of Ireland. In management positions, Irish Anglicans accounted for 43 per cent of bank officials, and Protestants as a whole actually possessed a 53 per cent rate of dominance. In no other occupation was Protestant influence so substantial. It stood in marked contrast to the 8 per cent level of minority influence among managers and owners in wholesale and retail trade. But this census category is a rather misleading indicator of high status, because it indistinguishably aggregated large department store owners with the vastly greater number of small shop-keepers and one-room publicans. The more revealing statistic is the healthy 32 per cent rate of minority influence among heads of commercial sections of business, since only large firms would require such a degree of specialization. In fact, Brian Inglis argued in his autobiography that the leading and most influential wholesalers in Dublin were predominantly Protestant before World War II.[7] For the country as a whole, his claim is not borne out by the census, but his usually penetrating observations cannot be dismissed with certainty.

After 1926 Irish Anglicans were again able to increase their position of privilege in the commercial world. In 1926, when there were many more small shops, table 11 shows that they were less likely than Catholics to be owners and managers in trade, but by 1971 their normal pattern of greater concentration or privilege prevailed in this category. As the total number of Church of Ireland managers and owners actually fell, table 12 makes it clear that their

TABLE 11

Denomination by Commercial Occupations, 1926–1971

	1926			1971		
	R.C.[a]	C. of I.[a]	I.D.[b]	I.D.[b]	C. of I.[a]	R.C.[a]
Owners, managers & publicans (whole-sale & retail)	47.6	40.1	−7.5	+3.8	49.9	46.1
Travellers & agents	6.1	21.4	+15.3	+11.9	25.0	13.1
Shop assistants & barmen	46.3	38.5	−7.8	−15.7	25.1	40.8
Total	100	100	∓15.3	∓15.7	100	100

[a]This refers to the percentage of male Church of Ireland commercial workers and the percentage of male Catholic workers who were in these three occupations.
[b]This measures by how much the percentage of male Irish Anglicans in these three commercial occupations is greater (+) or less (−) than the proportion of male Catholics in the same three occupations.

enhanced privilege was made possible by even greater rates of decline among minority salesmen and shop-assistants. This pattern of exceptional decline within lower status occupations was far from unique, since it was also responsible for the minority's increasing tendency to be concentrated in the professions and on larger farms. In other words, the greater privilege of Irish Anglicans in the 1970s was largely due to the diminishing size of their lower class, rather than to any great expansion of their numbers in higher class positions.

Table 12 also indicates that Church of Ireland influence among owners and managers in trade declined between 1926 and 1971. Although this trend is consistent with the general pattern established elsewhere, it does not tell us a great deal about changes in the higher levels of commerce, which may have been obscured by offsetting shifts among small shop-keepers and publicans. Fortunately, more compelling evidence of upper-class trends is available for the financial world. In 1972 *Hibernia* published a brief who's who of the upper echelons of the major Irish banks. On the basis of name and schooling, White estimated that approximately 25 per cent of the 200 senior managers and roughly 36 per cent of the 44 directors were Protestants.[8] These are very high figures for such a late date, but they must be contrasted with the 53 per cent rate of Protestant influence among the 960 bank officials listed in the 1926 census. The 244 individuals surveyed by White were obviously a

TABLE 12
Commercial Workers by Denomination, 1926–1971

	% C. of I.[a]		% Change 1926–71[b]	
	1926	1971	R.C.	C. of I.
Owners, managers, & publicans (whole-sale & retail)	8.1	5.8	+14.6	−13.5
Travellers & agents	22.6	9.8	+153.8	−18.5
Shop assistants & barmen	7.5	3.4	+4.2	−54.8
Total	9.1	5.4	+17.4	−30.4

[a]This refers to the percentage of all male commercial workers who were members of the Church of Ireland.
[b]This refers to the percentage change in the number of male Irish Anglicans and the number of male Catholics in these commercial occupations between 1926 and 1971.

much more exclusive and high-ranking group than the 1926 census enumeration of all bank officials. Since Protestant influence tended to be most pronounced at the highest occupational levels, there is every reason to believe that the Protestant proportion of senior bank officials and directors in 1926 was much higher than the census figure of 53 per cent. Cast in these terms, it is clear that there was a very appreciable decline in the degree of Protestant influence at the highest levels of the financial world. To be sure, White's data serve as a valuable reminder that Protestant influence had by no means disappeared. But we should not lose sight of the basic trend of convergence as Catholic influence rose and Protestant influence fell. As this situation developed, the class differences that remained seemed less and less important to either party.

Industry. Initially, industry played a relatively insignificant role in the economy. In 1926 its share of the gross domestic product was only 18 per cent and less than 17 per cent of the national work force was categorized as "producers, makers and repairers." Even the latter census category, which is the only one cross-classified by religion, gives an exaggerated impression of the numbers actually involved in industry because it included many service and craft occupations unconnected with industrial enterprises. Since most factories were also rather small and geared to the tiny home market, industry accounted for no more than 8 per cent of the nation's export trade in 1926.[9]

However, there were a small number of large concerns with extensive and profitable export markets. Three of the most prominent were Protestant firms. Guinness's and John Jameson respectively dominated the brewing and distilling industries and the third was Jacobs', the large Quaker-owned biscuit firm. It was not possible to obtain information on major firms throughout the country, but in the provincial city I have called Kingstown Protestants were agreed that they dominated the city's small industrial sector before World War II. At this time, five of the largest firms were owned by Protestants, and no Catholics could be remembered in their managerial ranks before the 1950s. Similarly, older employees of Guinness's in Dublin recalled that the great majority of managers and even most clerical workers were Protestants during this early period. This impressionistic evidence must be borne in mind when interpreting the census of 1926. In its producers, makers, and repairers category, Irish Anglicans were only 11 per cent of its highest-status occupational grouping, which included owners, managers, and sometimes foremen. Even in specific industrial activities, minority influence was not above 30 per cent in any area, although a rather singular concentration of Presbyterians and Methodists in printing did lead to a 48 per cent rate of Protestant influence. Church of Ireland managers and owners of large firms were probably swamped in the census by the approximately 50 per cent of firms that employed less than fifteen persons, and that accounted for a very low proportion of total employment and output.[10] Indeed, it is entirely possible that Protestants were the dominant force in this fledgling industrial sector. But once again, the fact that 88 per cent of Irish Anglicans were ordinary workers in 1926 thoroughly undermines any notion that they were all members of the economic elite.

From these meagre beginnings, Irish industry showed greater signs of expansion than any other sector of the economy. Between 1926 and 1958 manufacturing's share of exports rose from 8 to 25 per cent, and by 1974 it had more than doubled again to 55 per cent. As these figures indicate, industrialization took many years to become established. Under the protectionist policies initiated by de Valera in the early 1930s, industrial employment expanded quite rapidly for a few years by providing local manufactured goods for the small home market. But per capita productivity grew slowly and few of the new firms made any contribution to export trade. With the exception of another short burst after World War II, the even more sluggish pattern initiated by the war continued until the late 1950s when the government initiated a new set of economic policies.

Foreign investment then began to be encouraged; the export trade was made more appealing by various kinds of tax relief; and grants were provided for new industrial enterprises, especially those geared to the export market. With a view to free trade with Britain, the government also started to dismantle its protective tariffs – a process which culminated in Ireland's entry into the European Economic Community. In this new climate, the previous stagnation of the economy was rapidly reversed, with industry experiencing more sustained growth than ever before. Per capita incomes and industrial productivity increased rapidly; employment in industry rose by almost a third; and by 1973 industry finally outstripped agriculture as a source of employment. Ireland was still the poorest and least industrialized country in the EEC at the time of its entry in 1973, but this should not obscure the immensity of the changes that have occurred in recent years.[11]

Unfortunately, precise comparisons between 1926 and 1971 cannot be made as a result of changes in the census format. However, it would appear that the minority was highly successful in maintaining and actually increasing its relative position of privilege in industry. In 1971 less than 1 per cent of Catholics and more than 6 per cent of Irish Anglicans were listed in the census as managers, directors, and company secretaries. On the other hand, Church of Ireland labourers and workers in the broad producers, makers, and repairers category outnumbered their coreligionists in higher management by a ratio of two to one, whereas the Catholic ratio was at the far higher level of 22 to one. Although these figures were not confined exclusively to industrial occupations, they strongly suggest that the size of the Church of Ireland working class diminished considerably after 1926.

Over the same period, Irish Anglicans also succeeded in retaining a very substantial degree of influence for a community that composed just over 3 per cent of the total population of the country in 1971. According to the census of that year, 15 per cent of managers were still members of the Church of Ireland. Among senior managers, a small survey in 1972 indicated that 24 per cent were Protestants,[12] and another large survey of Dublin males in 1968 found that 25 per cent of those in its top-ranking stratum were non-Catholics.[13] These figures might lead one to think that little had really changed since the 1920s. But such a conclusion would be unwarranted because it does not take account of the marked economic growth of recent years. Although the managerial category in the census was not used until 1961, minority influence fell from 20 to 15 per cent over the next ten years. The social implications of this trend are much more apparent when we see that the number of Catholic managers, directors, and company secretaries increased by 52 per cent, whereas the number of Irish Anglicans in this category actually fell by 2 per cent. In fact, the 3,773 *new* Catholic managerial personnel who emerged in this short span outnumbered by almost two to one all Church of Ireland managers in 1971. Much the same sort of trend may also be observed in Hutchinson's detailed study of social mobility in Dublin. He found that over 70 per cent of the current members of the two highest strata came from backgrounds of lower social status. This very high rate of upward mobility was not, in his view, due to an exceptionally strong sense of equality in Irish society. In the main, he attributed it to recent economic growth which greatly expanded the opportunities for upward mobility by increasing the number of upper and middle-class positions. This was particularly true of the highest social strata, where 60 per cent of the current positions simply did not exist a generation ago. In the face of the expansion of the upper strata, non-Catholics were able to do little more than maintain their previous numbers because their overall population was declining. It follows that the great majority of these new positions in the upper class were filled by Catholics who, in effect, engulfed the older, non-Catholic elite. Hutchinson did not specifically document the mobility trends of Catholics and non-Catholics, but reasoning of this sort must surely lie behind his conclusion that "the erstwhile social dominance of non-Catholics is drawing to a close."[14]

Hutchinson's analysis of Dublin is confirmed by rather different information I collected on the degree of Protestant ownership in the provincial city of Kingstown. As late as 1966 eleven of the twenty-two "industries" listed in the city's guidebook were identified as Irish Protestant by members of the local community. Reflecting the low level of industrialization at even this late date, the term industrial was applied to enterprises as diverse as a large bakery and a seed and nursery business. As some of these firms had already become public companies by this time, local residents were not always certain of the precise degree of Protestant ownership. The management of six of the eleven firms was largely Protestant, and it is this core group which Protestants regarded as particularly their own. Since they were less than 3 per cent of the city's population, this represented a quite remarkable degree of influence. However, radical change occurred after 1967 when a new industrial estate was established on the edge of the city. With the added encouragement of tax incentives and government grants, a large number of new Irish and foreign manufacturing companies were attracted to the estate and to the surrounding area. By 1973 the local chamber of commerce listed thirty-eight firms in all, and by this time only ten were considered to be even nominally in the hands of Irish Protestants. In rough terms, this rapid industrial growth led to a very considerable dilution of Protestant influence, since the proportion of industries under their control had fallen from approximately 50 per cent in 1966 to 24 per cent in 1973.

Kingstown is a rather extreme example of Ireland's recent economic growth, and this sort of evidence is not as reliable as the census. Nevertheless, Kingstown does demonstrate in a concrete manner the recurrent theme of this chapter that minority influence was swamped by the enveloping growth of the Irish economy. With economic growth, the middle and upper classes expanded and Catholics were able to rise without displacing Irish Anglicans. As this happened, Catholics had less reason to feel envious and resentful, and the minority's past attitudes of fear and snobbery were steadily undermined. At the same time, as a result of the relatively high rate of decline among Irish Anglicans in the lower classes, their privileged status increased as they became somewhat more concentrated in the middle and upper classes. To some extent, this enhanced their sense of communality. But once again, the growth in the number and proportion of Catholics in the same two classes actually reduced the likelihood that Irish Anglicans would encounter one another for class reasons alone. Thus, in fact as well as in perception, class differences between the two communities were no longer as important a source of division.

THE DECLINE OF THE PROTESTANT FIRM

Until recently, most businesses in Ireland could be readily identified as either Protestant or Catholic. This state of affairs increased the risk of class conflict between the two communities. It did so because the existence of separate Protestant firms made the material advantages of the minority all that much more visible to Catholics. The tendency of these firms to favour their Protestant workers also ensured that middle and lower-class Protestants had many more opportunities for employment and promotion than if they had been forced to compete with Catholics in the same class position. These economic bonds across class lines played an important role in perpetuating the minority's privilege. As we have seen, it was the lower-class members of the Church of Ireland who experienced the greatest numerical decline after 1926. No doubt quite a few emigrated, but others were able to achieve a fair measure of upward mobility within the protective confines of Protestant firms. In other words, there were very practical reasons for the marked sense of economic superiority that once pervaded even the less advantaged sectors of the Church of Ireland community.

This discussion is principally concerned with changes in urban occupations, but it should not be forgotten that many Irish Anglicans were farmers. As most farms were run by the owner and his immediate family, a high degree of segregation was inevitable. Even so, the extent of their isolation should not be exaggerated. On large farms, Church of Ireland owners often relied on Catholic workers since few Protestant labourers were available. Prior to mechanization, smaller farmers often joined forces with local Catholics at the harvest and other peak periods in the agricultural year. In recent years, their tradition of neighbourliness has, if anything, grown stronger, although the need for cooperation has diminished. With mechanization, the demand for labourers declined, and even the harvest was more often than not handled by the farmer and his immediate family. At the same time, new contacts with Catholics were emerging through the increasing number and importance of various farming and marketing associations. On balance, as I propose to show in chapter 7, the two communities were being brought closer together, but the daily round of farming in the 1970s was still a far more segregated activity than most urban occupations.

As the census and other large surveys do not provide information on individual firms, the findings given here are based on the interviews I conducted in 1973 and 1974 within the six sample parishes. By including members of their immediate families, I was able to trace the occupational careers of seventy-nine urban members of the community. In order to differentiate between traditional and contemporary patterns of segregation, 1955 was chosen as a convenient dividing point which preceded the marked changes of the 1960s and yet included an acceptable number of informants. Of the thirty-six who entered the work force before 1955, 29 or 81 per cent found their first position within a firm where the great majority of their immediate co-workers were fellow Protestants. Only two worked for firms that were neither Protestant-owned or managed. There was also an important class difference within this small sample that deserves mention. Although all five manual workers were employed by Protestant or English firms, only one of the five worked primarily with other Protestants. In contrast, twenty-eight (90 per cent) of the thirty-one in white collar occupations took their first position within firms where their immediate co-workers were predominantly Protestant. Some were secretaries, clerks, or owners of small, entirely Protestant shops, businesses, and professional offices, and the rest were part of the mainly Protestant staff and management of larger commercial and industrial enterprises that relied heavily on Catholics in lower positions. Thus the two communities were not always sharply divided into separate firms. While Protestants were rarely employed in Catholic establishments, working-class Protestants often worked alongside Catholics. Within many Protestant firms, segregation was an internal matter of Protestant office workers and Catholic labourers, and in some cases only the managers were largely Protestant. With the top-heavy class structure of the minority, no other form of segregation was possible.

Considering how small the Church of Ireland community was, this represents a remarkable degree of segregation. It is only by examining its social context that one can understand how it survived for such a long time. The small size of so many Irish firms clearly facilitated segregation, although this was not a major factor since internal forms of segregation were maintained in even the largest Protestant firms. It was widely believed that Catholic firms would not look very favourably on a Protestant applicant, but in reality overt discrimination played an equally minor role in channelling the minority into Protestant firms. With the conspicuous exception of three individuals who felt that they had been refused employment in Catholic firms because of their religion, the great majority of those I interviewed had never considered looking beyond their own community. As there were so many Protestants well placed to provide employment, their voluntary segregation did not lead them to feel deprived. In fact, the many material benefits of preserving segregation played a major role in their support for such practices.

To most Protestants, segregation was an inevitable and natural state of affairs. As one of them put it, "Obviously your contacts were mainly Protestant. Qualifications did not matter so much then. You got your job through somebody." No doubt many Catholics were envious, but they too thought along much the same lines. In Dublin during the 1950s Humphries found that Catholics still subscribed to the view that "the greatest economic obligation of kinship in the city" was "to get a relative a job."[15] More recently, Jackson described this traditional and rural way of thinking as a system of "sponsored mobility," where those in positions of authority routinely promoted the interests of individuals to whom they felt under some social obligation.[16] The general outlook of the minority could not be more succinctly described. Hence the prevailing ideas of the day helped to create a climate where Catholics were at least prepared to tolerate, if not to condone, the segregationist tendencies of the minority.

Nevertheless, the resources available to the minority for gaining employment were far more extensive than those that most Catholics could hope to draw upon. Among the working class in particular, the parish church was often an important source of employment. During the late 1940s and 1950s, it was not uncommon for Protestant employers with vacant positions to inform the rector, who then announced this information from the pulpit as part of the regular Sunday service. In other cases, employers kept in touch with the leaders of the major youth organization in the poorer parishes, the Boys' Brigade, with the result that "the Captain always looked after his boys when they left." The Church of Ireland also ran an employment agency after 1925, and in 1944 the Dawson Employment Bureau was established for "employers and unemployed members of the Church of Ireland."[17] The leaders of the Boys' Brigade believed that Protestant employers were attracted to the young men of their parishes because they tended to be hard working, honest, reliable, and generally averse to the common Irish pastimes of horses and stout. This fundamentalist ethos of working-class parishes certainly existed at one time,[18] but its presence should not lead us to underestimate the way in which the parish served as an organized link with Protestant employers – and hence as a source of both economic security and religious commitment.

For those from more privileged backgrounds, family and other community connections were equally important in obtaining employment. Prior to World War II, applicants in banking were sometimes sponsored by a substantial depositor and a bank manager. The segregated social life of the minority normally ensured that both these resources were much more readily available to Protestants than Catholics. As one older banker recalled, few Catholic applicants would have had the good fortune to find that they were "in the same cricket club" as one of the men who conducted the interview. Since many managerial and professional skills at this time were acquired after entry into a firm, employers attached much less significance to pre-existing qualifications in selecting employees. What mattered were rather more subjective considerations, such as whether an employee would "fit in" and was of "sound character." Such a managerial style was obviously suited to the religiously selective inclinations of many Protestant employers. Of course, a secondary education was normally required for most middle-class positions. In such cases, Protestant secondary schools were the major institutional connection with Protestant firms. Through their well-established old-boy network, most headmasters found that "we had no difficulty finding places for our boys." The commercial courses offered in certain schools may well have strengthened the interest of Protestant employers, but the appeal was clearly restricted, for those headmasters interviewed could not recollect any Catholic firms enquiring after "our boys." Similarly, for women, there were secretarial colleges run by Miss Littlewood and Alexandra College, to name two of the more prominent, which again catered primarily to the Protestant business community. And at a later point in the careers of the middle class, the exclusive fellowship and social contacts of Freemasonry were widely regarded as being "crucial in business."

For younger members of the community, their choice of a Protestant firm was often an almost unconscious response to these wider educational and social divisions. However, underlying these insulating mechanisms was a rooted determination among many Protestant employers to avoid hiring Catholics whenever possible. Public evidence of this is understandably scarce. In one of its rare condemnations of "Protestant jobbery," the *Gazette* was quick to point out that "there are at least three parties to be reckoned with in a private business: the employer, the employee and the customer."[19] White found a small number of employment notices in the *Irish Times* during the 1920s which, despite the risk of arousing Catholic hostility, specifically requested Protestant applicants.[20] Although this was not very common, there were still many firms at a much later date in which "Protestants got in straight away." As so many expressed it, "what counted was what foot you dug with." The segregated institutional and social life usually enabled employers to exercise their preferences discreetly without requiring any public rejection of Catholics. Otherwise, positions were publicly advertised without reference to religion, but the result was normally much the same, for the practice in one insurance company was to identify Catholic applicants by their schooling, and these were "put aside." Since "jobs were scarce then" and "we could pick and choose," there was rarely any need to turn to the secondary list of Catholic applicants. Such practices may not have been applied universally, but there was widespread agreement that "we looked after our own then" as much as circumstances permitted.

By the 1970s the segregationist tendencies of the minority had undergone a very striking decline. In fact, only eighteen (24 per cent) of the seventy-six Irish Anglicans on whom information was collected in 1974 still worked primarily with other Protestants. For the period before 1955 the corresponding figure was 80 per cent. Of these eighteen individuals, seven were employed in small family businesses; five were independent professionals; and six were managers of small enterprises, though most of their clerical staff and virtually all of their workers were Catholics. In other words, segregation survived in only the smallest firms. Since blue-collar workers had not been much segregated in the past, the transformation was most marked among managers and clerical workers in medium and larger firms. In addition, 63 per cent now worked in firms that were owned or controlled by Protestants, and this was true of only 59 per cent of salaried employees. Again this represents a fundamental change from the 90 per cent whose first job in the years before 1955 was in a Protestant firm. Thus not only was the old tradition of the exclusively Protestant firm fading, but the minority was showing signs of a new willingness to take up careers within the Catholic world.

Within the offices of Protestant firms, desegregation tended to develop more rapidly among clerical workers than managers, although the actual timing and degree of extensive Catholic entry varied considerably. In Kingstown, for instance, half of the secretaries and clerks were Catholics in three of the major Protestant firms by the 1940s, whereas the largest and last company to hire a Catholic secretary did not do so until the 1950s. By 1974 two of the five major firms relied exclusively on Catholic clerical workers; two had one Protestant secretary; and the fifth employed five Protestants in its clerical staff of twenty-four. Among managers, on the other hand, there was far less change. All of the managers were Protestants in the mid-1950s, and this was still true of two of the firms in 1974. In one firm with five managers in the 1970s, a Catholic had been recruited as a sales and marketing manager in the 1960s; in another the Protestant proportion shifted from six of eight in 1965 to two of five in 1974; and in the remaining company, a Catholic had been appointed as a managing director in the 1970s. What happened within these five firms underlines the continuing success of Protestants in retaining their position of privilege, although their overall level of influence was greatly reduced by the recent influx of Catholic and foreign enterprises. These firms were also relatively small even by Irish standards. Nevertheless, in the quite intimate atmosphere of their offices, the average proportion of Protestants was only 19 per cent.

In the much larger Protestant community in Dublin, certain firms were able to retain their exclusively Protestant character for a longer period of time. In the central offices of two large and well-known firms, respondents had difficulty remembering any Catholics having been employed there up to and including the early 1960s. I was told that both these firms have since started to employ Catholics in much greater numbers, and by 1974 all but one of the fourteen clerks and secretaries I interviewed were in predominantly Catholic offices. The exception, as might be expected, was a small family-owned business. However, managers in insurance, the brewing industry, and the building trade – areas where Protestant involvement was traditionally high – were agreed that Catholics began to enter their offices in significant numbers during the latter part of the 1950s. Initially they took up rather junior positions, and then they were "gradually brought on – salesmen into the main office and that sort of thing." In 1974 only six of the thirty managers in my small sample dealt primarily with other Protestant managers in their daily activities. But since these changes were slow to take effect, another six more senior managers still found that their colleagues "at higher levels" remained largely Protestant. For the time being, there were very few Catholics in the senior management of many of the old Protestant firms, but their growing number of younger Catholic managers suggests that this will change in the future. Such trends must surely lie behind the striking finding of MacGreil that only 3 per cent of the over 2,000 Catholics he polled in 1973 felt that their religion was "a disadvantage ... in getting on in Dublin."[21] Had he conducted his survey thirty or even twenty years earlier, it is hard to imagine that he would have obtained similar results.

How, then, do we account for this very considerable weakening of the segregationist tendencies of the past? To begin with, the continuous shrinking of the Protestant community made it increasingly difficult for Protestant employers to recruit fellow Protestants, regardless of their personal preferences. The problem was simply that "we couldn't get Protestant workers." But if necessity was the original cause of recruiting Catholics, the steady growth of this practice ensured that segregationist convictions were undermined as the years passed. After 1945 there was also a growing feeling in a number of larger firms that the employment of Catholics in office and sales positions would be "good for business" and would "help to bring in the Catholic orders." A few older clerical workers remembered that there were increasing complaints from Catholic employees over their exclusion from office positions. They claimed that "we were made to feel we had to change." No doubt Catholic protests of this sort were voiced, but their importance should not be overestimated. After all, Catholic office workers had not been employed in many Protestant firms during the highly nationalistic period of the 1920s and 1930s when Catholic sensibilities had been all the more acute. Most managers were insistent that they did not alter their practices "from fear," and they stressed that "we were never boycotted." Nevertheless, there were sound economic reasons for their decision to start recruiting Catholics. Even with the slow economic growth of the years prior to the 1960s, Catholic business activities were expanding in number and strength, while the relative influence of Protestants was steadily diminishing. As this situation developed, Protestant firms had less and less to gain from maintaining their traditional exclusivism. In fact, their best interests now lay in fostering ever closer and more harmonious relations with the expanding Catholic business community. One obvious way of establishing these increasingly profitable links was to employ Catholics in managerial positions.

Another equally potent pressure associated with the accelerated economic growth of recent years was the increasing proportion of large business concerns and the parallel decline of small, family-owned enterprises.[22] As many Protestant firms expanded, the difficulty of retaining an exclusively Protestant staff became all the more acute. In some cases, the very existence of Protestant firms was undermined when expansion involved amalgamation with Catholic concerns. Perhaps the best-known example of this sort of development was the recent merger of the old Protestant establishment of John Jameson's with the Catholic firm of Power's and Cork Distilleries.[23] From my own enquiries, the trend is best illustrated by changes in the retail side of the Dublin dairy industry. Until the 1970s Dublin was served by a number of small dairies. One of the largest was owned and almost entirely managed by Protestants. In the early 1970s it amalgamated with a few of its Catholic competitors. The proportion of Protestants in the new central office was much the same as the four-to-twelve Protestant/Catholic ratio on the new board of directors. As this was such a recent change, the old divisions could still be discerned. In 1974, for instance, the heads of the old Protestant depots were still largely Protestant, while none were to be found in the Catholic depots. But after the merger, hiring for all but the lowest of positions was controlled by the mixed central office. In this new context, religious considerations could no longer predominate because neither Protestants nor Catholics possessed the privacy and organizational independence which had once enabled them to favour their coreligionists. A merger of this type did not directly alter the privileged and influential position of the individual Protestants involved, although their collective control was clearly weakened. Moreover, their continuing economic power was made less visible to the public eye by such mergers, and thereby provoked less social comment and friction.

These organizational changes were accompanied by a growing conviction that considerations of religion in hiring and promotion were neither proper nor economically sound in the modern business world. More than anything else, the emergence of such beliefs cut at the very core of the segregationist practices of the past. In some cases, these new notions were implemented simply because Protestants lost control of recruitment through amalgamations and take-overs. This pattern was especially evident in an English-owned manufacturing company which had retained a "Protestant only" policy among its roughly forty members of staff until as late as 1969. In that year, the parent company was purchased by another English firm. In order to assess their new acquisition, the new owners sent over management consultants who quickly replaced the Protestant manager and radically changed his employment practices. My informant had left by 1973 for a Catholic firm, but by this time "approximately one third of the staff, all of the travellers and many of the office girls" were Catholics.

However, the transformation of managerial policy was so widespread that it cannot be attributed solely to external pressures of the sort just mentioned. It is better seen as a product of the rapidly industrializing economy of the 1960s and 1970s which required an increasingly educated and technically skilled labour force in its pursuit of productivity and profit. The Irish Management Institute described it as "the beginning of a new era of planned growth, the time when 'the ice age melted ... people began to challenge established practices and the inflow of new ideas about management began to turn into a flood'."[24] In this changed atmosphere, no Protestant manager was prepared to justify or defend the selective recruitment practices of the past. Invariably, they now argued that "religion doesn't enter into it any more." These sweeping statements must be viewed with some suspicion, especially in relation to smaller firms, but there is more substantial evidence to suggest that much had changed. The most obvious is the fact that Catholics were now penetrating the managerial ranks of Protestant firms. Clergy and headmasters also claimed that calls from Protestant employers steadily declined over the 1960s, and by 1974 they had virtually died out. Reliance on the Dawson employment agency diminished so much that it eventually closed in 1972. Increasingly, employers were looking for technical and other educational qualifications that often could not be provided by the Protestant school system. "We were looking for a cost accountant who was trained," explained one manager, who, though he had been recruited in the old way, had recently hired a Catholic. "Certainly he was taken on merit. Before they came straight from school." To meet this demand, Protestant headmasters found that a growing proportion of their pupils were going on to vocational schools, technical colleges, and university. With the exception of Trinity, these institutions were not a part of the former old-boy network of the minority, and the formal qualifications they provided to Protestant and Catholic alike further increased the likelihood of open competition. Moreover, with the recent intake of Catholics into Trinity and Protestant secondary schools, even the more conservative managers were now more reluctant to turn to their old sources as they could no longer be assured of getting a Protestant. Taken together, these changes in the outlook and organization of Irish society ensured that Protestant employers grew less willing and less able to perpetuate the segregation of the past.

By making less visible the remaining privilege and influence of the minority, the demise of the exclusively Protestant firm contributed to the decline of class differences that was described earlier. The underlying causes of both these major developments were the shrinking size of the Church of Ireland community and the recent changes associated with economic growth and industrialization. Their immediate consequence was to undermine the economic divisions and tensions that once prevailed between the two communities. However, the latter economic trends of economic growth and industrialization also had ramifications far beyond the narrow concerns of this chapter. The wider implications of these trends cannot be explored here, but as we proceed it would be well to remember that the changes they wrought in the structure of Irish society helped to transform relations between Protestants and Catholics in areas as diverse as politics, education, and social life.

Church and Faith

The importance of ethnic and class differences should not lead us to underestimate the central role of church and faith in shaping relations between the two communities. Religion, after all, was the basic symbol of communal division. As other tensions began to fade, communal boundaries became increasingly dependent on the deep sense of religious identity felt by most Irishmen. As late as the early 1960s, Donald Connery, a perceptive American commentator, could rightly claim that "Religion matters more in Ireland than in any other country in the English-speaking world."[1] Twenty years later, it would still be difficult to quarrel with Connery's observation, but by this time the traditionally divisive character of religion was showing many signs of transformation and decline. Before examining these recent developments, we must first come to some understanding of the intense religious hostilities that pervaded the earlier period.

THE RELIGIOUS DIVIDE
BEFORE VATICAN II

The great importance most Irish Anglicans attached to matters of religion can be understood only in the light of the strongly Catholic environment in which they found themselves. On certain political matters – most notably the activities of the IRA – the Catholic laity were prepared to disregard the advice and the words of condemnation of their clergy. But elsewhere the largely secular state created by the treaty of 1921 was quickly moulded by both parties to reflect the Catholic identity of the great majority of the inhabitants. Although Protestant critics at times claimed that the Catholic church was the effective ruler of the country, J.H. Whyte's detailed research has shown that the Catholic hierarchy rarely involved itself directly in the legislative process.[2] In fact, there was little need for the church to interfere. As good Catholics, legislators and voters were themselves deeply committed to expressing their faith in the institutions and laws of the country. One crude manifestation of this commitment is to be found in the evidence of various surveys that a minimum of 80 per cent of Catholics attended mass on a weekly basis.[3] For the shrinking Church of Ireland community, the visible and disturbing result was that the number of Catholic religious increased by 43 per cent in the years prior to 1961 when the Catholic population was actually declining. But these statistics and legislative changes do not give an adequate picture of the intensely Catholic character of the country. The detailed reporting of ecclesiastical news, the daily Angelus on radio and television, photographs of the pope and religious pictures in private homes, the invariable prominence of Catholic clergy in public life, and the omnipresent collecting boxes for Catholic welfare and missionary activities – all these expressed a vividly Catholic ethos. In such a climate, even the most diffident of Irish Anglicans could not help but be acutely conscious of their separate and marginal status.

The attitude of the Catholic church towards non-Catholics before the Second Vatican Council can be best described as one of aggressive exclusivism. At the very least, Irish Anglicans were considered to be fundamentally in error in their religious thinking. Except for the purpose of conversion, contact with non-Catholics was officially discouraged on the grounds that it might threaten or contaminate the faith of the laity.[4] These attitudes were particularly evident in the treatment accorded to mixed marriages. As a rule, the Catholic church was reluctant to sanction their occurrence unless the non-Catholic partner converted to Catholicism. If conversion did not occur, permission was grudgingly granted only when the terms of the Ne Temere decree were met. Even then, the suspect character of the Protestant partner was still publicly affirmed by the common requirement that the wedding service be held in the sacristy rather than before the main altar of a Catholic church.[5] At this time, the Catholic church also insisted that its laity not attend Protestant church services. When a respected Protestant died, this rule created a not uncommon situation where those Catholics who wished to pay their last respects could do no more than stand outside the Protestant church while the burial service was being conducted. Thus even in those few situations where Catholics wished to reach across community boundaries, their efforts to do so were thwarted by the demands of their church.

However, the most consequential form of exclusivism stemmed from the Catholic church's insistence that its laity attend schools under its control. This expectation existed throughout the Catholic world, but Ireland was one of the few countries where the stricture extended to university level. This singular prohibition on attendance at Trinity College Dublin reminds us that the Catholic attitude to Protestants had a distinctively Irish thrust.[6] For most Catholics, both Trinity and the Church of Ireland were inextricably associated with the earler period of Protestant Ascendancy. The material and social advantages that had been conferred on Irish Anglicans at that time inevitably soured Catholic attitudes. Through their schooling in particular, there were very few Catholics who did not know of the penal law era when their ancestors and their church had suffered for devotion to their faith at the hands of the Protestant establishment. With this heritage, even sympathetic Catholic observers readily admitted that many of their older brethren could not have been convinced by "the Pope himself" that "Protestants can win salvation."[7]

Belief and ritual: Defending identity and pedigree. In the early 1930s a three-volume history of the Church of Ireland was produced at the specific request of the church's General Synod in order to serve "as a measure of defence against hostile propaganda."[8] What disturbed Irish Anglicans was the prevalent Catholic view that "The Church of Ireland has always been and still continues to be the Church of the English colony in Ireland."[9] Around the same time, a number of pamphlets were also written for "the ordinary members of our Church" in order "to supply answers to certain questions which constantly arise ... as regards the position and claims of our Church."[10] Similar pamphlets have been published from time to time for well over a century, but the greatest number appeared either in the period before and after disestablishment (1869) or in the late 1920s and 1930s. These were both times when Irish Anglicans were under strong pressure to redefine their sense of identity. In the earlier period, they were forced to reassess their relationship with the Church of England, and in the latter years they were confronted with the complete severing of the English connection and an even more ascendant Catholicism. As some of the pamphlets were used in schools and as many of the ideas they contained were often propounded from the pulpit before the 1960s, the historical interpretations they espoused had a wide currency. In many ways, they may be seen as a folk history of the Church of Ireland community. As such, they will not be judged for their historical accuracy. Their main value lies in the insight they provide into the minority's threatened sense of identity and the form of the religious response that was available.

The pamphlets stressed that the Church of Ireland could trace its origins back to the very beginnings of Christianity in Ireland. This theme of uniformity of doctrine with the early or "Primitive Church" is and was universal within Anglicanism. In the Irish context, it may be crudely described as involving the view that St Patrick was a Protestant. No other assertion was emphasized so heavily and none engendered greater controversy. In fact, many of the pamphlets in the 1930s were specifically written to counter Catholic ecclesiastics who had publicly "challenged the claim of the Church of Ireland to represent the Church of St. Patrick." The Church of Ireland arguments consisted of demonstrations that St Patrick's mission was not commissioned by Rome; that he and the early Irish church did not recognize the pope's authority; and that in all essentials of practice and doctrine, only the present-day Church of Ireland was in full conformity with the teaching of St Patrick. For these and other reasons that will follow, Irish Anglicans were insistent that only their church was justified in calling itself the Church of Ireland.

According to the pamphleteers, the initial independence of the Celtic period did not last. Just as the nationalist canon held that Ireland had suffered 700 years of foreign domination, so the minority argued that the Church of Ireland had undergone four centuries of subservience to Rome and an additional three centuries of English interference. This original autonomy was seen to be eroded in the twelfth century by a "Romanizing party" which eventually established the pope as the new head of the church and brought it into conformity with Roman practice. As this development preceded and overlapped with the Norman conquest of Ireland under Henry ii, it was often claimed that the Roman influence was introduced by Henry. As one writer put it, "The Church of Ireland resisted the Roman innovations but was no match for Rome backed by its ally England." Thus, in a neat reversal of contemporary nationalist thinking, the Church of Ireland portrayed Catholicism, and not itself, as the imposed and alien religion of the English. Indeed, some pamphleteers argued that since Henry's conquest had been sanctioned by the pope, it was the Catholic church, and again not their own, which was the antinational institution that had brought about the English conquest of Ireland.

Roman authority during the next 400 years was charged with introducing new and false doctrine for which there was no Patrician support; with supporting the English colony at the expense of the Irish; and with undermining the moral and physical fibre of the Irish church. In the opinion of the pamphleteers, this sorry state of affairs led the Irish people to embrace the principles of the Reformation and to "reject the Pope's supremacy." It followed, they claimed, that the Reformation did not bring about the creation of a new church but only the casting off of a much later imposition of Roman authority and doctrine. They also maintained that the great majority of the bishops and clergy accepted the terms of the Reformation and carried on as before. This contention was extremely important, for it was upon these grounds of episcopal and doctrinal continuity with the Celtic church that the Church of Ireland laid claim to the ancient cathedrals and churches of the country and rejected "the common assertion of Roman Catholics that the churches were taken from them." For the pamphleteers, it was the Catholic Church which deserved to be called a new church. They argued that its bishops were not part of the Irish episcopal succession but were new appointees of the pope and other foreign ecclesiastics. In the tendentious words of the pamphlet literature, "The present Roman mission dates from 1614. It is an Italian run mission both un-Irish and un-Apostolic in character."

Although the Church of Ireland was now free of Roman influence, it was characterized as suffering from the continued intervention of the English. Again, this was a crucial argument, for it enabled Irish Anglicans to explain many of the more embarrassing episodes of the seventeenth century. Their church's failure to retain the loyalty of the great mass of the Irish people was attributed to its inability to recruit Irish-speaking clergy and to the lack of an Irish prayer book and bible. But more than anything else, most writers stressed that the root cause of their church's failure lay in the renewed efforts of the English to conquer Ireland. Since the Reformation had already spread in England, "Everything ... which was anti-English became also anti-Reformation." Thus, in spite of the superior claims of the Church of Ireland, it was argued that "new emissaries of Rome" were able to take advantage of "Irish ignorance and Irish antipathies" – and "the great opportunity was lost." During this tumultuous period, the pamphleteers emphasized, "Cromwell and his Puritan soldiers were fanatical opponents alike of Roman Catholicism and Anglicanism." The Catholic community, they acknowledged, had suffered greatly at this time, but they stressed that their own church and laity had also experienced persecutions, massacres, and evictions under Charles I and James II. Eventually, of course, after almost 100 years of turmoil, "the Battle of the Boyne ... ended this menace to our Church."

The pamphleteers did not deny "the unfortunate policy" of the penal laws which followed, but they pointed out that these were only partly enforced and were modelled on similar laws against Protestants in France. They also emphasized that the penal era of the eighteenth century was a period when the Church of Ireland "was almost completely dominated by English political interests." This tendency to blame England for the excesses and inadequacies of their church developed into a much more explicitly anti-English stance in a pamphlet written in 1955: "The English Government, regarding Ireland as a colony, ... did not even trust Irish Protestants, and it showed this by filling all important posts, including ecclesiastical posts, by as many Englishmen as could be found willing to accept them, regardless of course of their degree of fitness for appointments. The Church of Ireland was, in fact, driven in upon itself by political conditions and became for a time little more than the Church of the English in Ireland." The pamphlet writers were agreed that during the following century, the physical and spiritual life of their church improved as more and more Irish bishops were appointed. However, only with disestablishment did the Church of Ireland again describe itself as entering an era of "independence like the ancient Celtic period." And since 1871 members of the Church of Ireland have been emphatic in their insistence that their church "is by no means the Church of England in Ireland."

Taken as a whole, such notions must have been particularly appealing to Irish Anglicans in the years after 1922. Besides furnishing justification in such sensitive matters as their occupancy of the old church buildings of the country, the pamphlets provided a view of the past that stressed their ancient and indigenous origins as an integral part of the country. Rather than apologizing for their British colonial heritage, they could ignore it by turning to the religious element in their ancestry. At times, they could even reverse the tables by accusing the Catholic majority of being the followers of a more recent and foreign religious tradition. Yet in stressing the religious aspect of their history and in defending themselves from the controversies of the past, the pamphlet writers tended to portray England as an alien and disruptive force in the history of their community and country. In so doing, the Church of Ireland itself played a part in weakening and discrediting the ethnic component of the minority's identity.

Irish Anglicans probably found it reassuring to know that they had at their disposal such a detailed defence of their past, but in day-to-day life they tended to express their religious identity in much less historical and abstract terms. They believed that what set them apart from their Catholic neighbours was their commitment to a distinctive body of religious values. Those most frequently cited were the values of individualism, freedom of conscience, honesty, reliability, and respect for the true historical record. The clear if rarely stated implication was that these attributes were less common among Catholics. Whether value differences of this sort once existed cannot be ascertained, but their role in defending the social position of the minority prior to the 1960s must be evident. The espousal of individualism helped to justify the lack of sympathy Irish Anglicans felt with developments in Irish society after 1922. Similarly, their commitment to the ideal of freedom of conscience served as an acceptable religious basis of opposition to the cultural traditions of the Catholic majority which they felt were being thrust upon them. Their stress upon the moral virtues of Protestantism no doubt helped Irish Anglicans to rationalize their economic advantages at a time when many Catholics were questioning their right to retain this privileged status. Closely allied to this, their emphasis on responsibility as a consequence of their faith was well suited to a community whose members occupied so many influential positions in the economy. Finally, their tendency to equate their religion with a sense of the true historical record enabled them to justify an attitude of critical and aloof suspicion towards those Catholics who questioned their right to consider themselves genuinely Irish.

Despite the obvious influence of their class and ethnic interests, Irish Anglicans believed that their values were derived primarily from their religion. However, there is little to be gained from an attempt to link these values to the formal theological principles of the Church of Ireland. In fact, an exercise of this sort would be misleading. The Thirty-nine Articles, which summarize the essential doctrines of Anglican churches throughout the world, have long emphasized a careful balancing of Protestant and Catholic principles – what Anglican theologians have described as a via media. But for Irish Anglicans, the essence of their faith centred on their strong affirmation of its Protestant and Reformed character. As was accurately observed, "The Irish layman does not think or call himself Anglican but 'Protestant' using the word in a sense now almost obsolete elsewhere."[11] He was Protestant because he protested against what he saw as the errors, accretions, contradictions, superstitions, and intolerance of Catholicism. It was his deep conviction that Catholicism was a false and debilitating faith that undermined the moral and intellectual fibre of its adherents. To prove this, he had at his disposal a tradition and a pamphlet literature which aggressively refuted and ridiculed Catholic doctrines on such matters as infallibility, papal supremacy, the cult of the Virgin Mary, and transubstantiation. When pressed, he would admit he was Catholic in the sense that he held his own religion to be in conformity with early Christianity, but it is a term that was used primarily by the clergy and the theologically sophisticated. Indeed, in the intensely Catholic environment in which Irish Anglicans found themselves, it was almost inevitable that they should feel compelled to suppress the Catholic element in Anglicanism. And since they tended to perceive Catholicism as the inferior religion of a peasantry, their denial of the Catholic component of their own faith must also be seen as a symbolic assertion of their determination never to sink into what they regarded as being a "lower civilisation."[12]

These anti-Catholic sentiments were held with such conviction that a largely lay movement was initiated at the time of disestablishment to purge the Church of Ireland of all manifestations of "Popery."[13] For a few years, there was intense debate as to how the church should use its newly acquired freedom. Some were opposed to any change, whereas many others simply wanted to ensure that the Anglo-Catholic movement of the Church of England should not take hold in Ireland. There was also a group with more extreme views who wished to lead their church into a new union with all the Protestant denominations in Ireland by altering those practices and doctrines to which the Dissenters objected – thereby, in effect, removing the Church of Ireland from the Anglican communion. In the event, no significant change of doctrine was implemented. The bishops were especially resistant to any possibility of their church becoming "only a Protestant sect,"[14] and most laity were reluctant to support any measure that might increase the already widening gulf between themselves and England. However, this groundswell of Protestantism did bring about a number of changes in the rules regulating the conduct of church services. These distinctive canons, which remained virtually unchanged until the 1960s, deserve particular attention. More than any other aspect of the minority's religious tradition, the canons concretely expressed in regular communal activity the deeply Protestant character of the Church of Ireland.

Essentially, the canons ensured that the potential similarities of Anglican and Catholic liturgy would be suppressed within the service of the Church of Ireland. Thus crosses of any kind were not permitted on, behind, or above the communion table, and stringent rules required that it be a plain wooden structure with no more than a simple covering. The clear purpose was to differentiate it as much as possible from the often more ornate altar used in Catholic services. In a similar vein, lamps and candles were not permitted "except for the purposes of giving light;" incense was prohibited; and bells were not allowed to be rung "during the time of Divine Service." Significantly enough, the canons used the term minister rather than that of priest, which was used in the Thirty-nine Articles and in the Catholic church. This distinction was further underlined by the requirement that ministers not be allowed to wear any of the rich ecclesiastical vestments used by Anglo-Catholics and Catholic priests. With the apparent intent of ensuring that there should be no evidence of idolatry, the canons stipulated that the minister should not "bow or do any act of obeisance to the Lord's Table, or anything there or thereon." During the central section of the service of Holy Communion, the minister was instructed to stand at the north side of the communion table and not in front of it, as was done in other parts of the Anglican communion and in the Catholic church. Moreover, in order to symbolize the Church of Ireland's rejection of the Catholic doctrine of transubstantiation, it was specifically required of the minister that he not "elevate" the paten or cup "beyond what is necessary for the taking of the same" into his hands.[15] Finally, any remaining similarities to Catholic ritual not covered by the canons were further reduced by informal custom. This was most evident in the secondary role accorded to the normally central service of Holy Communion. It was common practice to hold it either early in the morning when few attended, or after the major Sunday service of Morning Prayer. In the latter case, the vast majority of those attending Morning Prayer walked out of the church during a short interval before the start of Holy Communion. At least with Morning Prayer, there could be no doubt that a Protestant service was being conducted.

In order to protect the unambiguously Protestant character of the church's ritual, the canons called for the setting up of a court of clergy and laity in any case of ritual impropriety. If they wished, the laity were entitled to initiate complaints on their own, and the court was empowered to suspend any clergyman who resisted its judgment. Since 1922 only two rather atypical parishes in Dublin with high church traditions have been involved in court proceedings. However, rather than indicating lay indifference on the matter, this low level of litigation should be seen a sign of the strength and unanimity of lay conviction.[16] With a society of laymen "always ready to prosecute anyone"[17] who broke the law, both the letter and the spirit of the canons were observed almost universally in the years prior to the 1960s. Of course, most Anglican clergy educated in Ireland probably accepted the anti-Catholic sentiments that lay behind the regulations. But any clergyman who might still have been inclined to resist these social and legal pressures quickly discovered that he was subject to the even more compelling power of the laity in the making of ecclesiastical appointments. As one cleric observed, "The faintest alteration in doctrine or ceremonial from that to which they have become accustomed may constitute a fatal bar. A rumour of churchmanship of a certain type will stop his promotion for the rest of his life, or so long as he remains in Ireland."[18] In short, the canons of the Church of Ireland created an effective mechanism for the expression of the minority's strongly felt Protestant identity, while through its pamphlets the church provided a much needed interpretation of the minority's heritage.

Church and clergy: The guardians of communal boundaries. With the collapse of unionist organizations after 1922 and the increasing scarcity of Protestant politicians, community leadership and organization became the major responsibility of the Church of Ireland and its clergy. At the national level, these tasks were supervised by the church's General Synod during its four-day annual meeting. It devoted much of its time to the internal affairs of the church, but it also heard reports and made decisions on such matters as education and social services. Since these important areas of social life were largely organized along denominational lines before the 1960s, the General Synod was a very considerable force in the everyday lives of the laity. Especially in the field of education, its committees negotiated with the government whenever Protestant interests appeared to be threatened, and they proved to be quite willing to criticize the government's Irish language policy. But in many other areas – most notably political relations with Britain and the growing Catholic character of the state – church spokesmen were usually reluctant to voice publicly the grievances of their laity. According to the *Gazette,* many believed that the Church of Ireland "should refrain from drawing too much attention to herself lest such attention should result in material or social disadvantage." In the same editorial, the *Gazette* went on to state that it "did not for one moment believe that any such result would follow,"[19] but thinking of this sort undoubtedly lay behind this public quiescence. The net result was that the General Synod and the clergy served primarily as rather cautious leaders within the confines of their own community.

In 1978 the General Synod contained all bishops in an ex-officio capacity and 648 elected members on the basis of two laymen for every clerical representative.[20] General Synodsmen were elected according to predetermined quotas by the diocesan synods of the twelve united dioceses into which the Church of Ireland was divided. Although approximately 80 per cent of all Irish Anglicans lived in Northern Ireland by the 1970s, the South retained a much stronger influence in the General Synod than this demographic differential suggests. Diocesan boundaries did not coincide fully with the border, but in 1974 those dioceses predominantly within the Republic still accounted for just over 50 per cent of the voting strength of the General Synod. Prior to 1968 the southern dioceses controlled 61 per cent of the votes, and before 1945 they held a majority of 71 per cent.[21] The southern influence was also strengthened by the continued use of Dublin, rather than Belfast, as the site of the General Synod and as the administrative centre of the church. Even in 1978, 64 per cent of the General Synod's powerful Standing Committee was made up of members from the South. The growing electoral power of the northern dioceses in the General Synod suggests that it will become increasingly dominated by northern interests. This trend may also explain in part why a more critical and outspoken attitude began to be expressed by the General Synod during the 1970s. However, in the earlier period with which we are now concerned, the General Synod was well able to voice the particular needs of the minority in the South.

Below the General Synod were the diocesan synods which also met annually to deal with administrative and social issues arising within their own areas. These synods were normally made up of two laymen for every clergyman from each of the parishes within the diocese or group of dioceses under the authority of a bishop. At the annual meeting of the Easter vestry where the diocesan synodsmen were appointed, elections were held for the twelve to eighteen members of the select vestry who assisted the clergyman in the running of the parish. In the normal course of events, there was not much competition for places on the select vestry. In small rural parishes, this still meant that many families were represented on the select vestry. In larger urban parishes, on the other hand, lay leadership tended to be confined to a smaller group of especially active parishioners, although most laity had a strong interest in any important decision made by their select vestry. As these various bodies devoted most of their time to rather dry matters of finance and administration, it would be a mistake to think that their deliberations were avidly followed by the laity. Nevertheless, this three-tiered system of government did provide a geographically wide-ranging and extensively lay-orientated form of national integration.

Within these decision-making structures, the power of the laity was extensive but by no means complete. On all matters before the General Synod, a consensus of two-thirds of the bishops with a written explanation was sufficient to block any measure supported by the clerical and lay representatives. Similarly, at the diocesan level, the bishop could insist that any measure he disagreed with be submitted to the General Synod for a final decision. The bishops rarely exercised these powers, but it was much more common for the clergy and laity to vote separately in both the General and diocesan synods. This was permitted whenever ten members of either "order" indicated their wish to do so. In such cases, a majority of both orders was necessary for the ratification of any decision. This delicate system of checks and balances was also to be found at the parish level. Most notably, the laity possessed what amounted to a veto in the appointment of their clergyman, although they could not impose their will on the diocesan representatives who were also involved in the selection procedure. Moreover, once instituted, the clergyman could not be removed simply on the request of the parish laity. On matters concerning doctrine and the ordering of services, the clergyman was subject only to the authority of his bishop, but he could not ignore the indirect power of the laity in making ecclesiastical appointments and in initiating court proceedings at any sign of ritual deviance. In the running of the day-to-day affairs of the parish, the select vestry was empowered to override the wishes of their clergyman. This mainly applied to the use of parish funds, but the select vestry also held the crucial authority to dictate the membership requirements of the various associations which made use of parish facilities. With this power, the vestry was able to exercise centralized control over any club or group of parishioners which might wish to violate the segregated character of parish social life.

Despite all these constraints, the clergy were the major leaders of their church and community after 1922. They were, after all, the full-time professionals in the field with the time and experience necessary for the task. Prior to the 1960s the great majority were also university-educated men. To some extent, this set them apart from the laity in certain rural and working-class parishes, but it added to their authority and it enabled them to deal comfortably with the laity whose backgrounds were far more privileged. The man who stood out as the principal representative and voice of the church during the first forty years after independence was J.A.F. Gregg.

Between 1920 and 1938 he was archbishop of Dublin, and for the next twenty years he occupied the See of Armagh and served as the head of the entire church.[22] Gregg rarely commented in public on political matters, but he did attempt to guide the laity in their difficult adjustment to the new state. Although he felt a strong personal attachment to Britain and empire, he stressed the pragmatic necessity of offering "to the Irish Free State ... our loyalty and goodwill."[23] Reflecting his ambivalent feelings, he argued that the minority had a duty to accept the new regime precisely because it had been established by a treaty with the British government. This "derivative loyalty" did not escape the criticism of the Catholic press,[24] but it was a policy which he pursued with great consistency. Speaking to Protestants as much as Catholics, he condemned those "who think of us as an alien minority."[25] Again at the General Synod of 1939, he reiterated his belief that he and his community had "an identity genuinely Irish," although he emphasized that it was "not necessary to be Gaelic in order to be Irish."[26] For these reasons, he urged that Gaelic revival could not and should not be the essential cause of division between minority and majority. This determination to play down the importance of ethnic differences was most evident in Gregg's handling of the short-lived controversy over state prayers. For some years after 1922, prayers during Sunday services for the monarch, royal family, and Commonwealth had served as a rallying point for the minority's fading British allegiances. The use of these prayers had been justified on the grounds that Ireland was still part of the Commonwealth which was formally headed by the king. But when the Republic of Ireland Act came into effect in 1949, this rationale no longer existed. At the following General Synod, Gregg successfully argued that "in our prayers, above all, there must be reality."[27] And since that date state prayers in the Republic have been concerned only with the president and government of Ireland, whereas in Northern Ireland prayers for the queen continue to this day.

What pressed most heavily on the morale of the community was the census evidence of their continuing numerical decline. In the face of this trend and their discredited ethnic allegiance, Gregg stressed that "If we are to hold our ground, we need to remember that, ultimately and fundamentally, it is the difference in our religious outlook and pre-suppositions that give our community its character."[28] As members of a small community, he felt that they were under great pressure – "on sociological grounds" – which could be overcome only by "our organized and conscious will ... to stand upon our defence."[29] In this vein, he chided the laity for their small families, their unwillingness to marry, and their late age of marriage. However, the theme Gregg most emphasized was the danger and injustice of mixed marriages under the Ne Temere decree. Unlike their class and ethnic differences with Catholics, here was an issue where Irish Anglicans could see themselves as the aggrieved party – and hence could justify their desire to maintain their separateness. On behalf of all the bishops, Gregg outlined the advice of the church unequivocally at the General Synod of 1946: "... it is hard to prevent such marriages from taking place now and then. But it is desirable that every effort should be made by the parents and friends of our young people to discourage them. And the right time to do it is, not when an intimacy has been formed and love has sprung up, but at an earlier stage, so that young people, before their hearts are captivated, may understand that close friendships (which may ripen into love) should not be formed with those of a different faith. ... The Church which cannot count on a younger generation is doomed to early extinction."[30]

This practical concern with communal survival was strongly reinforced by the intensely anti-Catholic thrust of the pamphlet literature to which Gregg and other clergy contributed. Their outspoken hostility to Catholicism was perhaps most clearly reflected in the pastoral letter by all the Church of Ireland bishops on "The Roman Catholic Dogma of the Assumption" of the Virgin Mary. To underline their feelings on the matter, this official statement was read by the clergy in every parish church throughout the country during Morning Prayer on 12 December 1950. In the letter, the bishops informed their laity that the new Catholic doctrine contained "no historical evidence whatsoever," was "heretical," and stemmed from "a sectarian organisation" which "misrepresents the Catholic faith and exposes it to ridicule." While statements of this sort and most pamphlets did not commend an explicit strategy of exclusivism, their frequent criticism of "Roman error" and their emphasis on the Church of Ireland as the sole representative of St Patrick's faith obviously provided a powerful set of justifications for such behaviour. Thus on the grounds of preserving the purity of their faith and a continuing body of believers, the clergy at this time consistently espoused a policy of social segregation and isolation.

At the parish level, the clergy were well able to practise what they preached. As may be seen from table 13, the minority received an exceptional amount of clerical care. This was true even by the high standards of Irish Catholicism. In 1926 and 1971 religious professionals were somewhat more common within the Catholic community because of their large number of nuns and brothers. But if we focus exclusively on clergymen, who were most likely to be involved in parochial work, we find that Irish Anglicans were actually more "priest ridden" than Catholics on both these occasions. In all but a handful of large Dublin parishes, this meant that the clergy were intimately familiar with most of their parishioners. Formal parish visiting usually did not occur more than twice a year, but through parish activities contact between clergy and laity tended to be much more frequent. Within this parish network, the clergyman had three major responsibilities. First, he and his wife played a prominent role in running the many organized activities connected with the parish. As well as supervising women's guilds, Sunday school, and the like, the clergyman normally managed the local school; he was often called upon to be chairman of local badminton, tennis, and other recreational clubs frequented by his parishioners; and he was expected to provide and supervise segregated dances for the unmarried young adults in his parish. Second, the clergyman acted as a social worker who channelled the philanthropy of his more affluent parishioners within community boundaries. When needed, he administered poor relief which was obtained either from within the parish or from national bodies such as "The Association for the Relief of Distressed Protestants." Clergy also served quite often as informal employment agents, and at times they were called upon to be marriage brokers, seeking suitable Protestant partners through the *Gazette*, diocesan magazines, or other clerical colleagues. Third, the clergyman functioned as a link between the local parish and the national community. This included activities as diverse as the assistance of applicants for places in Protestant schools; the location of Protestant homes and hostels for young people moving to the city for work; the placing of the elderly in Protestant geriatric institutions; and the arrangement of medical care in a Protestant hospital. Together, all these various activities ensured that the parish was at the very centre of the minority's segregated social life and that the clergyman was the principal guardian of its well-defined boundaries.

ORGANIZATIONAL PROBLEMS:
A GENTEEL DECLINE

It would not be an exaggeration to claim that the very existence of a separate Church of Ireland community hinged on the continued presence of this national system of parish churches and resident clergy. The local church and the clergyman were especially impor-

TABLE 13
Church of Ireland Clergy and Parishes, 1926–1971

	1926	1936	1946	1961	1971
Number of clergy	776	700	648	517	428
Number of parishes	657	574	534	387	325
Laity per clergyman	212	207	193	201	228
Laity per parish	250	252	234	269	301
% Population decline in preceding census period		−11.7	−13.9	−16.7	−6.1
% Decline in number of parishes preceding census period		−12.6	−7.0	−27.5	−16.0
% Decline in number of clergy preceding census period		−9.8	−7.4	−19.8	−17.2

tant to the laity in sparsely populated rural areas where they served as a visible and reassuring symbol that Irish Anglicans were not just a scattered collection of individuals but a living and organized community. Table 13 indicates that the number of clergy and parishes diminished considerably after 1926, but it is equally evident that the clergy-laity ratio and the average size of parish remained low and virtually unchanged until 1961. As late as 1965 the average parish in the diocese of Dublin contained fewer then 600 parishioners, while in rural dioceses the typical parish ranged from 129 souls in the southwest to a high of 286 in Cavan.[31] After that date the number of clergy and parishes began to decline at a faster rate than that which was occurring within the community as a whole. But even with a 25 per cent decline in parochial clergy between 1965 and 1977, there was still roughly one parochial clergyman for every 300 laymen in the latter year,[32] and this does not take into account the clergy involved in other activities. Given the small, scattered, and shrinking Church of Ireland population, it is quite remarkable that such an intensive system of parochial care should have survived.

The ability of the church to support this impressive array of clergy was in large measure due to its very healthy financial position. This wealth, in turn, stemmed more from the generosity of previous generations than it did from the weekly and annual donations of the laity. It may be remembered that the church had built up a capital fund of over four million pounds from the settlement provided by the British government at disestablishment in 1871. Around the same time, the laity also made substantial contributions, and this tradition of leaving bequests to the church has continued to the present day. By 1978 the church controlled a capital fund of over £18,000,000 which provided it with an income of £2,000,000 after the deduction of administrative costs. Some of this capital was for the general use of the church, but by far the greater part consisted of a large number of individual bequests and trusts that had been donated to specific parishes and dioceses. Of this latter portion, approximately two-thirds was tied to the southern dioceses.[33] Despite this apparent affluence, much concern was expressed during the 1940s that the church might soon be impoverished by the combined effects of inflation and the diminishing value of old investments at fixed and low rates of return. The crisis was temporarily circumvented by a decision in 1947 that enabled the Representative Church Body of the Church of Ireland to transfer half the money in its care to riskier, but much more profitable, ordinary or preference shares.[34] With this financial rearrangement, the church's investment income had doubled by the 1970s. After meeting all the legally prescribed terms of its various bequests, it found itself with approximately £600,000 to allocate as it wished. Besides clerical pension funds and a variety of administrative costs, this surplus money was used to supplement the salaries of the clergy in the small southern and western dioceses and to subsidize a number of social services in the Republic.[35]

Some idea of the overall importance of the church's inherited wealth may be gained from Archbishop Gregg's estimate in 1947 that "only about a quarter of the stipends paid to the clergy come from the living. The other threequarter is interest on the accumulations left by those who went before us."[36] For more recent times, the financial records of the six parishes where interviews were conducted tell a similar tale. In 1973 only the two Dublin parishes allocated sufficient money from current lay donations to cover the salaries of their clergy, and in one of these parishes 39 per cent of this cost was covered by local parish endowments. In fact, the total amount of lay giving was much greater, for the many other costs involved in the running of the parish were borne exclusively by the laity. This was also true of the other four parishes, but here parochial cash contributions to central sources for the incomes of their clergy were less than the clerical salaries provided by those sources. In the most affluent of these parishes, local investment income exceeded the funds required from central sources and was used for this purpose. In the others, cash donations accounted for between 15 to 61 per cent of the clergyman's income. Even with these subsidies, most parishes had difficulty in generating even a little more than the limited funds expected of them by central sources. It seems clear, then, that many rural parishes would have had great difficulty in retaining a resident clergyman with all the organizational implications of his presence, had it not been for the church's well husbanded and substantial inheritance.

Despite the protection afforded by this inheritance, the church once again began to encounter organizational problems during the 1970s. A major cause was the rapid inflation of these years which consistently exceeded the growth of the church's investment income. In 1976, for instance, the increase in its income amounted to no more than half of the rise in the consumer price index.[37] In order to cope with this pressure, the church was forced to terminate its support of a number of social services. It also found it necessary to cut by 66 per cent the supplementary grants it had once made for clerical incomes in southern dioceses.[38] These cutbacks did not affect the income derived from bequests tied to various parishes and dioceses, but all parishes were forced to raise the level of their lay contributions in order to meet the rising costs involved in maintaining their buildings and in supporting their clergy. The financial difficulties of parishes varied enormously, as some were much better endowed than others. In general, however, smaller rural parishes were most threatened by inflation, since there were so few laity to absorb additional costs. Increasingly, many of these parishes found that the only means of retaining a clergyman was to join with other parishes in the same situation. As table 13 shows, this was not a new development, but now the cause was financial rather than the old pressure of population decline. The magnitude of the problem can be seen in the 1975 decision of the diocese of Cork to reduce the number of its clergy and parishes by 30 per cent at the same time that it demanded up to 50 per cent increases in the financial contributions of its laity.[39]

On the whole, the laity recognized the rationality of these larger groupings, but they found it very difficult to discard old loyalties. In many rural parishes, which were themselves the product of earlier amalgamations, a laity of rarely more than 200 were often dispersed among three, four, and sometimes more churches on an average Sunday. With the loss of their own resident clergyman, the laity in the outlying parishes became less financially and socially involved, and their attendance at church tended to decline. In the larger urban areas, many of the same patterns emerged among the numerous small churches to be found within the city centre. Their demise was also accelerated by the recent flight of the laity to the suburbs. Thus the church found itself in the doubly burdensome position of being under pressure to build new churches at precisely the same time that its resources were being drained by support for so many old and unneeded buildings. For obvious reasons, most of the large suburban parishes were best able to deal with the increased costs of inflation. But even these growing parishes found it difficult to carry on old traditions, for curates were increasingly difficult to obtain and this reduced the once familiar contact between clergy and laity.

As late as the mid-1970s very few parishes in the Republic actually lacked a clergyman for other than financial reasons. After 1945 church leaders occasionally pointed out that the declining value of clerical incomes was deterring young men from taking up careers in the church, but in this earlier period they were mainly concerned with the educational and personal qualifications of the candidates.[40] The church responded to the initial decline in vocations among university graduates by establishing a diploma course in the 1960s for men without university degrees, and another program with stronger connections to Trinity (though still not requiring a secular degree) was set up in the mid-1970s. Although these measures did not fully stem the long-term decline in ordinands, few saw it as a serious problem because the fall in vocations tended to be offset by the diminishing number of parishes and laity. However, the cumulative effect of the trend became apparent in 1974, when figures were published indicating that 24 per cent of the clergy in both the North and the South were over the age of sixty.[41] In 1978 the problem was found to be even more serious, for revised figures showed that 39 per cent of the clergy in the Republic were over sixty and a little over two-thirds were over fifty.[42] In 1975 a report to the General Synod estimated that if current levels of ordinations continued the entire Church of Ireland would lose 151 of its 598 clergy in the next ten years. Even this figure, the report admitted, was misleading because at current levels of recruitment an existing shortage of curates in large parishes was expected to absorb all the new curates ordained between 1975 and 1984.[43] Since most of these large understaffed parishes were in the North, there is every reason to believe that the shortage of clergy will be felt most strongly in the South, and especially in sparsely populated regions with financial problems.

However, the effect of these recent organizational difficulties on the state of the Church of Ireland should not be exaggerated. To meet some of its problems, the General Synod in 1974 introduced an auxiliary ministry of laymen who were empowered to conduct certain church services.[44] Although this meant that the role of guardian of the community's boundaries was becoming a part-time occupation, it created the possibility of keeping many small churches open that might otherwise have closed. It is also possible that clerical vocations may begin to grow again, and it should be remembered that the church's inherited wealth and affluent laity still give it much potential strength. Even in rural areas, the growing inability of amalgamated parishes to serve as centres of social life was largely due to the persistence of old parish loyalties and their falling population. Moreover, with the radical drop in emigration during the 1970s, this latter demographic pressure is likely to diminish. None of these considerations lessens the manpower and financial problems that may arise in the future, but at the end of the 1970s these new pressures had not yet seriously affected the church. For the time being, the Church of Ireland retained a national parochial system and a low clergy-laity ratio capable of preserving communal boundaries. It follows that we must look primarily to the changing attitudes of clergy and laity in order to account for the recent decline in the strength of the religious divide.

ECUMENISM

Except for the occasional outburst of hostile rhetoric, relations between the Church of Ireland and the Catholic church were virtually nonexistent prior to the Second Vatican Council. To the Home Reunion Committee of the Church of Ireland, there was no alternative, since "the old unity policy of the Church of Rome is that of complete absorption into its own system."[45] However, there was a much more ecumenical spirit among the Protestant churches. Ever since 1905 the General Synod has heard and discussed annual reports on various ecumenical endeavours among Protestants. Between 1930 and 1935 the General Synod entered into formal unity talks with the Presbyterian church, and since 1968 these official negotiations have been revived and expanded to include Methodists as well as Presbyterians.[46] To date, no agreed blueprint for unity has been achieved, but the lengthy discussions are indicative of the much closer relations that have always prevailed between the main Protestant churches. At a local level, there has rarely been any opposition to marriages between Protestants of different denominations. Schools, recreational associations, and parish activities have long been mutually open. In some parts of the country, dwindling nonconformist parishes have joined Church of Ireland parishes when their numbers became too small to survive independently. In Waterford, the Church of Ireland donated an unused church to the

Presbyterians, and in Dublin it agreed to share another of its churches with the Methodists.[47] This local disregard for divisions within Protestantism has not brought about unity, largely because of the complexity of the theological problems involved and the failure to achieve it in Britain – always an important role model for the Church of Ireland. In 1979 the prospect of formal unity between the Church of Ireland and the Catholic church was even slimmer, but this should not lead us to underestimate the impact of ecumenism on relations between the two communities.

The new era was initiated in 1966 when the Catholic archbishop of Dublin invited his Church of Ireland counterpart and many other Protestant clergy to an ecumenical meeting at the Mansion House. In recognition of the momentous character of the occasion, the president, the Taoiseach, and a host of other public dignitaries attended, and the proceedings were broadcast on television. At the meeting, an empty chair was left on the platform where a number of Catholic ecclesiastics were seated, but the Church of Ireland archbishop found himself occupying a seat in the body of the hall. The address was highly conservative, stressing the obstacles to unity, and the expected joint blessing at the end never occurred.[48] For the *Gazette*, "The most promising feature ... of the whole affair lay in the disappointment expressed openly by Roman Catholic clergy and laity after the meeting."[49] However, this hardly promising beginning was followed by an increasing number of much more genuinely ecumenical meetings and gestures. A major development was the decision of the Catholic hierarchy in 1966 to permit attendance at non-Catholic church services.[50] This led to such highly publicized events as the attendance of the new Catholic archbishop of Dublin at a citizenship service in the Church of Ireland cathedral of Christ Church. Again numerous politicians and representatives of various churches and official bodies were present, but this time the two archbishops joined together for a blessing at the end of the service.[51] At parish level, shared annual services for unity and for peace were introduced in many parts of the Republic. Local clergy and their respective hierarchies also began to meet and to consult with one another to a greater extent than ever before. This period of public reconciliation culminated in 1973 when the leaders of all the major Irish churches attended a much-heralded conference at Dundalk that committed itself to dealing with a wide range of ecumenical topics and common social concerns.[52] And since that date, the meeting has become a regular event in the Irish ecclesiastical calendar.

In the area of liturgy or ritual, this movement away from

traditional attitudes was symbolized by the 1964 decision of the General Synod to permit the use of crosses on or behind the communion table.[53] Later, many of the prohibitions against bowing and making the sign of the cross during services were removed. Similarly, the "north end" prescriptions, which had once so differentiated the Catholic and Anglican liturgies, were made much less precise.[54] Of even greater significance was the admission by a liturgical committee that a number of clergy had adopted the "westward" position prior to the acceptance of the above change by the General Synod.[55] In the past, such an obvious violation of the canons would have probably led to complaints before the court of the General Synod. But by the 1960s there was no sign of any sustained protest. At the same time, the introduction of the vernacular and the increasing use of hymns in the Catholic liturgy after Vatican II accentuated the similarities in the services of the two religions. And through hearsay and the occasional personal experience, the laity were coming to realize that their respective faiths were much less alien than many had once thought.

These liturgical changes were only one aspect of a much more general tendency to deemphasize the historical and theological controversies of the past which had once justified the minority's exclusivist stance. By the early 1970s the anti-Catholic themes of the previously mentioned pamphlets were rarely propounded by the clergy from the pulpit. The same pamphlets were no longer part of the religious education provided in the vast majority of schools, and few of them could be found in Dublin bookstores by this time. Since the 1960s only one new pamphlet, written by the dean of St Patrick's, could be considered as carrying on the abrasive style of the earlier years.[56] In its place, the clergy tended to lay much greater stress on the themes of tolerance and understanding in the church's attitude towards Catholicism. At the General Synod in 1977, the archbishop of Armagh was still prepared to condemn any suggestion "that the Anglican Reformation came into being because of the lust of Henry VIII," but he was equally willing to chide his fellow Protestants for making "simplistic and erroneous statements ... about the Papacy ... and Roman Catholic theology." "We must," he stressed, "have done with shallow superficialities and appreciate the motives, the complexities, the whole theological and historical background which lie behind the tragic divisions of Christianity."[57] Church leaders also argued that their church had "a special part to play in the reunion movement"[58] as "a bridge-church committed to the reconciliation of the catholic-type and protestant-type communities."[59] In effect, they were placing a new emphasis on the once dormant Catholic element in their own tradition. "In the past," as one country clergyman explained, "our emphasis was on the faults of the Roman Catholic Church. We emphasized our Protestant heritage. Now we emphasize our Catholic heritage."

Ecumenism had an equally profound influence on the leadership of the Church of Ireland clergy at the parish level. Prior to the 1960s they were largely on the periphery of even the most secular of local activities, whereas the Catholic clergy normally played a prominent role. In part this was because the Church of Ireland clergy were reluctant to involve themselves in situations where Catholics were bound to predominate, but it also stemmed from the fact that few invitations were forthcoming. However, this changed radically in the years following Vatican II. On the Catholic side, the recollection of a Catholic curate in a rural parish clearly illustrates the transformation. As a child, he recalled that he had been severely admonished by his parish priest to keep well away from the local Protestant church where the second marriage of a divorced Protestant was taking place. But several years ago the curate discovered that the same Protestant divorcée, who had once been so shunned, was now invited to read the lesson at an ecumenical service in the local Catholic church. Although not all Catholic clergy were as prepared to encourage ecumenical gestures of this sort, MacGreil's survey in Dublin found that the great majority of the Catholic laity (84 per cent) were in favour of church unity.[60] In these changed circumstances, the Church of Ireland clergy was inundated as never before with invitations to take part in the public affairs of the Catholic community. These included attendance at dinner dances of local associations, joint blessing of new buildings, and involvement in local hospitals, vocational educational bodies, meals on wheels, and the like. In effect, ecumenism created a situation in which the clergy were now providing their laity with an example of the propriety of social involvement in the Catholic world. Interestingly enough, this was most true of the clergy in the provincial towns and the countryside, who were most likely to have the time and energy to devote to affairs outside their own community. In a paradoxical manner, the very conservatism of rural areas also meant that the laity were more inclined to follow the lead of their clergy – even though this involved breaking old traditions. In the more anonymous and secular atmosphere of Dublin, the laity were less conscious of their clergy's behaviour, and the clergy themselves tended to be more caught up in the day-to-day round of their large parishes. Even so, opportunities for ecumenical involvement among the Dublin clergy increased considerably after the mid-1960s.

Despite the widespread influence of ecumenism, both clergy and laity were extremely ambivalent in their attitude towards it. This was particularly true of the working-class and rural members of the community, who retained a rooted suspicion of "the holy water, Virgin Mary, incense and all." Elsewhere, the doctrinal objections of the past were rarely mentioned, and among the young the old debates and controversies were now often unknown. However, the great majority remained fundamentally opposed to the ultimate goal of ecumenism – namely, church unity. Since some felt that the Catholic church had not responded as positively to the ecumenical movement as had the Church of Ireland, they resented what they saw as a situation where "we do all the giving." Most simply found the idea of formal unity inconceivable, and they identified the mixed marriage laws of Catholicism as the current obstacle to the further pursuit of this distant goal. Above all, what shaped their thinking was their "nagging fear" that with their small numbers they would be "swamped" and "lose our identity" if unity ever became a reality.

Nevertheless, MacGreil's survey showed that 75 per cent of Protestants in Dublin continued to favour the principle of unity with the Catholic Church,[61] and in other parts of the country I found that many Irish Anglicans were equally unwilling to reject the ideal of ecumenism. They valued ecumenism because it fostered "better and closer relations with Catholics," because they felt they could "mix more freely now," and because it undermined the traditional view of them as alien and dangerous heretics. The conflict in Northern Ireland undoubtedly strengthened their support for ecumenism, for they saw ecumenical services as a way of publicly affirming their solidarity with Catholics in these anxious times. But more than this was involved. The ecumenical principles of tolerance, respect, and understanding were also the principles upon which Irish Anglicans sought recognition of their divergent values and their right to a place in the public life of the country. In other words, the laity's attraction to ecumenism was as much a response to the internal affairs of the Republic as it was to the northern conflict. For MacGreil, the willingness of Catholics and Protestants alike to embrace the principles of church unity suggested that both were moving toward what he called a position of "partial pluralism."[62] On the Catholic side, MacGreil may have underestimated the resistance of conservatives to the more tolerant and less exclusivist outlook of ecumenism, but at least the new stance did not call into question the existence of the Catholic community. Within the much smaller group of Irish Anglicans, on the other hand, their attraction to ecumenism created a far greater dilemma, because their desire for public integration posed a threat to the more private forms of social segregation upon which their very survival had long been based. Thus, in a rather uneasy manner, the Church of Ireland laity supported ecumenical rhetoric and its public manifestations while retaining reservations about its systematic application.

Among the clergy, attitudes to ecumenism were equally mixed. They were quick to point out that their new activities were not "a sellout,"[63] and they repeatedly condemned the Catholic requirements in mixed marriages as a "roadblock"[64] in ecumenical relations. As awareness of the increasing frequency of mixed marriages spread during the 1970s, the bishops began to require their clergy to press for the rights of the Protestant partner when counselling prospective partners in mixed marriages.[65] According to Bishop Caird, "Anglicans" would not "be happy until complete freedom of conscience in regard to the children is fully recognized."[66] Since the Catholic church showed no sign of meeting this demand, an increasing number of voices were raised in the committees and meetings of the General Synod, criticizing "the un-reality of Inter-Church dialogue."[67] It was precisely in this sort of climate that Archbishop McAdoo and Dean Griffin produced their new pamphlets on the distinctive features of Anglicanism; Griffin's contribution, in particular, revived many of the old debates with Catholicism that had so preoccupied the earlier generation of pamphleteers.

Nevertheless, this retreat from the uncritical ecumenism of the late 1960s did not represent simply a reversion to the rigid exclusivism of the pre-1960 era. On mixed marriages, for instance, the clergy did not advise that efforts should be made to prevent their occurrence, as Archbishop Gregg had once done. Instead, they sought the removal of the very factor – namely, the Catholic promises – which was now the laity's principal reason for opposing mixed marriage. Similarly, Griffin's renewed emphasis on "where we stand" was portrayed as a necessary step in the pursuit of the "desired unity of the Christian Church."[68] To McAdoo, this was "no paradox," for he felt that there was "an inner logic in people being totally committed to their own Church and at the same time wishing to reach out in understanding and fellowship."[69] For the committed members of his church, McAdoo's advice may yet prove to be sound. But in the face of so many mixed marriages and an increasingly indifferent laity, even this qualified support for ecumenical principles may seem rather surprising. In part it existed because many genuinely believed that the ecumenical movement was a reflection of the will of God. Like the laity, they also saw ecumenism as a means of furthering peace in Northern Ireland and of pressing the Catholic church in the South to confront the injustices they felt in such matters as mixed marriages. Added to this was the fact that at the local level many clergy were strongly attracted to ecumenical activities because of the opportunities for progressive leadership and wider prestige that such participation provided. Moreover, many were acutely conscious that their traditionally isolationist stance had failed to halt the population decline of the past, and was now often poorly received by the younger members of their parishes. Indeed, far from giving in to feelings of resignation and apathy, a number of clergy were coming to believe that through a more outgoing policy their church might now actually be able to convert mixed marriages into gains rather than losses. For all these reasons, then, the clergy continued to support ecumenism despite their fears and reservations. And by doing so, they played a major part in undermining the isolationist stance and exclusivist ideology which had once been so characteristic of the Church of Ireland and its laity.

SECULARIZATION

In other western countries, sociologists have tended to view ecumenism as being largely due to the growth of secularization. In essence, they have portrayed ecumenism as an effort by the churches to reduce competition and to coordinate activities in the face of an increasingly indifferent world.[70] On the surface, reasoning of this sort would appear to have little applicability to Ireland. Due to the Northern Ireland conflict and the external impetus of the Second Vatican Council, it might be argued that in Ireland ecumenism was much less dependent than elsewhere on the pressure of secularization. Indeed some might argue that secularization was not yet an established force in Ireland, since various large surveys in the 1970s showed that a full 90 per cent of Catholics continued to attend mass on a weekly basis.[71] In the light of such statistics, it would be foolhardy to suggest that secularization was at anything more than a very early and incomplete stage. However, even this modest claim requires a clear understanding of what is meant by this often misunderstood term. To draw upon two standard definitions, secularization may be best thought of as a process of "privatization,"[72] whereby "sectors of society and culture are removed from the domination of religious institutions and their symbols."[73] This is usually, but not always, accompanied by diminishing involvement in the organizational structures of church and parish. When put in these terms, secularization need not imply that questions of ultimate meaning and purpose in life will necessarily disappear. Nor does it deny that the moral prescriptions of religion may continue to shape the behaviour of individuals in a personal and direct manner. For the most part, secularization must be seen as a process that occurs at the social or group level. Above all, it refers to a contraction in the range of public and communal situations in which religious organizations and the concerns they espouse are deemed to have a socially binding influence.

The provision of social welfare facilities was one of the two major areas – the other was education – in which denominational structures once played an important role in the formal organization of Irish society. Many of these bodies were still to be found in the 1970s, but by this time they were showing signs of losing both their financial independence and their denominational character. These trends can be observed in the recent history of the Adelaide Hospital in Dublin.[74] It deserves particular attention because it was the last of the hospitals in the Republic "which Protestants may call their own."[75] Even in 1970, its nineteenth charter continued to exclude Catholics from its board, senior positions, and subscriber membership, and it still maintained the only Protestant nursing school in the Republic. Until approximately the end of the 1940s, virtually all of its staff and bed patients were Protestants. Although the state was by no means averse to the principle of denominational control, the highly exclusivist character of the Adelaide was greatly assisted by its independence of all government assistance. Besides endowments and fees, the remainder of its financial needs were met by individual donations and by subscriptions and annual collections from many Church of Ireland parishes. As a rule, only subscriber members or those whom they recommended were admitted for in-hospital treatment. As this prerogative often fell into the hands of the clergy, the Adelaide was made available to all sections of the Church of Ireland community.

After the establishment of the Irish Sweepstakes in 1930, the government used this new source of revenue to provide funds for the voluntary hospitals. Most of the others readily accepted the government's offer, but the Adelaide refused to participate. It did so on the grounds that it could not, as a matter of principle, accept funds collected by the immoral method of profiteering from horse-racing. However, underlying this decision was also the rather more pragmatic concern that "with the money will come the interference of those who administer it."[76] Despite these fears, increasing costs combined with a relatively static income created a growing deficit which could not be overcome by various appeals to the Protestant community. In the face of this pressure, the Adelaide eventually accepted a limited measure of state funding under a newly expanded health scheme that was introduced in 1953. It was also at this time that the Adelaide first began to admit a significant though still small number of Catholics for regular, in-hospital treatment. But it was not until 1961 that its still deteriorating finances forced it to join the other voluntary hospitals in accepting large-scale government support. This terminated the special right of parishes and subscriber members to hospital beds, although the privilege was not formally removed until a decision of the board in 1971. In 1974 the board decided to rescind denominational requirements in the making of senior appointments, and it was considering whether it could legally alter its charter to admit Catholics into its own ranks. In that year, all of the board, the great majority of consultants, about a third of the remaining doctors, approximately 75 per cent of the nurses, and roughly half of the patients were still Protestants. It is likely that the Adelaide will retain a certain Protestant ethos for some time to come but it is equally evident that these recent developments have substantially undermined its financial independence, its formally exclusivist character, and its organizational links with the Church of Ireland. At the same time, the clergy were finding that their laity were becoming less suspicious of the other Irish hospitals as the general quality of hospital care throughout the country improved under the more generous grants and medical schemes introduced by the government in the 1960s. Under these changed circumstances, it was becoming increasingly uncommon for anyone other than the elderly to insist upon making use only of the Adelaide's facilities.

With its limited funds, the state showed little interest in actually closing established denominational services. However, the recent experience of the Church of Ireland Social Service suggests that the future of these other denominational bodies was far from certain. As the church's major welfare agency in the Republic, the Service dealt with such matters as illegitimacy, adoption, marital and family problems, assistance to the elderly, and the like. Until the 1960s it was run on a voluntary basis with no other financial support than that provided by the Church of Ireland and individual donations. In the early 1970s it followed the lead of the state by expanding its services and by appointing a full-time director and two trained social workers. Although this further weakened its already precarious finances, the situation was temporarily resolved by the government agreeing to provide an annual grant to cover approximately a third of the Service's running costs. None of this would appear to indicate the growth of secularization, but there were other signs that precisely such a trend was emerging. This can be seen most clearly in the Service's dealings with unmarried mothers who were a major element in its case-load. Before the mid-1960s most unmarried mothers were put in touch with the Service by their local clergyman. Yet by the 1970s social workers in the organization found that an increasing number of unmarried mothers first turned to their doctor or another agency, and only then were they referred to the Church of Ireland Social Service. This apparent growth of a secular tendency was compounded in 1970 by the closure of the Bethany Home, which had once been the major facility for Protestant women in need of institutional care. At around the same time, the Service's importance was additionally undermined by the government's decision to provide its own direct grants to unmarried mothers for living and housing expenses. Depending on how the Service's statistics are interpreted, the result was that its case-load diminished by between 25 to 50 per cent in the 1970s, while its expanded bureaucracy created ever higher costs. All this indicated that the days of the Service were numbered, although the final blow was actually delivered by the Church of Ireland when it reduced and then withdrew its subsidy in the face of its own financial problems. Since the state was not prepared to take up the additional burden, the Church of Ireland Social Service was forced to cease operations at the end of 1977.[77] Although similar financial difficulties beset other denominational services, a number of small Protestant institutions for the aged continued to survive in the mid-1970s. Nevertheless, as the Irish electorate came to expect an ever wider range of free social services, the general trend was inevitably one of growing state involvement in a field that had once been largely organized along denominational lines.

Finally, on the question of lay support for the church, reliable estimates for past rates of church attendance are not available, but the clergy were generally agreed that regular participation was the norm until twenty-five years ago. The eighty-three lay members of the community whom I interviewed claimed that they and their families all attended church regularly when they were young. But by 1973 only 55 per cent reported weekly attendance. The remainder usually identified the 1960s as the period when they began to lose interest. Because of the urban bias and small size of this sample, the figure of 55 per cent may not be entirely trustworthy. However, I obtained a significantly lower estimate from church records of weekly attendance at services and Sunday School within the six parishes surveyed. Again adjustment must be made for the larger size of the urban parishes. When this is done the parish data suggest a national rate of about 45 per cent over the winter of 1973–74. In the three largely rural parishes, the figure was 51 per cent, although the clergy and financial records indicated that very few families were completely uninvolved with their parishes. In contrast, weekly attendance in the three urban parishes was only 35 per cent, and financial records showed that slightly less than 50 per cent of families made regular contributions. These urban figures are rather lower than the self-reported findings of MacGreil's sample of 132 Protestants, which produced a weekly rate of 49 per cent and a monthly rate of 66 per cent.[78] On the other hand, the combined population of almost 4,000 in the three urban parishes, the less subjective character of the information, and the confirming evidence of the financial records all suggest that MacGreil's figure may be somewhat inflated. Overall, it would appear from these various estimates that parochial involvement, especially in urban areas, was far from universal and was probably declining.

Religion was still a far more vital force in Ireland during the 1970s than in most other western countries. But in the ferment of the last fifteen years, the spread of ecumenical rhetoric provided a religious rationale for ignoring the Church of Ireland's isolationist traditions and it ensured that younger Irish Anglicans were less likely to be imbued with the insular outlook and divisive justifications of the past. At the same time, there were signs that secularization was beginning to emerge. Diminishing rates of church attendance, an emerging shortage of clergy, and secular pressures on denominational social services were all indications of this trend. However, these few examples do not adequately tap the full scope and implications of secularization. In order to do so, we must turn to the remaining areas of Church of Ireland community life.

CHAPTER SIX

Education

Next to the church, the other major cornerstone of the Church of Ireland community was its segregated system of education. At an early age, children occasionally developed friendships with neighbouring Catholics, but to the relief of most parents the beginning of school usually weaned them from these unfortunate tendencies. As they went their separate ways, they were imbued with the unthinking prejudices and historical memories of their own tradition, and when they emerged from the educational system not a few found that they could never be completely comfortable with "the other side." In its heyday, this deeply divisive system extended from primary school through to university.

Its origins, it may be recalled, can be traced back to the last century when the rising forces of nationalism and Catholicism combined to prevent the rather half-hearted efforts of the government to introduce nondenominational education. At independence, the principle of denominational control was quickly reaffirmed by the new government. However, the protection afforded to the minority by this decision was largely a by-product of the government's desire to conform to the teachings of the Catholic church. From the Catholic viewpoint, the major purpose of education was to inculcate children with the Catholic faith necessary for fulfilment in this world and salvation in the next. As the guardians of their faith, the clergy believed that they were obliged to be involved directly in the administration and provision of education. Neither state secular education nor interdenominational facilities with separate religious instruction were regarded as acceptable alternatives. From the rest of Irish society there was little argument, and successive ministers of education bent over backwards to demonstrate publicly their support for their church's stand. Even into the 1970s the Catholic church went out of its way to make it clear that its thinking had not been altered by either ecumenism or the conflict in Northern Ireland, while the politicians showed little interest in further confrontation after their difficulties over contraception.[1] Nonetheless, industrialization and urbanization were placing the nineteenth-century, denominational character of Irish education under increasing strain as the years passed. And here as elsewhere, the forces of change in Irish society impinged most heavily on Protestants.

PRIMARY SCHOOLS

Clerical control and de facto segregation were and are most pronounced at the primary school level, or at what are called national schools. With the exception of the Dalkey School Project (which will be described later) and a few other schools vested in the minister of education, the 3,600 national schools in 1978 were all under the patronage of one or other of the churches.[2] The catchment area for most schools was based on parish boundaries, and the local clergyman was normally the manager of the school. In the mid-1970s, new boards of management were created which allowed for some representation of parents and teachers, but the patron still nominated a majority of the members and the rector usually carried on as the chairman of the board.[3] In this capacity, the rector and lay representatives on the board were responsible for the appointment of teachers, for all administrative decisions, and for any correspondence with the state Department of Education. Financially, the manager and hence the select vestry and the entire parish were required to maintain their school buildings and to contribute a portion of any building costs, while the state paid for any remaining capital expenditures and for the salaries of teachers. Many parishes found it necessary to supplement the rather meagre state grants for school supplies, and some levied small fees in order to provide a broader curriculum than that which the state was prepared to support. In practice, the day-to-day involvement of the clergy varied according to their personal inclinations, although most were a familiar presence by virtue of their administrative responsibilities and their participation in religious education and morning prayers. All this ensured that church, clergy, and parishioners were intimately involved in the running of the parish school. Technically, the rules of the Department of Education stipulated that no child could be forced to take part in religious instruction, but in this situation very few parents were prepared to consider anything other than a school of their own faith.[4]

The final element in this segregated system was the Church of

Ireland Training College for teachers. After 1922 it trained teachers from all Protestant denominations, and the state was its sole source of financial support. With the blessing of the government, its principals were Church of Ireland clergymen before 1977, and the latest appointee was a layman who had previously been the secretary of the Church of Ireland's Board of Education. Both he and his predecessor had submitted the names of a few Catholic student applicants for approval by the government, but in 1978 all of those accepted by the state were still Protestants. The students tended to come from rural and poorer backgrounds where a traditional and intense type of Protestantism was most likely to be found. Although some of their more academic courses were taken at Trinity, many of a more practical nature were conducted within the protective confines of the college, which normally required its students to live in residence. In the 1970s the less insular outlook spreading throughout the entire Protestant community inevitably had its effect. One symptom of this change was that a substantial minority of Catholic pupils were now being admitted to the model school attached to the college. However, for most of the period with which we are concerned, the college's recruitment patterns, its policy of segregation, and its isolation from much of Dublin life combined to give it a strongly Protestant ethos.[5]

Given this high degree of institutional independence, it might be thought that separate schooling would have been readily available for any Protestant who sought it. Eventually, this turned out to be largely true, but in the 1920s many schools went through a period when they encountered considerable difficulty in retaining a Protestant teacher. According to the Board of Education, the shortage was "so grave as to menace seriously the existence of many schools in the South."[6] Part of the problem was that "a large number" of teachers transferred to Northern Ireland at independence. Like other Protestant civil servants who emigrated, they were concerned about the future security of their incomes and pensions. The board also stressed that many left because they refused to learn the Irish language and to administer the highly nationalistic curriculum required by the new state. At the same time, there was a marked drop in the number of candidates accepted by the Church of Ireland Training College. For the most part, this was due to the unwillingness and inability of Protestant candidates to meet the new standards of proficiency in Irish which were now required for admission to any teachers' training college. The fact that so many one-teacher schools served the small Protestant community made the situation all the worse, for the departure of a teacher often meant the closure of the school and not simply the enlargement of existing classes. To resolve this problem, the government agreed that lower standards of Irish would be accepted for entrance into the Church of Ireland Training College. Thus only ten of the 115 who took the entrance examination were successful in 1926, but forty-eight were allowed to enter the college. As roughly fifty new teachers were needed annually, the crisis was temporarily averted. In the same year a more permanent solution was achieved by the establishment of an Irish-speaking preparatory college attached to the main college. Once in operation, the future supply of Protestant teachers was secured. By 1930, thirty-three of the thirty-eight student teachers needed that year were admitted to the main college with the necessary leaving certificate in Irish, and by 1936 all of the graduating class held the Irish certificate.[7]

In the long run, the more dangerous threat to the Protestant school system lay in the minority's small, scattered, and diminishing population. According to government regulations, state aid in the 1950s was terminated for any school with an average enrolment of fewer than twenty pupils, and in 1965 this cut-off point was raised to twenty-four. Had these rules been stringently applied, the number of schools under Church of Ireland management would have been sharply reduced, for approximately half of them consistently fell below the lower level of twenty pupils. However, a stay of execution was made possible by additional regulations which were obviously designed with Protestants in mind. Provided "appropriate religious instruction" was "not available to the children of a particular denomination ... within reasonable distance of their homes," the state in 1965 was prepared to support a school with only twelve pupils, and it would not close a school unless its enrolment fell below eight for two consecutive years.[8] And prior to this, the government minimums were set at ten and seven pupils respectively.[9]

Even these generous provisions were not sufficient to guarantee segregated schooling for all Protestants in rural areas. In the early 1930s the Board of Education estimated that between 1,300 and 1,500 Protestant children were "out of reach of suitable education." By 1933 the board was using its own financial resources to transport 650 Protestant children to nearby Protestant schools, but it claimed that it was incapable of providing for the remainder.[10] As this was the depression era and the affected children often came from small farms in the west, many of their parents may not have been able to afford the relatively small sums involved. On these grounds, church authorities in 1929 began to press the government for some kind of financial relief. After four years of negotiations, it eventually agreed to pay half the costs of any transport scheme involving more than five children, while the remainder would be taken up by diocesan and parochial sources. In practice, the state's contribution normally amounted to about a third, but in the climate of the day it is remarkable that Catholics were prepared to countenance any subsidy that largely benefited Irish Anglicans, who still tended to be regarded as overly privileged descendants of the old Ascendancy. It is, of course, quite likely that the government was primarily motivated by its wish to appear consistent in meeting the demands of the Catholic church for denominational control. The fact remains that these various special rules played a major part in enabling approximately 95 per cent of Church of Ireland children to attend their own schools during the 1950s.[12]

After 1965 both the board and the Department of Education began to encourage the creation of larger central schools which they now believed were preferable on educational grounds, although the minister made it clear that he continued to regard Protestants as a special case.[13] For the most part, this new policy was offset by the government's decision in 1967 to provide a more comprehensive and generous transportation scheme which paid the entire cost of groups of over five and offered a 50 per cent grant for smaller ones.[14] In 1978 only one of the six parishes lacked its own separate school. The exception was the parish in the southwest which was so depleted in numbers and so large in size that its few school-age children had been forced to attend three different Catholic schools for many years. However, for the much greater number of Irish Anglicans in the midlands, in the border counties, and on the east coast, population decline and the government's policy of consolidation did not have the same effect. Although many small schools were being closed, the children in the other two parishes continued to attend centralized Protestant schools. In fact the extended use of transportation facilities which made this possible may have actually increased the extent of segregation in these areas. Thus children living on the borders of the Ulster parish in my sample had been forced to attend mixed schools before the 1960s, whereas in 1974 all but two were being transported to the central Protestant school. If the population decline of the past were to continue, even busing would soon be insufficient to keep many rural schools open. But this prospect now seems much less likely, since emigration has recently declined and the number of Irish Anglicans under the age of ten actually rose during the 1960s. With the exception of the more remote parts of the country, most rural Protestants during the 1970s were still able to exercise their strong preference for their own schools.

Except where a few temporary shortages occurred in the newer suburbs, Irish Anglicans in the larger urban areas had little difficulty in gaining access to a Protestant school, and the clergy were agreed that the overwhelming number never considered Catholic schools. However, a new pressure emerged in the 1970s when Catholics started to apply for places in Protestant national schools. By 1978 about 30 per cent of the pupils were Catholics in one rural school, although it appears to have been relatively atypical, for other rural schools in the surrounding area rarely contained more than a handful of Catholics. By all accounts, the bulk of the demand came from the rising, Catholic middle class in the larger towns and cities. In Dublin, a survey by the Catholic church in 1973 found that from 5 to 15 per cent of the pupils in sixteen Protestant schools were Catholic, [15] while the rector of another parish was quite happy to allow the numbers of Catholics to rise to 25 per cent of his school. [16] The number of Catholic admissions usually depended on the attitude of the local clergyman and on the extent to which there was a demand for places from parishioners. Thus the largest urban parish in my survey, containing many young married couples had only thirty-four Catholics in its school of over 500, although there may well have been a few more hidden in its list of eighty-six Christians or non-Christians. This could not be described as a major invasion, but here – as in the other schools with a more significant Catholic intake – only a fraction of Catholic applicants were actually accepted.

The tensions and the rather uneasy state of exclusion which lay behind this surge of Catholic interest were brought out most clearly in Dalkey. As the old village became incorporated into the suburban sprawl of Dublin, the Church of Ireland proportion of pupils entering their parish's rapidly growing national school fell from 82 per cent in 1960 to 30 per cent in 1970. By this later date, the remaining 70 per cent included children from other Protestant denominations, but an increasing number were Catholics whose parents were young professionals buying new homes in the area. As the school expanded, the select vestry began to grow apprehensive because it found itself encumbered with an ever larger financial responsibility for a school in which the majority of the children and their parents were no longer contributing parishioners. In order to share these costs, a Parent-Teacher Association was formed which then began to press for the creation of a much larger school of 300 explicitly based on multidenominational principles. This added to the financial fears of the select vestry, which insisted in 1969 that the PTA be responsible for the parish's contribution to the building costs of the planned new school. At the same time, the prospect of this enlarged role for the PTA and its multidenominational goal intensified the concern of the rector and the select vestry that they were losing control of their parish school. Eventually the rector reasserted his managerial powers in 1973 by stopping all future growth and by insisting that he would personally oversee all future applications so as to give first priority to his own parishioners. His actions ensured that the school remained under the control of the parish, but the resulting uproar was so intense that he resigned not long afterwards and left the ministry.[17]

As White has pointed out, "the PTA was at war not with the parish but with the whole national school system"[18] and its implicit assumption that schools should be linked to church and parish. However, it was soon discovered that the Department of Education's regulations did not prevent it from supporting a school unconnected to any church. On this basis, a number of disgruntled parents of all denominations formed the Dalkey School Project in 1975. Their aim was to set up separate, parentally-controlled schools throughout the country in which there would be equal access for all denominations and religious instruction for any who so desired it. Their more immediate objective, however, was to establish such a school in the Dalkey area. With a membership of around 300 and with surveys indicating that a substantial majority of parents of school-age children preferred a multidenominational school, the DSP put pressure on the government to support their efforts. After lengthy negotiations, the government acquiesced, and Dalkey's multidenominational school was opened in 1978. At around the same time, religiously mixed associations with similar goals were formed in Marley Grange, Firhouse, and Bray, but in 1979 only the Dalkey School Project was in operation.[19]

In the immediate future, these fledgling efforts at integration are most unlikely to lead to major changes in the national school system. The Catholic church made it clear that it remained opposed to anything other than the current system of direct denominational control, and it went out of its way to court support from the Church of Ireland.[20] The stance of the Church of Ireland was also essentially conservative, although it did reflect to a greater extent the uncertainties and secular inclinations of its laity. This vacillating state of mind was most clearly evident in the 1974 statement by the church's Board of Education. In reaction to the northern conflict, the board declared that it would "welcome ... agreed experiments towards encouraging integration in education on the understanding that denominational interests would be respected."[21] At the same time, the statement made it clear that concrete moves towards integration in the South were "largely precluded" because of the church's small numbers, the Catholic position on mixed marriages, and the lack of a real alternative to denominational schools. In 1978 a much stronger proposal favouring integrated education was put before the General Synod, but after much debate a decision was avoided by shelving the proposal for further discussion. The opposition was led by Dr McAdoo, the archbishop of Dublin. While he supported the qualified terms of the 1974 statement, he argued that church schools should be retained because they were a necessary defence against secularism and because ecumenical advance was best achieved when all parties were imbued with a firm knowledge of their own faith and traditions. For McAdoo, integration should be confined to such activities as the "twinning" of schools for the purpose of interschool visits, discussions, and the like.[22] It is this singular consensus among Catholic and Anglican church leaders that accounts for the unwillingness of the state to tamper with their formal powers. However, neither the emerging reality of Irish education nor the attitudes of all Irishmen were fully in line with the official views of their churches. This will become more apparent at the secondary education level. But even in primary schools, urban and middle-class Irish Anglicans were now admitting small numbers of Catholics to their schools, and some were cooperating with Catholics in a much more whole-hearted endeavour to create alternatives to denominational education.

SECONDARY SCHOOLS

The secondary schools existing in 1922 were all privately owned institutions which had been established without any assistance from the state. With few exceptions they were affiliated to one or another of the churches. Although the new Department of Education made extensive changes in the curriculum, it did not interfere with the principles of private and denominational control.[23] (After 1930 the state did extend its system of vocational schools, but the Catholic church soon established its influence as the clergy were often chairmen of the local Vocational Education Committees.)[24] Ownership of the diverse collection of Protestant schools was vested in their respective boards of governors which normally included both clergy and laity. For the most part, they were rather small, drab institutions which lacked the ruling class assumptions of the English public school, although few doubted their superiority to their Catholic counterparts. Apart from the several schools under The Incorporated Society for Promoting Protestant Schools in

Ireland, there was little coordination among them. Under their various charters, approximately half required that their governors be members of the Church of Ireland, while others were controlled by the Quakers, Methodists, and Presbyterians.[25] Thus most schools had a specific denominational allegiance, although their teachers and students were usually drawn from all the Protestant churches. Administratively, the independence of the schools from one another and from the state underwent no significant change over the next forty years.

For many years after 1922, state funds for secondary education were extremely scanty. In 1924 a new grant for each pupil was introduced, and the government agreed to supplement the salaries of a specified number of "recognised" teachers over and above a minimum required from the school. These new regulations, which applied to both Protestant and Catholic schools, were a marked improvement on what had gone before, but all other expenditures were still the responsibility of the school.[26] Under the new system, state grants in 1928 amounted to less than 15 per cent of the running costs incurred by the schools of the Incorporated Society.[27] Independence, then, had its price, although in earlier years Protestants were able to offset the state's frugality by relying on income from endowments. To use the example of the Incorporated Society again, parents in 1928 paid for 56 per cent of their children's education and endowments covered another 31 per cent. But as a result of inflation, the real value of this legacy declined to such an extent that by 1965 a special committee of the General Synod was claiming that endowments were "of negligible significance for solving the financial difficulties of our schools."[28] By 1971 endowments accounted for less than 4 per cent of the costs incurred by the Incorporated Society, and headmasters insisted that a similar situation prevailed in most other schools.

To some extent the situation was worse for Catholics in that they were poorer and they usually lacked the protective, if temporary, cushion of endowments. However, in other crucial respects, education was a more costly enterprise for Protestants. Lacking the services of religious orders, Protestant schools were forced to employ lay teachers who needed and expected the full salaries stipulated by the state. In contrast, "religious" teachers often used their government increments to subsidize the running costs of their schools, and the government regulation that schools must use their own resources to provide a basic salary for all recognized lay teachers was not applied to recognized teachers from religious orders.[29] The financial burden for Protestant parents and schools was also greater because so many students were out of reach of cheaper day schools. Some would probably have attended a boarding school no matter where they lived, but this was certainly not true of the 42 per cent of pupils in Protestant schools who were boarders in the early 1960s. In addition, the large number of small Protestant schools was itself a source of much inefficiency, unnecessary duplication, and harmful competition. Their problems were then further compounded by the government's policy of favouring larger schools through allowing them a more favourable student-teacher ratio. Since it was prepared to support only two recognized teachers in a school with fewer than eighty pupils, the eleven Protestant schools (out of a total of forty) below this figure were compelled to hire additional teachers entirely at their own expense. Indeed, this was true of most Protestant schools as the government scales did not take account of the extra teachers required for boarders. In 1964 the state agreed to provide building grants for schools that had 150 pupils or were building to accommodate that number, but again twenty-six Protestant schools were unable to take advantage of the offer because they were below this minimum level. The net result was that most Protestant schools were in a "deplorable" physical condition by the 1960s, and many were in "urgent need" of financial assistance if they were "to continue let alone improve."[30]

Had these conditions been allowed to continue, the Advisory Committee to the General Synod gloomily predicted that they "would be forcing the Protestant children of the future to occupy the role of second class citizens."[31] Even allowing for some rhetorical exaggeration, their fears seemed well grounded. Much as it went against the grain of local loyalties and traditions, they urged that the only solution lay in a substantial reduction in the number of their schools. Under the Secondary Education Committee set up shortly afterwards to administer these policies of closure and amalgamation, the number of Protestant schools declined from forty-three in 1965 to around twenty-five in 1978. However, this drastic reorganization did not weaken the Protestant school system as much as many had anticipated. By 1975 the number of school places under Protestant control had actually grown by almost 20 per cent,[32] and enrolment at most of the schools that remained was over the 150 pupils required by the government for building grants. When combined with the sale of old properties and financial appeals to parents, these new monies enabled most schools to introduce extensive physical improvements and in some cases entirely new schools were constructed. Although Protestants were still unhappy with the lack of building grants for boarding facilities, the transformation was on such a scale that the SEC in the 1970s readily acknowledged that its earlier description of decay and decline was no longer warranted.[33]

At around the same time, the government became more involved than ever before in the direct provision and financing of secondary schooling. The first sign of this change was the 1963 decision of the state to provide a limited number of comprehensive schools in areas where no secondary schools were available. This program was superseded by others as the years passed, but in 1966 three of these original comprehensives were opened. One of them, in Cootehill, County Cavan, was in an area where 10 to 15 per cent of the population was Protestant. In 1973 Protestants amounted to roughly the same proportion of the student body – even though one of the three members of the local board of management was a Catholic priest.[34]

The second and more far-reaching decision was made in 1966 when Donagh O'Malley, the minister of education, proposed a scheme to provide free secondary education. As he was not prepared to interfere with the principle of denominational ownership, he offered an annual grant of £25 a pupil to any academic secondary school which agreed to suspend all fees in return. Most Catholic schools were able to take advantage of O'Malley's offer, since their fees were less than £25, but Protestants were effectively excluded because the great majority of their schools required fees in excess of this figure. As might be expected, the Secondary Education Committee was less than happy with this arrangement. After negotiations, the government agreed to a compromise by offering the SEC a block grant for day pupils of £70,000 which it was to administer according to a means test of its own devising. This sum was based on the proportion of Catholics entitled to free education. In 1968 the same basic grant of £25 was extended to cheaper boarding schools, which resulted in an additional £60,000 being made available for Protestant boarders.[35] For the year 1978–79 the total grant had risen to over half a million pounds.[36]

Technically, these revised arrangements were more than equitable since Protestants were in receipt of more money than they were entitled to under a strict interpretation of the original scheme. However, they remained deeply dissatisfied, and some claimed that the existing provisions subjected them to an unintended but nonetheless real form of discrimination. Their basic complaint was that the purpose of the scheme – namely, the provision of free secondary education – was fulfilled for Catholics, but not for themselves.[37] Thus, for the school year 1973–74, the maximum boarding grant of £180 was slightly more than half the average fee of £351, while for day pupils the average fee of £127 was considerably more than the maximum grant of £70. In some of the cheaper schools, the maximum grants were very close to the fees charged, but even here Protestants, unlike Catholics, were subject to a means test. And this means test was very rigorous, for 40 per cent of day pupils in Protestant schools received no grant at all, while for boarders the figure was 59 per cent.[38] With the increasingly heavy rate of inflation experienced during and after the second half of the 1970s, there is every reason to believe that the financial pressures on Protestant parents have grown more severe.

Given the state's commitment to free education within a denominational context, Protestants felt they were entitled to their own free and separate facilities, even if this cost more than for Catholics. In an attempt to satisfy this demand, the Department of Education established four free comprehensives for Protestants during the early 1970s. Two were in Dublin, and the other two were in Cork City and Donegal. Prior to the take-over by the state, all four had been independently-owned Protestant schools. Since they were the products of earlier amalgamations, the result was that nine of the forty-three schools listed in 1965 were transferred to state hands. Formally they were owned by the state, were entirely reliant on government funding, and hence were nondenominational in character. In reality, they remained under the control of the Protestant community and they continued to regard service to Protestants as their first priority. The teaching staff carried on as before and three of the five members of the local boards of management were nominees of the resident Church of Ireland bishop or archbishop. Once in operation, the four comprehensives provided free schooling for 23 per cent of the pupils in school under Protestant control,[39] while the remainder were still obliged to pay their fees and then look to the SEC in the hope of some relief.

At the same time, the extensive changes being introduced in the Catholic system gave Protestants little reason to desert their own schools. With growing enrolments and a 50 per cent decline in vocations in the ten years prior to 1978, the day-to-day influence of the teaching orders inevitably declined,[40] but their rights of ownership and managerial control were not altered. In fact, the state appeared willing to give extensive powers to the Catholic church in its new system of community schools, which were to combine existing vocational and academic schools into a single unit to serve the entire community. In the original scheme of 1970, the Catholic bishops were to appoint four of the six members to the schools' boards of management. This proposal was quickly buried in a storm of protest, including the objection of Protestants that it was depriving them of access to what had previously been the non-denominational vocational system.[41] Although over twenty-five community schools were in operation by the end of the 1970s and more were planned, there was still no agreement on their charter or deed of trust. By the middle of the decade, opposition came from the teachers' unions and the VECs which resented the still considerable powers offered the Catholic church in later government proposals.[42] According to the latest revisions of 1979, the participating religious orders were to have three of ten positions on the boards of management; they were allowed to reserve a limited number of teaching positions for their own exclusive use; they were to have a strong voice in the hiring of all other teachers; and a faith and morals clause was retained which required that a teacher could not "advertently or consistently seek to undermine the religious belief or practice of any pupil."[43] It would, of course, be remiss to ignore the internal rumblings of discontent that prevented an early agreement. On the other hand, such a blueprint for the future can only be described as highly denominational, and the same could also be said of the Protestant school system. However, this analysis of official structures does not confront the central issue of whether they continued to be successful in segregating Protestant from Catholic. When this question is raised, a rather different picture emerges.

By all accounts, there was always the occasional "Christian Brother Protestant" before 1945, and there was also a slightly larger number who attended vocational schools. At that time, dire necessity was considered to be the only legitimate grounds for such deviant behaviour, and even then it was regarded with much suspicion by many Protestants. The state-run vocational schools tended to be seen as somewhat more acceptable, although in practice the demography of the country and the pervasive influence of the Catholic church ensured that they had an almost equally Catholic ethos. For the rest of the Protestant community, those capable of paying fees or sufficiently able to win a scholarship went to a Protestant school, while many simply left national school and moved directly into a Protestant working environment. These traditional patterns began to fall apart after 1945 as educational standards rose with industrialization and increasing affluence. Unpublished national surveys of primary school leavers by the Board of Education (table 14) show that Irish Anglicans responded by becoming almost universally involved in secondary education. As might be expected, their participation in Protestant schools

TABLE 14

Secondary School Choices of Church of Ireland Primary School
Leavers, 1961 and 1970

	June 1961	June 1970
Total number	1,200	1,014
% Attend Protestant secondary school	45	59.3
% Attend vocational school	16.8	22.5
% Attend Roman Catholic secondary school	4.2	13.6
% Attend no secondary school	34.1	4.8

grew, but at the same time their attendance at Catholic schools
increased to 21 per cent in 1961 and then to 36 per cent in 1970. In
fact, this latter figure can be raised to 38 per cent if we exclude the
very small number in 1970 who did not pursue any form of secondary
education.

Increased attendance at Catholic schools was largely confined to
the smaller towns and countryside where the small and scattered
Protestant community was incapable of supporting its own day
schools. Previously many rural Protestants, who had not been able
to afford boarding fees, had managed to get by without any form of
secondary education. When this was no longer possible, they found
that they had no other choice but to turn to vocational schools and
then later to Catholic academic schools with a full secondary
curriculum. Thus as Irish Anglicans outside of Dublin increased
their attendance at secondary school from 63 per cent in 1961 to 94
per cent in 1970, those entering Catholic schools almost doubled
from 26 to 45 per cent, while the percentage in their own schools rose
from 37 to 49 per cent. In contrast, 87 per cent of Church of Ireland
primary school leavers in 1970 within the diocese of Dublin were
still able to find places in Protestant schools, and those who did not
tended to live in the outlying parts of the diocese.

These differences probably grew more marked during the 1970s.
Within both Dublin parishes surveyed, all but a handful interested
in vocational training went on to one or other of the Protestant
secondary schools which now included the two free comprehensives. In the provincial town with a Protestant day school, the great
majority of parents were also prepared to pay the necessary fees,
although a few parents were finding free Catholic schools increasingly attractive. Elsewhere, a completely different situation prevailed. In the Ulster parish surveyed, only one of fourteen who left
primary school in 1974 entered a Protestant school, while in the

more affluent midlands parish 50 per cent of the children still did so. Thereafter, old loyalties were subject to further strain as boarding fees rose from an average of £350 in 1974 to as much as £1,000 in 1978. It is, of course, difficult to ascertain what constitutes an intolerable financial burden, although one clergyman from the midlands estimated that approximately a third of his twenty-three parishioners at Catholic schools in 1978 could have been sent to Protestant schools had the parents wished. Thus in the face of necessity and ever more common practice, what had once been socially taboo was becoming increasingly acceptable, and with the rhetoric of ecumenism and toleration there was much to justify it. Church of Ireland clergy were usually given every assistance when they requested facilities to provide religious education in the local Catholic schools. However, the clergy regarded their weekly tour of Catholic schools as an irksome and time-consuming responsibility with little practical value. Indeed, an hour or an hour and a half a week of separate religious instruction cannot have been a very effective antidote to the day-to-day experience of mixing with Catholics in all other activities.

The breakdown of segregation was by no means confined to the forced attendance of Protestants at Catholic schools. Within Protestant schools, an early symptom was the increasing reliance on Catholic teachers. Although a few Catholics had been employed for many years, a general shortage of Protestant teachers did not emerge until after 1945. From that point on, the annual reports of the Board of Education repeatedly bewailed this apparently insoluble problem. A few special scholarships were created at Trinity and there was much talk of improving salaries, but in 1965 the Advisory Committee on Education reported that 25 per cent of teachers were Catholics in the thirty-four schools that responded to its enquiries. In 1974 my own survey of six different Protestant schools found that 24 per cent were Catholics, and a further check in 1978 revealed that their number had risen to 30 per cent. The Catholic proportion varied from school to school with the greatest concentrations occurring in a small rural boarding school (42 per cent) and in a Dublin comprehensive (34 per cent), while at the Cork comprehensive fully half of the staff were Catholics.[44] At the other end of the scale was the most socially exclusive of all the schools (11 per cent), which was limited by the relative scarcity of Catholics with the appropriate West Briton style. And in between were the boarding and day schools in Dublin catering to the middle class where 27 per cent were Catholics.

Until recently, Catholic teachers were hired with much much reluctance and only after all other avenues had been explored.

Besides a few drill masters, most Catholics had been initially re-cruited because few if any Protestants were able to teach the much hated Irish language. It was not, however, a major deterrent to the profession, since only one or two specialist teachers were required to be fully competent in Irish.[45] The isolation and shabby living quarters of many rural schools may also have discouraged some Protestants, but the fundamental reason was simply economic. It may be remembered that the small size of Protestant schools forced them to employ many teachers who were not entitled to govern-ment salaries. As the remuneration for these officially unrecognized positions was abysmally low, Protestants were understandably reluctant to accept them.[46] Moreover, even the rather better paid salaries of recognized teachers appeared less attractive to Protes-tants than to Catholics because the greater economic privilege of the former led them to expect a higher standard of living. With their many contacts in the Protestant business community, young Protestant university graduates found it much easier than did their Catholic counterparts to pursue the more lucrative careers in industry and commerce. In consequence, teaching failed to attract recruits. The problem became all the worse after 1945 because continuing emigration reduced the supply of Protestant teachers at a time when more teachers were needed to meet the growing demand of Protestants for secondary education.[47] In effect, a situation arose in which Protestants could not and would not provide the manpower for their separate school system. Out of necessity, headmasters turned to the much larger supply of Catholic teachers.

By the 1970s this chronic shortage had changed the thinking of headmasters in that all of them professed that teaching ability and educational considerations were their "paramount" concern in looking for a teacher. In fact, the Dublin comprehensive, which had formally committed itself to becoming a multidenominational school, was no longer considering religion in hiring, and I was told that a few other schools were following a similar policy. Yet when pressed, the headmasters in the other five schools acknowledged that "all things being equal we would prefer one of our own." In the future, they may be able to exercise this preference, for they claimed that the supply of Protestant teachers was starting to improve. Should this occur, it would still take some time to displace the now established body of Catholic teachers. It also seems clear that the ability of the schools to transmit a traditional Protestant outlook must have suffered over the last twenty years, when between a third and a quarter of those entrusted with the task were Catholics.

While necessity was the major impetus behind the two last-mentioned developments, the same could not be said of the recent admission of Catholic pupils into Protestant schools. Once again, it was not an entirely new trend. In the 1920s the Catholic archbishop of Dublin and the *Catholic Buletin* vehemently condemned "the servile frame of mind" that sent upwards of 100 Catholic children to "Protestant and godless secondary schools."[48] This figure may have been an exaggeration, but in either case the number did not grow significantly over the next forty years, for the headmasters in the six schools surveyed reported that they had no more than a handful of Catholic pupils until the late 1960s. Then suddenly their numbers began to grow. By 1974, 14 per cent of the pupils were Catholics and in 1978 this had grown to 19 per cent. At about the same time, another larger survey of fifteen Protestant schools strongly confirmed the accuracy of the latter figure, for it found that their 1,150 Catholic pupils also amounted to exactly 19 per cent of the combined student population.[49] Within my own smaller sample, the greatest increase occurred at the free comprehensive, which saw its Catholic proportion rise from 3 per cent in 1971 to 33 per cent in 1974, thereafter levelling off to 34 per cent in 1978. In the independent Dublin schools catering mainly to the middle and upper classes, the increase in Catholic enrolment was not quite as marked, although the number still rose steadily from one or two per cent in 1970 to between 12 and 15 per cent in 1978. Significantly enough, in 1978 only 4 per cent were Catholics within the two smallest private schools which traditionally served poorer Protestants in Dublin and the midlands. However, integration was not confined exclusively to Dublin, for I was reliably informed that a third of the pupils were Catholics in another private and more prosperous school in County Cork.

For primary as well as secondary schools, there were very similar reasons behind this sudden surge in Catholic interest. In part, Catholics were drawn to Protestant schools because their classes tended to be smaller, because they were seen to be a little less rough, and because they were thought to provide a somewhat more progressive education. As White has perceptively observed, religious segregation gave Protestant primary schools a form of class protection that was not readily available to Catholics unless they were willing to pay for it.[50] At secondary schools, both Catholics and Protestants were forced to pay for the privilege of class segregation, but Catholic schools with high prestige were in short supply and Protestant schools may have retained a certain mystique from their ascendancy past. The attractions of class and status should not be underestimated, but they were evidently not the only factors at work, since they had existed long before the recent growth in Catholic applications. Some parents may have been reacting to the conflict in Northern Ireland, and it seems likely that others were looking for a more secular education than they had received as children. Despite their church's continued insistence that their children be educated in Catholic schools, MacGreil's large Dublin survey in 1973 found that 78 per cent of his predominantly Catholic sample favoured "interdenominational mixed free community schools."[51] Catholics with these aspirations were understandably reluctant to send their children either to the traditional Catholic academic school, or to any of the large national schools in the cities which were still often run by religious orders. Even the new community schools were by no means secular institutions, and they could never hope to have more than a very small percentage of Protestants. In contrast, Protestant schools were staffed almost entirely by lay people; they had a good mix of both Catholic and Protestant teachers; and the demography of the country offered a real possibility of creating a genuinely interdenominational ethos. Moreover, as we shall see, Protestant schools devoted much less time to religious matters, and some were making a conscious effort to provide an integrated curriculum in religious education.

With the conspicuous exception of the two poorer ones, the Protestant schools were inundated with far more Catholic applications than they were prepared to accept. Had they wished, the free Protestant comprehensives in Dublin and Cork could have become entirely Catholic schools in a few years, while the private schools for the middle class encountered an almost equally large barrage of Catholic applications. In an age of ecumenism, a conflict-ridden Ulster, and an emerging secular outlook, Protestant schools were prepared to do their part in fostering a measure of integration. In fact, the free comprehensives had been set up with the specific intent of increasing Catholic admissions to between 20 to 25 per cent of their enrolment. By 1978 there were also a few independent Protestant schools that were forthrightly proclaiming their conversion to multi- or interdenominational principles, but the remainder were rather more reticent. In the face of this overwhelming Catholic demand, the other private schools usually imposed a quota on Catholic day pupils and refused to admit Catholic boarders, although this last barrier was beginning to fall in a few schools. The great majority of Protestant schools, including the comprehensives, were not prepared to open their doors fully to Catholics on the ground that their first responsibility was to Protestants who usually had no other alternative than a school controlled by the Catholic church. Of course, their more fundamental fear was that a completely open door policy would lead to their total absorption within the Catholic world. Nonetheless, the limited integration which they were allowing inevitably diluted their Protestant ethos and encouraged a familiarity with Catholics that was virtually unknown to previous generations of Protestants.

TRINITY COLLEGE DUBLIN

It may be recalled that Trinity joined the other major Protestant institutions in offering its loyalty to the new government in 1922, but like the rest of the community its attachment to Britain and its distrust of Irish nationalism were much slower to fade. According to a later provost of the college, during the next thirty years Trinity remained "very uncertain of itself" and largely "out of touch."[52] Indeed, these rather discreet phrases do not do justice to the atmosphere of resentful alienation that still prevailed. When the opportunity arose, its undergraduates defiantly sang "God Save the King"; and it was said that on Armistice Day a few brave students placed a razor behind their lapel in the hope that someone might try to remove the red poppies they wore. In view of its ascendancy background, its long exclusion of Catholics, and its vocal opposition at Westminster to the nationalist cause, such incidents did little more than confirm the already ingrained tendency of most Catholics to regard Trinity as an alien, antinational institution. The Catholic hierarchy in 1927 then further underlined Trinity's marginality by reiterating their disapproval of non-Catholic colleges and by forbidding their clergy to recommend attendance, although they did not go so far as to impose a complete ban on the laity.[53] There are no accurate figures on the religious background of students at this time, but estimates placed the proportion of Catholics at between 10 and 25 per cent.[54] The state, for its part, did not interfere with Trinity in any way. To compensate for lands sold by the college as a result of the land acts, it agreed to provide an annual income of £3,000, and it gave an additional lump sum of £5,000 to make up for income lost during the Civil War.[55] But other than these small sums, Trinity relied almost exclusively on its own fees and endowments until 1947. And as the years passed, the college grew increasingly impoverished, its buildings began to decay, and its reputation as an international centre of learning seemed in serious danger.

Had the governing body or board of Trinity asked the government for more assistance during the 1920s or 1930s, it is open to debate whether it would have been successful. The generally equitable treatment of Protestants in other areas might have been interpreted as a promising sign, but the fact is that Trinity was not prepared to make such an overture. The members of the board were elderly men whose formative years had passed during the pre-independence era. With this sort of background, their inclination was to avoid any rebuff from upstart nationalists. Above all, they feared that government funding might compromise their prized independence. At a minimum, they expected that they would be required to introduce Irish as a compulsory subject in the entrance examinations, and much more dire consequences were probably anticipated by those who had fought and defeated the proposal of the early 1900s that Trinity and University College Dublin should combine in some sort of federated University of Dublin. Despite these fears, financial necessity and pressure from the junior fellows finally forced the board to overcome its scruples. In 1947 it approached the government with a request for £35,000 to which the minister of finance readily agreed without requiring any conditions in return. After that date, the level of government funding steadily grew, buildings were repaired, new ones were added, and the financial worries of the prewar years receded. By 1964 half of the college's income of £814,000 was derived from government grants, and by 1973 it had a budget of just under four million pounds, with the state providing 78 per cent of the total.[56]

Trinity's enrolment also began to expand after the war, but this early sign of revival did little to alter its image as an alien institution, since the bulk of its growth stemmed from a temporary influx of foreigners. At its peak in 1961, only 39 per cent of the college's students were from the Republic; another 14 per cent were Northerners; and the remaining 47 per cent were foreigners, of whom the largest single group (34 per cent) were British. In contrast, a full 90 per cent of students just prior to the war had come from the thirty-two counties and only 6 per cent had been British. Thus, in a very literal sense, the British character of Trinity was being strengthened at a time when British influence was starting to fade elsewhere within the Protestant community.

Not long afterwards, Trinity was sharply criticized by the government's Commission on Higher Education for expanding beyond the demand of its Irish constituency. The charge was technically correct, although in fairness it should be pointed out that the colleges of the National University – unlike Trinity – were able to grow at this time with an enrolment drawn almost exclusively from the Republic. At the commission's hearings, the provost went out of his way to stress that Trinity had long given first priority to Irish applicants; that it was now "anxious to integrate itself in the national life"; and that it did "not want Trinity to be regarded as a Protestant institution for Protestant students." In fact, with the steady decline of the southern Protestant community, its future as a Protestant body was less than secure. The college believed that its failure to attract sufficient Irish students was largely due to the ever more rigorous restrictions on Catholic entry imposed by the Catholic hierarchy. Even allowing for some exaggeration in Trinity's claims that it had weaned itself from its British leanings, there was still a sound basis for its complaint. In 1944 the Catholic archbishop of Dublin for the first time explicitly forbade the laity of his diocese to attend Trinity without his special permission, and in 1956 this decree was extended throughout Ireland.[57] Although the age-old ethnic, religious, and class hostilities behind the ban cannot be ignored, it is noteworthy that Bishop Philbin, on behalf of the hierarchy, stressed that they were no longer motivated by such sentiments. Instead, he argued that they now objected to Trinity's "neutral and secular character, its strong Protestant traditions having given ground to an uncommitted attitude in which currents of opinion more radically opposed to Catholicism may exert considerable influence."[58] But for the time being, the hierarchy had little to fear, since the Catholic proportion of new students ranged from 20 to 29 per cent during the 1950s, and in 1961 dropped to a postwar low of 16 per cent.

This state of partly reluctant and ultimately untenable isolation from the rest of Irish society finally began to decline during the 1960s. Despite the fact that the college's numbers continued to rise over the decade, the proportion of non-Irish students fell from 47 per cent in 1961 to 32 per cent in 1966. By 1970 only 11 per cent of the new students were foreigners and in that year 73 per cent were residents of the Republic. According to F.S.L. Lyons, then senior tutor, this remarkable transformation was in part due to the "strenuous efforts" of college authorities to recruit Irish applicants.[59] They, in turn, were probably stirred by their increasing reliance on state funds and by the censure they received from the Commission on Higher Education for their past admissions policy. Some officials may also have been thoroughly frightened when the minister of education in 1967 issued his short-lived proposal that Trinity and UCD should amalgamate. In addition, the accelerating rate of industrialization and the growing affluence of these years undoubtedly helped to stimulate Irish interest in university education. However, with the continuing decline in the Protestant population, none of these developments would have had much effect had it not been for a new willingness on the part of the Catholic laity to disregard their church's ban on Trinity. Among new students, the proportion of Catholics rose from its low point of 16 per cent in 1961 to 35 per cent in 1967. In 1970, when the hierarchy decided to withdraw its increasingly ineffectual ban, the newly appointed Catholic chaplain estimated that the proportion had grown to almost 40 per cent of all full-time students. Then in 1973 more reliable college statistics put the figure at around 59 per cent, and by 1978 this had grown to 66 per cent.

Within the college, the Church of Ireland chapel was opened in 1973 to all denominations, which have since made regular use of its facilities. In 1978 Trinity established a nondenominational course in theology, and throughout the 1970s the students appeared to attach little importance to the religion of their peers. According to Protestant headmasters, the bulk of their students still opted for Trinity whenever possible, although they did note that some were now being drawn to the recently established Colleges of Technology. This may change in the future, but the very considerable degree of integration now prevailing at the university level was still largely a matter of Catholic penetration into the Protestant world. With its markedly secular character, Trinity's Catholic majority could not be described as representing a victory for traditional Catholicism.

THE CURRICULUM AND PROTESTANT IDENTITY

A *"national tone."* Prior to 1900 the textbooks of the national schools made little reference to the history and culture of Ireland, and the Irish language, though not actively oppressed, was largely ignored. Such topics, it was feared, might fan religious antipathies and stir revolutionary fervour. Displaying the almost unconscious arrogance of the day, the authorities deemed it best to focus on British history and culture in order, as one of the earliest commissioners of the National Board put it, to transform every pupil into "a happy English child."[60] For Protestants, this colonial mentality was ideally suited to preserve their British identity, while to Catholic nationalists it was little more than a policy of cultural genocide. In retrospect, it would be simplistic to attribute the decline of Gaelic civilization solely to the educational system, but reasoning of this sort did pervade the views of the emerging nationalist leadership. Like many nationalist movements, they were convinced that full independence could be achieved only when they were able to overthrow the cultural as well as the political domination of

Britain. Hence one of their first acts upon gaining power was to introduce extensive and revolutionary changes in the curriculum.

"The chief function of Irish educational policy," declared the Free State's first minister of education, "is to conserve and develop Irish nationality."[61] To this end, national conferences of educationalists held in 1921 and 1926 called for a strengthening of "the national fibre by giving the language, history, music and traditions of Ireland their natural place in the life of the schools." The explicit corollary was that reference to English culture and tradition should be reduced as much as possible. In the national schools, only Irish history was to be taught, with the specific intent of "inculcating national pride and self respect" and of "showing that the Irish race has fulfilled a great mission in the advancement of civilisation." Similarly, the history courses of secondary schools devoted most of their time to Ireland, and initially they excluded all mention of England in their listing of European topics. Perhaps the clearest indication of this anti-English bias was to be found in the instruction issued to national schools that "reading in English for the higher standards should be directed to the works of European authors" so that "English authors, as such, should have just the limited place due to English literature among all the European literatures."[62]

The issue which was a cornerstone of the nationalist movement, and which most obsessed the Department of Education, was, of course, the attempt to use the schools as the chief means of restoring Irish to the status of the national language. This objective, it may be remembered, was enshrined in the constitutions of 1922 and 1937. At secondary schools, Irish was made a compulsory subject which students were required to pass in order to obtain both the intermediate and leaving certificates. All state grants depended on the provision of Irish instruction, and financial bonuses were offered to schools that taught through the medium of Irish. These regulations were rigorous enough, but far greater pressure was put on the national schools. Here a minimum of one hour of the four and a half hours of daily instruction was to be devoted to Irish; all teaching was to be in Irish during the first two years of infant classes, provided the teacher was sufficiently qualified; at the higher levels, Irish was to be used as the medium of instruction as far as possible; and after 1934 English was entirely excluded from the curriculum for infants.[63] In a country where English was the mother-tongue of 90 per cent of the children, these measures were very strong medicine.[64]

No other government policy provoked such widespread and sustained criticism from Protestants. For forty years, the annual reports of the Church of Ireland's Board of Education repeatedly condemned the compulsory and restrictive character of the regulations. As we saw in chapter three, the minority regarded Irish as an alien, primitive, and anachronistic language with no roots in their own English-speaking tradition. Although many Protestants were not prepared to express such views in public, reticence in defending their British allegiance did not dampen their protest. In the main, they argued on the pragmatic ground that the heavy emphasis on Irish reduced the amount of time available for other more important subjects, had no practical value, and was doing little to further a true revival in the everyday use of Irish. In particular, they stressed that educational standards were being eroded by the misguided effort to teach through a language which pupils did not understand. Similar views were also put forward by the Irish National Teachers' Organization in 1941. In 1966 an independent and quite sophisticated piece of research vindicated many of their claims when it found that the great amount of time devoted to Irish was responsible for the lower standard of education among Irish primary school children compared with their counterparts in England.[65] But arguments of this sort, especially when they came from Protestants, had no appreciable influence on the government before 1945.

Catholics as well as Protestants were initially hampered by a shortage of qualified teachers, but for obvious reasons Irish was slower to take hold in Protestant schools. In fact, older Protestants in rural areas recalled that some of their schools taught no Irish whatsoever during the 1920s and early 1930s. Through summer courses and the establishment of the Irish-speaking preparatory colleges, the situation slowly improved so that by 1940 88 per cent of all teachers and 73 per cent of Protestants were appropriately qualified.[66] According to older teachers, retirements and the introduction of financial penalties for the unqualified ensured that the remainder were eventually qualified. Even so, neither teachers nor managers were inclined to do anything more than meet the letter of the law, especially when it came to teaching other subjects through Irish. The attitude in Catholic schools was undoubtedly more positive, although the difference should not be exaggerated. At the height of the language revival in the 1930s, the typical primary school in the country continued to teach most subjects in English beyond infant classes.[67]

By the 1940s a similar pattern of embittered acquiescence prevailed in secondary schools. The problem of obtaining Irish teachers was never as acute because only one teacher was required for each school, although the High School in Dublin did not obtain a satisfactory teacher of Irish until 1936.[68] Through the 1940s, and even into the 1950s in some cases, headmasters acknowledged that passing Irish remained "a problem." But once again the pragmatism of Protestants eventually reasserted itself, since most schools could not ignore the need to obtain government grants and examination results. As one headmaster put it, "we accepted Irish but with rather bad grace." Little more was involved, for they rarely if ever used Irish as a language of instruction, whereas 64 per cent of the nation's schools did so in 1941.[69]

By the 1970s the previous antipathy towards Irish had been replaced by an attitude of indifference. Only one of the headmasters I interviewed was an ardent language enthusiast, but they all accepted it as a legitimate part of the curriculum and they claimed that parental animosity was a thing of the past. However, not all the change had been on one side. As early as 1941, the INTO indicated that parents and teachers throughout the country were unhappy with the extreme rigour of government regulations. No immediate change was introduced, but in the following years there was a slow easing of the pressure on the schools. In 1948 English was readmitted as a subject in infant classes. In 1965 the Department of Education advised that Irish not be used as a medium of instruction in the lower levels of the national schools, and by the 1970s the amount of time devoted to its study had been reduced. Similarly, the proportion of secondary schools teaching in Irish diminished from 64 per cent in 1941 to less than 10 per cent in the late 1960s.[70] Then in 1973 the government ceased to demand that candidates must pass in Irish in order to be awarded the intermediate and leaving certificates. These measures silenced many of the initial objections of Protestants, and they confirm my earlier argument that Catholic commitment to Gaelic revival was on the decline. In this new atmosphere, Irish has simply become a non-issue.

In many ways, the "national tone" required of the rest of the curriculum was much more instrumental in fostering a sense of Irish identity within Protestant schools. In particular, the almost exclusive concern with Irish affairs in the new history courses stood in marked contrast to the British orientation of Protestant schools before independence. It also differed radically from the situation in Northern Ireland where Protestant children were brought up to look to Britain and its capital as their essential frame of reference, while Catholics were steeped in the struggles of their ancestors with Britain.[71] In broad terms, the shared curriculum of the South had three general consequences. First, the absence of any concerted focus on British history meant that Protestants were no longer exposed in any systematic way to the glories of empire with which they had once so clearly associated themselves. Second, although Britain could not be ignored, the emphasis was on her activities of conquest and foreign domination. Cast in such terms, the British connection came to be seen as embarrassing, if not worthy of condemnation. And third, the focus on Irish history brought out the long involvement and many achievements of Protestants in Ireland. Indeed, through the examples of Wolfe Tone, Davis, and Parnell, Protestant children were led to discover that Protestants had also made their contribution to the nationalist struggle. In short, the new curriculum brought out the dormant Irish context of their history, and it belittled their British allegiance by neglect and by the presentation of Britain's oppressive role in Ireland.

This is not to say that Protestant children were immediately transformed into committed nationalists. Within the protective confines of their schools, the strong British loyalties of older teachers raised prior to independence undoubtedly coloured their interpretation of the curriculum required by the state. The passive resistance of the schools is perhaps best illustrated by their refusal to take up the Gaelic games which were played so extensively in Catholic schools. The insular and "exaggerated nationalism" of many of the school texts with their "stress on war and hatred of the enemy" may also have alienated young Protestant readers at the same time that it weakened their British sympathies.[72] As one teacher recalled of his school days in the 1930s, "We would not sing God Save the King but neither would we sing the Soldier's Song." A transitional stage of this sort may well have been inevitable, but not all texts suffered from these excesses and there was sufficient choice for the worst to be avoided. In fact, the Church of Ireland commissioned a primary school history which was then approved by the Department of Education in 1945.[73] While it could not be described as a pro-British apologetic, its stress on church history did reflect the growing propensity of Protestants to look to their religion as the basis of their identity.

Yet no matter what text was used, the essential thrust of the new curriculum could not be circumvented. In both primary and secondary schools, inspectors were there to ensure that the appropriate material was covered, and at secondary schools there was always the awareness that examinations were set and marked by the state. More importantly, the teachers I interviewed who had entered the profession in the 1930s and 1940s claimed that most of their generation was committed to weaning pupils from their attachment to Britain. Like the Church of Ireland and the *Irish*

Times, they believed that survival in independent Ireland was possible only through a whole-hearted recognition of their Irish origins and identity. These aspirations were greatly encouraged in the 1960s when public criticism led to the publication of a new and more objective series of history textbooks.[74] The changed attitude of the state is best conveyed by the introductory comments on the teaching of history in the new primary school curriculum: "The picture of events which the child carries from the classroom should be true to the facts and unspoiled by special pleadings of any kind. It should in particular represent fairly the contributions of all creeds and classes to the evolution of modern Ireland."[75] The emphasis on Irish matters still remained strong, but with this more tolerant outlook the earlier ambivalence of Protestants largely disappeared. The exception was the most socially exclusive Protestant secondary school in the Republic which had the unique habit of recruiting its headmasters from England. Here the attitude still prevailed that "we don't belong to anybody" and that "we don't have to salute any flag at dawn." But in the others, headmasters and teachers were insistent that there was universal support for their commitment to "make our boys truly Irish and see their careers in Ireland." "Being Irish," they all agreed, "is something we take for granted," and they claimed that this has been so since roughly the beginning of the 1950s.

Religious education. When it came to the defence of their religious heritage, Protestants seemed to be on far firmer ground. Just as the state afforded the churches extensive administrative powers, so too did it go out of its way to reassure them that religious education should have a central place in their schools and that they should have control of its content.[76] This should have provided sufficient protection, but in the early 1920s the Board of Education was moved to complain bitterly that school readers prescribed by the government contained references to Catholic beliefs and imagery. It was especially distressed by books in the Irish language, for there was little Protestant literature in the field and many of the stock phrases in Irish referred to Catholic saints and Catholic interpretations of the afterlife. At the General Synod of 1923, it was claimed that "there were Inspectors demanding that these doctrines should be taught to and repeated by Church of Ireland children."[77] It is possible that Protestants were occasionally subject to pressures of this sort, although it is quite likely that their protest was also linked to their intense aversion to the Irish language. While few Protestants seriously believed that the state was surreptitiously attempting to convert them to Catholicism,[78] here was an issue like that of mixed marriages where they felt safe in voicing their discontent. The result was that an angry deputation was soon sent to the minister of education, who readily promised that "no Protestant should be subjected to teaching of which his Church did not approve."[79] In 1927 their fears were further appeased when a new series of readers was published which excluded all the expressions to which the board had objected.[80] Over the next thirty-five years, the board continued to criticize later editions of readers, but the few offensive phrases that were found were little more than a minor irritant which could be ignored with the full blessing of the state.

Within the schools, the treatment accorded to religion varied considerably. In primary schools, it was a central part of the curriculum. Normally, half an hour a day was devoted to religious education, and the day was usually started with a few prayers and a hymn. As the children were young, the emphasis was strongly biblical, although some doctrine was taught through the study of the catechism. The teachers, it may be remembered, tended to come from rural and poorer backgrounds where a greater intrinsic importance was attached to religious convictions and distinctions than was the case in other parts of the community. The heavy stress which they naturally placed on religion was also strengthened by the General Synod examinations which were held annually in most schools before the 1960s. Regardless of their personal convictions, teachers treated the examinations seriously because this was the only situation in which Protestants could compete solely with each other and without the frustration of the Irish language. The presence of the latter in state examinations meant that neither teachers nor parents regarded them as a true measure of a child's ability, but the Synod examinations were quite another matter. After much preparation, a flock of clergy usually descended on the parish to administer the examinations, and a half-day holiday was called to celebrate their completion. The occasion was widely regarded as one of the major events in the school year.

In secondary schools, the preservation of their Protestant heritage was regarded as an equally important responsibility, but it tended to be expressed in a rather different way. In the day-to-day life of the schools, Protestantism was presented in terms of a commitment to independent and critical thinking, moral rectitude, and personal responsibility. As noted in chapter 5, these values were linked to the class and ethnic interests of Protestants, and it bears repetition that their portrayal as distinctively Protestant carried the usually unstated implication that Catholics did not subscribe to or meet these standards. In large measure, the schools focused on the moral and social superiority of the Protestant way of life rather than on matters of personal faith and salvation. Of course, it was all true, but too much religion, especially of an openly spiritual nature, was seen to have a certain suspect and even Catholic character. In this climate – and perhaps because of it – religious education per se received a relatively small amount of attention. Schools varied, but only two or three of the more than forty classes a week were usually set aside for religious instruction. Prior to the 1960s sections of the Old and New Testaments were studied in depth, and a much greater emphasis was placed on church doctrine and history than in the national schools. Built into much of the latter material were the acrimonious debates with Catholicism that were so often expressed in the pamphlet literature. No doubt the details of episcopal continuity at the Reformation or the logical fallacies of infallibility seemed rather dry fare to many teenagers. As one writer in the 1940s recalled, pamphlets such as "'Roman Claims' and 'Ireland and Her Church' were learnt in the same disinterested manner as Virgil IV and VI or Euclid VI and VII."[81] Nevertheless, the significance of religious education should not be underestimated, for it provided Protestants with the intellectual basis for their claim to a distinctive Irish identity and for their conviction of superiority. In general, a rather unemotional view prevailed that religion was taught because it was good for one, because it clarified who one was, and because it was a necessary defence against an inferior, hostile, and erroneous Catholicism.

As the forces of secularization and ecumenism emerged, the schools, like so many other parts of the community, began to question the importance and character of their religious identity. One of the first manifestations of this change was the 1965 decision to terminate the General Synod examinations. They were reintroduced on a voluntary basis in 1968, but only a minority of schools made use of them in the 1970s. In the mid-1960s, new curricula were also introduced in both primary and secondary schools, and in 1973 a committee of the General Synod published a major revaluation of religious education in the schools. In its report, the committee repeatedly stressed that this was an "increasingly secularist age," in which "most pupils ... regard the teaching of religion as being boring and irrelevant to the problems of their maturing lives." It warned that there was danger in spending "too much time explaining our ecclesiastical positions," since "A high proportion of the pupils in our Irish schools seem to be dissatisfied with the historical record and present performance of the Irish churches to the degree that many are beginning to ignore the existence of the churches." Hence the committee advised that the objective of the past, "to instruct the pupils in the Christian faith," was "no longer an adequate or appropriate aim." The new purpose was "not to indoctrinate but to explore." To this end it recommended that "The syllabus must also include other religions and ideologies which will be studied as sympathetically and as objectively as possible." Such a change, it acknowledged, "would seem to lead away from the denominational teaching of the past."[82]

During the later 1970s, this report led to the publication of a new set of guidelines which elaborated and extended the changes of the 1960s. At primary schools, denominational instruction was now largely absent, although a brief treatment of the creed and catechism was still retained in the second half of the final year. In secondary schools, the new instructions to teachers furthered the movement away from church doctrine and tendentious church history which had started in the 1960s. Under the new guidelines, the first three years were devoted to an historical and contextual analysis of the Bible and early Christianity. In the last three years, nine units of study were drawn up, of which only one dealt with Church of Ireland doctrine. New units now included such topics as comparative religion, poverty in the Third World, secular philosophies (marxism and humanism), and human relationships. In this last unit, the sensitive issue of mixed marriages was raised, but the notes for teachers suggested that "while the difficulties ... must be faced, it is important for the teacher to take a positive attitude." All this additional material meant that Irish church history was confined to one unit, which was now presented in conjunction with a detailed treatment of the growth of ecumenism both within and outside Ireland. The ecclesiological and liturgical differences of the Reformation were not to be ignored, but the spirit of the new curriculum may be gathered from the advice that any of the Thirty-nine Articles considered "hurtful to other Christians" should be "deplored in an age in which the Church of Ireland is committed to ecumenism."[83]

By the mid-1970s this stress on being Christian rather than being Protestant was evident in all schools, although the extent to which they were prepared to embrace this new notion varied. At the national schools, and especially in rural areas, the teachers, like the communities they served, still retained a strong sense of their Protestantism; while in Dublin there was a much more explicit commitment "to make our pupils decent Christians and not just good members of the Church of Ireland." Over the same period, some voices were raised, claiming that the standard and status of religious education throughout the country had been lowered by the abolition of the General Synod examinations.[84] Without the spur of competition and the threat of invidious comparisons, this does seem likely, although it is difficult to prove conclusively. In rural dioceses, some of the old customs were still retained, for some bishops continued to conduct annual tours of their national schools in which they administered a rather informal test of the children's religious knowledge. However, on one such tour which I joined I could find little to quarrel with in the glum observation of the bishop that he might as well have been asking the children about the Bhagavad Gita as the New Testament.

In secondary schools, only two of the headmasters I interviewed were openly committed to a "feeling of being Christian that is not tied down denominationally." But there were other indications that precisely such a trend was emerging. In all schools, the modified versions of the official Church of Ireland curriculum which were now being used shared its cursory attention to doctrine and its ecumenical emphasis. According to a report by the Dublin Diocesan Board of Education, religious education was now a "Cinderella subject" which provided "at best patchy Church teaching."[85] The Protestant ethos of the schools was also being eroded by the presence of a substantial number of Catholic teachers and an almost equally large percentage of Catholic pupils. Moreover, all four of the schools with a significant intake of Catholic pupils, as well as others in a similar situation, were now providing various forms of integrated religious education. There were exceptions,[86] and sometimes integration meant little more than insisting that the Church of Ireland curriculum was so "broadly based" as to be acceptable to all denominations – though there was more than a grain of truth in this latter claim. Elsewhere there was a much more thorough commitment to integration, which ranged from completely shared classes and a common curriculum to situations in which separate doctrinal instruction was provided along with mixed classes in other areas of religion.

These experiments appeared to be firmly rooted. In 1973 the Catholic Church complained to a number of Protestant secondary schools that it was being denied access to its pupils. Although this caused considerable consternation, all six schools in 1978 were still refusing to alter their existing arrangements in religious education because they claimed that most parents supported their efforts at integration.[87] The old values of individualism, personal responsibility, and the like were still espoused, but for all of the above reasons they were now much less likely to be defended as particularly Protestant in origin and character. It would be a mistake to think that all teachers welcomed this "apathy in our teaching of Anglicanism," and Archbishop McAdoo publicly complained that many parents were as distressed as he was at the lack of doctrinal instruction in most schools.[88] This conservative reaction may grow in the future, but it is highly questionable whether it can overcome the developments of the last decade and a half. According to concerned teachers, their pupils now attached "little importance to being Protestant," and the teachers readily conceded that they were "fighting to hold on to things that are being lost by neglect." Under these conditions, a new generation of Protestants was emerging who were far more familiar with Catholics than were their parents and who could see far less reason for maintaining their separateness.

CHAPTER SEVEN

Community Life

During the interviews I conducted in 1973 and 1974 within the six parishes selected for intensive study, I came to realize that there was no single or uniform style of segregation shared by all Protestants. Religious, ethnic, and overall class differences everywhere played some part in shaping their outlook and behaviour, but the importance and ramifications of these three basic divisions varied substantially from one part of the community to another. This internal social diversity was compounded by regional peculiarities, by varying degrees of population density, and by the marked difference between rural and urban ways of life. Although every parish had its unique qualities, it seemed to me that they could be reduced to four basic types. Each type perceived its identity in a different fashion, each related to its Catholic neighbours in a correspondingly different manner, and each responded in a different way to the various changes at the national level described in previous chapters.

FARMERS AND RURAL TOWNSMEN

The rural minority's relatively low mixed marriage rate of 20 to 25 per cent[1] suggests that it was more committed than any other part of the community to preserving its identity and separate communal existence. However, it should not be assumed that rural Protestants were more isolated or cut off from their Catholic neighbours than were their urban counterparts. In fact, in some respects, frequent and familiar contact with Catholics was a much more firmly established tradition in rural areas. Due to the small size of their community, most Protestant shopkeepers, doctors, lawyers, and the like were forced to rely on Catholic customers; and as in any rural area, their business relations tended to be enduring and far from impersonal. Especially prior to mechanization, Protestant farmers often cooperated with their Catholic neighbours at busy times of the year, and they regularly encountered one another at cattle markets, the creamery, and the cooperative. Even in the border counties, Protestants "couldn't live without our Catholic neighbours," who were often "a great help" when sickness or other crises disrupted the daily round of farming. And further south of the border, mutual aid and contact of this sort was all the more common, since Protestants were much more widely dispersed. Demographic necessity may have been the root cause of these practices, but they were also facilitated by the greater social homogeneity and shared interest of neighbours in rural as opposed to urban areas. And once established, they became an accepted tradition in their own right.

The extent and character of this familiarity should not be misunderstood, for underlying it, and in part stemming from it, was once much greater friction than ever existed in urban areas. It is impossible to prove this beyond a shadow of a doubt, but most of the serious tensions related to me in interviews and the great majority of publicly documented cases of overt conflict (e.g., during the Civil War, the Dunbar-Harrison case, and the incident at Fethard-on-Sea) occurred in rural areas. Three different incidents illustrate the various reasons for the rural minority's propensity to be cautious in dealing with Catholics. The first arose during the early 1950s when a Church of Ireland committee was formed to publicize the Protestant view on such matters as the Tilson case and the Mother and Child Act. It may be remembered that many Protestants considered the final decisions on these two issues to be discriminatory, because they were based on Catholic moral precepts which took no account of the divergent interests of the minority. When the committee made public its implicit criticism of the power of the Catholic church, its activities caused an especially strong stir in one rural parish whose rector was a member of the committee. Parishioners recalled that when they went down to the creamery to deliver their milk, their Catholic neighbours "would be talking over it and then they would hush." Being so few in number, the parishioners deeply resented their rector's behaviour, which they feared "would lead to an argument" that they could never hope to win. Although harsh words were exchanged over their milk carts, there was disagreement over whether anyone was physically assaulted. All stressed that this sort of incident "wouldn't happen now," for they felt that Catholics have grown less sensitive to any questioning or criticism of the power of the Catholic church. Catholics, as they put it, "don't mind the priest like they once did," and we have seen some evidence in the political arena to support this view. But even twenty years later, none of the older members of the parish had forgotten this time when "we used to be threatened."

The second incident was much more recent and was directly connected with "the troubles" in Northern Ireland. After "Bloody Sunday" in 1972, when a number of Catholics in Northern Ireland were shot by British troops, services of prayer were held in both Protestant and Catholic churches in many parts of the Republic. In rural areas, in particular, where actions could be readily observed, most Protestants made a point of attending their local church if a service was held. As one of these services in a Church of Ireland church started, a group of men, who appeared by their clothing to be members of the IRA, slipped into the back of the church. They sat quietly throughout the service. When it was over, they lined both sides of the path leading out of the church as the parishioners emerged. Nothing else happened after the service. Nor, as I have noted earlier, was there any evidence of a concerted campaign of intimidation throughout the country, although other incidents did occur.[2] Many Catholics in the area immediately went out of their way to let the minority know how atypical and repugnant they considered such behaviour to be. To the best of my knowledge, no other incident since that time has led Catholics to focus their frustration over the North so obviously on southern Protestants. But at a time of crisis like this, even the actions of a small number of Catholics inevitably accentuated the minority's underlying sense of vulnerability and separateness. And unalleviated by the anonymity of the city, the fears of the rural minority were all the more intense.

The third source of friction revolved around mixed marriages, although their increasing frequency and the recent evidence that Catholics were becoming more willing to marry in Protestant churches may have softened the minority's indignation. At a minimum, most rural Protestants would have shared with the middle class a sense of "terrible disappointment" at seeing their son or daughter "let us down" by doing what they themselves could neither do nor condone. But far more than this was involved in rural areas, for the entire community was acutely aware that a mixed marriage might well mean the loss of a family farm or business to "the other side." Such an event created a much more serious and visible threat to the very existence of most small and already struggling rural parishes than it did to the typically larger and more anonymous urban parish. There is little point in perpetuating the myth that Catholic girls were encouraged to seduce young Protestant men into marriages that robbed them of their virtue, wealth, and faith. On the other hand, there can be little doubt that Catholics derived considerable satisfaction at hearing of a Catholic purchase of or marriage into a Protestant farm or business. In one rural parish, for instance, the Catholic curate acknowledged that on a number of occasions he had been taken aside by some of his older parishioners who asked: "Did you hear of such a place; 'tis grand we got it back." A similar attitude might also be inferred from another more recent incident in a different part of the country, which occurred when the son of a Protestant farmer married a Catholic girl. After the wedding in the Catholic church, the wedding party toured the area, especially around the Protestant farms, honking their horns in celebration. In fact, it was far from certain whether the largely Catholic wedding party intended their gesture as friendly or taunting, but it is perhaps understandable that the latter interpretation was placed upon it by some local Protestants.

Prior to the 1960s, when the tensions between the two communities were much stronger, rural Protestants maintained polite but very distant relations with most Catholics. While they knew their Catholic neighbours far better than did urban Protestants, to mix socially at this time was quite another matter. Their overall superiority in class terms must have strengthened their sense of separateness and solidarity, but they did not involve themselves in segregated class-based associations in the way the urban middle class did. Nor were British traditions and loyalties as central a part of their lives, although their sympathies in this regard were certainly stronger than those of their Catholic neighbours. For the most part, their sense of identity and communal life revolved around religion and parish.

The one major exception to this rule was the Orange Lodge, which was essentially a northern institution. In the late 1960s a senior lodge official in the South estimated that there were about a thousand members in the Republic outside of Donegal. In the South as a whole, Orangeism was dying, and its principal building in Dublin, the Fowler Hall, was now being rented to its arch enemy, the government of the Republic.[3] However, local Orange lodges were once a vital part of the social life of Protestants in all three of the border counties. In the particular parish surveyed, all but a few shopkeepers, who did not wish to be associated for business purposes, had once been active members. Until approximately the beginning of the 1960s, the lodge's meetings, band competitions, and social events provided "all the outing you got then" other than those run by the parish. And since parish activities were usually dry, the toleration of drink at lodge activities gave them a much more festive atmosphere. Not unexpectedly, the overt anti-Catholicism of the Orange Lodge and its commitment to preserving Protestant dominance were not especially welcome in independent Ireland. After "a wee bit of trouble" during a "Twelfth Walk" held in county Leitrim in the 1930s, local lodges in the area decided to go to the greater security of Northern Ireland for the major marches of the year. As late as 1974, special services were still being held in some parish churches prior to the annual marches in July and August, but since the 1930s the attending Orangemen have not donned their sashes or unfurled their banners until they were safely inside the church.

In recent years, support of Orangeism has undergone a radical decline. Of six nearby lodges which had been active in the 1950s, three were closed by 1974, and two were reduced to a handful of members with only a nominal involvement. The one really surviving lodge was meeting far less frequently, and its membership was down to about a third of its active roll in the early 1960s. In part this was due to the steady decline in the total Protestant population over the last forty years. The intense rivalries between the many old lodges compounded their problems, for members of dying lodges often gave up their membership rather than combine forces with members of other lodges in the same position. In the parish surveyed, the rector, who had been raised further south, was personally opposed to the hostile rhetoric and strong British loyalties of Orangeism. After a real battle with his laity in the mid-1960s over the annual services in July and August, a compromise was reached whereby clergy from outside the parish were invited to lead the service. Thereafter, attendance at the services steadily declined. Although the other clergy did not share his strong views, the very fact that one man could make a difference was an indication of how fragile and hesitant loyalty to Orangeism had become. Indeed, from the beginning of the 1960s, older Orangemen admitted that the younger men, though they had often been involved as children, were becoming much less committed. The final blow came in 1969 with the outbreak of violence in Northern Ireland. From that point on, "fellows" were "afraid to be seen going down" to their lodges, and by 1974 none of the still active lodges in the region were prepared to send a contingent to the North for the annual celebrations. To some extent the demise of Orangeism was offset by parishioners shifting to the local Masonic lodge, but its restricted appeal to the more prestigious and affluent of Protestants meant that it did not integrate the entire community in the way the Orange Lodge had once done.

Both in the border counties and in the rest of the countryside, rural Protestants remained much more attached to their churches. In 1974 church services and other parochial activities were more widely supported in rural than urban areas, although there were fewer parish organizations because rural Protestants generally tended to be less associationally minded. At the extreme was the small, widely scattered, and remote parish in the southwest which had been unable to sustain any kind of regularly organized activity for many years. But in the midlands and border counties the great majority of married women were members of the Mothers' Union, and their menfolk were often on the select vestry of one of the small churches in their combined parishes. Teenagers and young adults were less likely to be involved in any kind of organization, but those who were invariably participated in parish clubs. Since these activities usually attracted limited age groups from an already small population, their very existence was indicative of a strong segregationist tendency. This is well illustrated by the parish badminton club in the midlands parish. On any given night in 1974, there were rarely more than seven or eight in attendance, but the members refused to join forces with a much larger Catholic club, even though they both shared the same premises. And similarly on the border, the experimental effort of the parish's badminton club of twenty-four to merge with the larger Catholic club failed after a year, when the Protestant members decided to withdraw for fear of losing their identity.

The great strength of rural Protestants lay in their continued efforts to provide segregated opportunities for unmarried adults to meet one another. These facilities have been absent in the remoter parts of the country for many years, but in 1974 there were regular Protestant dances as well as other recreational activities in two of the rural parishes surveyed. In the border parish, dances were held in an Orange lodge every six weeks; weekly dances took place in a market town some twenty miles away; and various parishes intermittently organized socials throughout the year. The midlands parish no longer ran its own socials in 1974, but it lay on the fringe of a circuit of Protestant dances that moved each week from one parish to another. Ranging in age from the early teens to well into middle age, 300 or more Protestants were regularly in attendance. With the loan of a family car, small groups drove as far as seventy miles to attend, and the occasions were widely recognized as "marriage markets." In pursuit of this goal, the local organizing committees provided subsidized busing each week to bring back eligible Protestant girls working in Dublin, so that they would provide a balance for the excess of males in this predominantly farming region. At one of the dances which I attended, two burly but very amiable young farmers politely demanded that each entrant sign his name and parish. They assured me that no more than half a dozen of those attending could be Catholics, although I later learned that they were not as effective at keeping out Catholics as they claimed. Nevertheless, it was this network of Protestant dances and the attitudes which underlay them that were the major reasons for the comparatively low rate of mixed marriages among the rural minority.

Of course, the fact that mixed marriages were growing in rural areas suggests that here too the tensions and divisions of the past were on the decline. This was most apparent in the increased participation of Protestants in local associations that had once been almost exclusively Catholic in membership. After 1945 farmers' organizations (e.g., the Irish Farmers' Association, Irish Country-women's Association, and Macra na Feirma) and cooperatives proliferated in number and in the frequency of their meetings and activities. If only for economic reasons, most Protestant farmers had joined by 1974, and in both of the larger rural parishes their numbers on local committees slightly exceeded their proportion of the total population. With the growth of self-confidence and prosperity in the 1960s, a local development association, a branch of the Red Cross, and a Chamber of Commerce were established in the border parish. Although Protestants were initially somewhat wary of joining, they soon overcame their scruples with the encouragement of their rector and were active participants by 1974. Similar developments were equally evident in many other parts of the midlands. Moreover, Protestants throughout the country were again drawn into contact with Catholics through their involvement in new, nondenominational services for the aged and other needy groups. And in the depressed and depopulated parish in the southwest, two Protestants joined the eleven-member community council that had been set up to combat the social and economic problems shared by both religious groups. In all these ways, the South differed from rural Northern Ireland where avowedly secular organizations of this sort usually failed to play the same integrative role. Since they were largely composed of the more established and affluent residents of the North, they effectively excluded all but a very small number of the Catholic minority.[4] In contrast, the same class bias in these organizations in the Republic actually helped to attract Protestants, and with their small numbers it was inevitable that they would find themselves in the minority.

With their limited charitable and economic interests, these new associations did not provide as intimate an atmosphere as that found at a parish social. But whether it was through polite conversation at the meeting itself, a more informal drink at a nearby pub afterwards, or the more festive atmosphere of the annual dinner dance, the two sides were brought closer together than ever before. The closer and more harmonious relations that resulted were to be seen in the experience of a Church of Ireland fund-raising committee in the midlands parish during the early 1970s. According to government regulations, the parish was obliged to provide a certain proportion of the capital costs incurred in the building of a new parish school. In its endeavours to raise this money, the committee successfully solicited support from the local cooperative and from some of the Catholic merchants. It also ran a highly successful dinner dance as another fund-raising effort, and this too was supported by Catholics as well as Protestants. As one local farmer acknowledged, "It wouldn't have happened when I was a boy."

This more outgoing attitude among older Protestants inevitably had its parallels among the young. A crucial development here was the increasingly common practice of enrolling Protestant children at vocational or Catholic secondary schools, where they acquired a familiarity with Catholics that was far greater than that of their parents. In marked contrast to the behaviour of previous generations, it was also becoming common for unmarried adults and young married couples to go out to local bars and hotels for drinks and musical entertainment. At the same time, the clergy claimed that more and more of their young people were attending local public dances which had the added attractions of bar facilities and better-known bands. For the moment, younger Protestants continued to follow their parents' wishes by attending their own dances. But with the emergence of so many new situations where young and old mixed with Catholics, it may well become increasingly difficult to sustain the more private forms of segregation that still survived.

Over the same period, there was also a decline in the intensity of Protestant social life. Until about 1945 there had been many more socials and other forms of recreation organized by both of the larger rural parishes surveyed. Most of the constituent churches in what became the present-day amalgamated parish had once held at least one social of its own a year, and most of the churches had once sponsored a table tennis club in a league of Protestant parishes. Within close proximity to the current geographic boundaries of the midlands parish, there had been approximately ten socials a year in the late 1940s, but by 1974 they had fallen to two. Besides its struggling badminton club, only one of its outlying churches by this later date kept up a small table tennis club which no longer competed with any other parish. Both the border parish and other parishes in the midlands were more successful in retaining a wider umbrella of parochial organizations, but here too those in the outlying churches were less involved in the now centralized organizations of the parish. And at a more informal level, it was widely believed, there had previously been much more visiting among members of the parish, whereas many now found that they often did not meet one another "between Sundays."

The advent of television, the increased affluence of recent years, and a dwindling population all contributed to this decline in solidarity, but recent difficulties at Protestant dances suggest that more than this was involved. In the border parish, for instance, the weekly dances that had once been held at the Masonic Hall in the centre of the town were stopped because "no one would stand at the door any longer" to prevent Catholics from entering. Similarly, the rector of the midlands parish closed his parish's twice-yearly dances in 1970 because he did not wish to give offence to "the outsiders" who "started to come." At a local circuit dance a few years later, one of the Protestant doormen, who delivered milk in the area, had some of his bottles overturned the morning after he ejected a Catholic from the dance. No more than fifty attended the following dance, although their numbers rose within a few months to close to their previous level. Elsewhere on the circuit, the laity who manned the door became increasingly reluctant to refuse entry to Catholics whom they were now more likely to meet in other situations. By the mid-1970s, I was told, a "fair few" Catholics were attending all the dances. But at one of the dances on the circuit, this practice seemed to have been halted in 1977 when the young, newly appointed rector began to attend the dances so that he could personally explain to any Catholic wishing to enter the Protestant objection to the Catholic church's laws on mixed marriages. His apparent success would not have been possible without the tacit support of his parishioners. However, they were not prepared to make this stand on their own, and one might reasonably question whether many of the now aging body of clergy would be prepared to lead their laity in this way.

With the exception of the new and rather confusing situation that arose when a Protestant brought a Catholic friend to one of the dances, rural Protestants were generally agreed that Catholic interest in their dances was due to simple curiosity, stimulated, at times, by "a few jars." Although there was far less agreement over whether these encounters have become more frequent in recent years, it is possible that this has occurred. Indeed, it seems likely that Catholics have grown less prone to think in segregationist terms as they have begun to intermingle with Protestants in other public situations. In the 1970s, rural Protestants remained committed to their parishes and to the preservation of a substantial measure of segregation in the more intimate areas of their social lives. Nevertheless, their community boundaries were growing more fragile and their segregationist convictions were starting to waver in the face of the more open attitude of Catholics. When to these developments is added their own greater willingness to mix with Catholics in activities not directly connected with their parishes, it is not surprising to find that the number of mixed marriages was increasing.

WEST BRITONS

Ever since 1922, as indeed for many years prior to independence, West Britons have been by far the smallest group within the Protestant community. They may be loosely regarded as the present-day descendants of the Ascendancy, although in many cases their genealogical links with the old land-owning aristocracy were either obscure or totallly lacking by the 1960s and 1970s. The events leading up to and spanning independence had, of course, thoroughly broken their political and economic control of the country. Moreover, their numbers had been drastically reduced between 1916 and 1923, when so many became embroiled in violence, were intimidated, saw their houses burned, and then finally fled the country. Those who remained after 1922 were for a time able to preserve much of their old way of life and some remained quite wealthy, but they were well aware that the country was now firmly in the hands of Catholics who would tolerate no interference from their former masters. In the post-1922 era, the continuity of the West Britons with their ascendancy past consisted primarily of their social isolation from the rest of Irish society and their markedly English cultural traditions. To use the terminology of this book, their distinctive characteristic now lay in their heavy emphasis on the ethnic element of their identity. In this, they remained visibly separate not only from the Catholic majority but from the remainder of the Protestant community.

In the years between independence and World War II, small pockets of West Briton society were to be found in both urban and rural areas. In his autobiography, Brian Inglis provides a vivid portrayal of his West Briton youth in Malahide, an old village and suburb of Dublin. His "set" included retired officers in the British armed forces and colonial service, higher professionals, and those in higher management and shareholding positions in the larger Dublin firms. The dividing line was based not simply on income but on whether one's position was in an old-established firm, and on whether that firm was in wholesale or retail trade. Those involved in trade were socially unacceptable, whereas others with much lower incomes were readily accepted if they had the right sort of upbringing, or preferably if they could lay claim to titled connections.[5] In rural areas, the "county" or West Briton world consisted of large landowners, gentlemen farmers, the Church of Ireland clergymen, and at times some of the local professionals. Here too income was not the sole consideration, for some of the more substantial Protestant farmers were not considered part of the county set if their education, lifestyle, and interests were too firmly rooted in their parish and in Ireland. After 1945 the ranks of the West Britons were swelled by a small trickle of Englishmen and displaced ex-colonials who wished to avoid the welfare state and higher taxes of a Labour government, and who saw rural Ireland as a cheaper and more hospitable environment in which they might pursue the ways of the gentry.

The distinctively English cultural style of the West Britons was sustained and made evident in a number of ways. The most obvious was their accent, and if a Irish influence could be detected by a discerning ear, this distinction was rarely apparent to the Catholic majority. Children might acquire a local Irish accent from the servants, but the usual sojourn in an English boarding school invariably eradicated this unfortunate mark. For many years, it was common for them to spend some time working or soldiering in England prior to taking up a position in a family firm. For those returning to a family farm or estate, a stay at Cirencester, an English agricultural college, was a frequent choice; but Gurteen, the Methodist agricultural college attended by the more affluent of the rural Protestants, held little attraction for West Britons. Even for those who returned directly to Trinity, its aloof and elitist stance, its strong British sympathies, its longstanding tradition of service within the British Empire, and its large intake of English students between 1945 and 1960 all helped to keep alive their affinity with England. The closeness of this connection is perhaps best conveyed by the fact that five of the seven West Briton men whom I interviewed had English wives. Yet these various examples do not do justice to the deep English conditioning which imbued all aspects of their lives from their dress to their "reflex reactions in all manner of social circumstances,"[6] and which in turn created an immense barrier between themselves and the rest of Irish society.

The social life of the West Britons retained a marked insularity until about 1945. In these prewar years, Irish society was seen as essentially a two-class system in which "Catholics were people one did not talk to." Indeed, they tended to regard Catholics "as if they were Blacks," but this did not mean that they felt any sense of hostility, for the vast social distance between the two groups ensured that "relations with our servants were always very good." Servants, workmen, and shop-assistants were mainly Catholic, and if they were Protestant they were treated much the same. One of the focal points of Inglis's set in Malahide was the weekly Church of Ireland service, where "the week's social occasions could be arranged."[7] The other was the nearby golf club, which took care, "other things being equal, that families 'in trade' and Roman Catholics were excluded."[8] A similar situation prevailed in the West Briton county world, where it seemed that "there were two of everything." Here, their golf club, which had been privately owned by one of the gentry, had been sold to the town in the late 1920s, but they were still able to maintain their own tennis and boating clubs – the town's club, of course, being a sailing club, while the county's was a yacht club. For the men, there was also a club in the central market town which served as a common gathering point in this more leisurely era, when "people would come into town by horse and spend all day." And within this closed social network, there was a great deal of visiting and many private parties, dances, tennis afternoons, and the like. If there was any contact with the rest of society, it was usually through the widely shared passion of Irish countryfolk for hunting. But once again, at the major social event of the hunting season, the Hunt Ball, "At least 90 per cent of the group we went with were Protestants, although it wasn't something we thought of."

Religion was an integral part of their lives, but it did not have the all-consuming importance for the West Britons that it had for most other Protestants at this time. Financially and in terms of church attendance, they were usually loyal supporters of their parish, and in rural areas in particular one or two from their ranks were normally invited to serve on the select vestry. It was common for West Briton ladies to devote much time, energy, and leadership to the annual bazaar and other major events of the year, and a few became heavily involved in the national leadership of the Mothers' Union. Yet all were agreed that "our lives never revolved around the parish," since this would have involved mixing with the less affluent members of the parish, a relationship which would have been equally uncomfortable for both parties. Most simply never considered participating in the badminton and other recreational activities of the parish, but some recalled that as children they "were not allowed to mix" with the rest of the parishioners. Indeed, they had little opportunity, for even prior to going away to boarding school most of the young West Britons were sent to private schools rather than the local Protestant national school.

The barrier was clearly one of class and status. In the men's club of the county set, "businessmen couldn't get in," and it was said that this applied with equal force to both Catholics and Protestants. Similarly, Inglis recalled that a prosperous shop-keeper and active member of his parish, whose daughter had been captain of the ladies team at Trinity, was nonetheless refused membership in Inglis's club because of his background in trade.[9] Such rigorous exclusivity may have been possible in the larger West Briton community around Dublin, but in the rest of the country this class boundary was not drawn so rigorously. As another Protestant from a "well-to-do" shop-keeper's background recollected of his youth before the war, "my religion alone ... was sufficient to secure for me entry into the homes of the landed gentry and titled persons dwelling within a fifteen-mile radius of the town." His apparently superior education and his admitted abilities as a "promising raconteur and a tennis player" probably set him apart from most of his Protestant peers.[10] But it is most unlikely that such attributes in a Catholic with a similar background would have been sufficient to gain him entry into the West Briton world.

The corollary of all this is that the West Briton world contained a small proportion of what were known as "Castle Catholics." These were Catholics whose social and cultural backgrounds were indistinguishable from that of the West Britons. Although the rest of the Protestant community regarded them with some suspicion, the West Britons usually had no compunction in treating them as fellow gentry. Of course, Irish history had ensured that the great majority of West Britons were Protestants, and in most of their clubs "there were never more than one or two Roman Catholics." But in certain circumstances the West Britons were prepared to subordinate religious considerations to those of ethnicity and status. In no other part of the Protestant community was this true at this time.

The closed world of the West Britons went into further decline in the years after 1945. The major cause appears to have been their high rate of emigration, although there are no conclusive statistics to prove that they emigrated more frequently than other Protestants. With their English accents and elitist traditions, there is every reason to believe that they were made to feel especially unwelcome by the Catholic majority, and their educational and career links with England made it all the easier for them to leave. The markedly anti-Irish ethos of the one secondary school in the south favoured by the West Britons also did little to encourage them to stay. According to the records of its old boys' association, about 50 per cent of those entering the school in 1945 subsequently emigrated. This was significantly higher than the already heavy emigration rate for the minority as a whole between 1945 and 1960. Thereafter, greater prosperity reduced emigration throughout the country, but in the seven West Briton families I interviewed six of their fourteen children over the age of twenty-one had emigrated by 1974. All six had left after 1960.

Those who remained responded to this demographic pressure in two ways. One was a rooted unwillingness to make any form of compromise with the rising Catholic majority. Rather than alter its traditional recruitment practices, the men's club supported by the rural West Britons was simply closed in the early 1950s, although in fairness it should be added that this symbol of a more leisured and traditional era had become something of an anachronism with the growing use of the motor car. However, this was not true of the tennis club, which "the county people wanted to sell" when it became clear that they could no longer keep going on their own. At the rector's insistence, the premises were eventually given to the club run by the town, but most of the West Briton members resigned. In 1974 only one parishioner was a member of the new amalgamated club.

The other, more common response was the decision "to broaden our social base to survive." Symptomatic of this trend was the experience of a yacht club which was widely regarded as a West Briton bastion until the 1950s. By this time, its membership had dropped so severely that it was "down to three sailing clubs." Faced with the threat of imminent collapse, the club's committee made a conscious decision in 1955 "to get Catholic members" by admitting all who could afford to join, although radical change did not occur until the more prosperous 1960s. This opened the door to the remainder of the Protestant community, but by 1974 only three of the seven members of the club's committee and approximately a third of the now 300 club members were Protestants. At the same time, there was a radical decline in the frequency of the more informal linkages of tennis afternoons and "at home days" which had once been so characteristic of West Briton life. Inglis described the West Britons in Dublin as having reached "a tacit clubbable understanding" with Catholics by the late 1950s. "The two groups fused together in golf clubs and yacht clubs, drank together in bars and even entertained each other at cocktail parties learning to avoid confrontation."[11] These changes were somewhat slower to emerge in rural areas, but here too the end result was much the same. By the mid-1970s, all that remained of the former West Briton world were their integrated clubs and their equally mixed cocktail circuits of higher professionals, large farmers, and business executives. Class, they now claimed, was the basis on which they selected their friends, and though they continued to support their parishes they remained as distant as ever from the rest of their fellow parishioners. But when I pressed the matter, all admitted that "most of our close friends are Protestants" and that "our dinner parties are mainly Protestant."

Despite the many changes in their organized social life, there was a far less appreciable decline in their cultural visibility and sense of marginality. All of those over the age of forty still retained obviously anglicized accents. They claimed that they thought of themselves as more whole-heartedly Irish than the previous generation, but it was only among these older West Britons that I heard the rather defensive qualification, "I suppose we are really Anglo-Irish." In a 1964 community survey in County Cork, this persisting sense of marginality was brought home to John Jackson when a West Briton, who was contacted in the course of a survey, argued that his family "should not be included because 'it's not meant for people like us' – even though they had been resident in the same house in the same district for three generations."[12] In a similar vein, J. Morris encountered a "youngish Anglo-Irish landowner" who expressed great indignation at any questioning of his Irish identity, since he could trace his Irish ancestry back some 400 years. Yet Morris "wasn't at all sure, for I knew that he travelled on a British passport, had a son at Eton and spends a large part of his time in London."[13] These two examples may be rather extreme, for all of the West Britons I interviewed were now firmly based in Ireland. In their own way, they were also making some effort to break with past tradition. The headmasters of the two most expensive Protestant secondary schools said that they were now receiving an increasing number of applications from parents who had been educated abroad. In fact, only six of the seventeen children in the seven West Briton families interviewed had been educated in England, whereas all of their fathers had done so. However, the school most commonly selected by the West Britons, with its English headmaster and ingrained tendency to look to England, was less than fully successful in changing the anglicized demeanour and hyphenated sense of nationality upon which the alienation of the West Britons was based. With this sort of background and education, even the young remained highly sensitive to what they regarded as the common Catholic view that "well, you're not really Irish, are you?" In short, what remained of the world of the West Britons were scattered but still marginal individuals.

THE URBAN LOWER CLASSES

Although true poverty was much more common among Catholics, Dublin contained a number of Church of Ireland parishes in which a substantial proportion of the members were lower-middle or working class in origin. The shop-keepers, artisans, blue-collar workers, and clerks in the parish I have called Lower Lansdowne once formed a significant part of the urban Protestant community. However, their numbers have declined at an especially rapid rate since 1922. A high rate of emigration after World War II was partly responsible, and it was compounded by the movement of their upwardly mobile children into newer, middle-class suburbs. The latter trend is likely to continue in the future, but this group's survival in the 1970s was principally threatened by an approximately 44 per cent rate of mixed marriages. This figure, which was based on a sample of fifty, would appear to be confirmed in its general accuracy by a recent estimate that one of every two engagements was to a Catholic in the socially similar parish of North Strand.[14] Whichever figure is used, both were significantly higher than the mixed marriage rates for either the rural minority or the Protestant middle class.

What set the parishioners of Lower Lansdowne apart and made them such "a distinctive layer in Dublin society" was that "their whole social life centered not on the Empire or Ireland or Dublin, but on the parish."[15] It almost goes without saying that "the majority of people were more British minded" during the 1920s and 1930s, but they soon learned "to live without the British connection." Their narrow world view, their limited opportunities to involve themselves in the running of the empire, their heavy Irish accents, and their many contacts with Catholics in the work world all contributed to the early disappearance of their British allegiance. But the significance of this trend should not be exaggerated, since mixed marriages were extremely rare at that time. Again, and for obvious reasons, the class-based associations of the West Britons and the urban middle class never played as important a part in their lives, although class-tinged attitudes of aloofness and superiority were not entirely absent. "The working-class Protestant," claimed a small shopkeeper, "was always that little bit more refined trying to keep up with the other members of his Church." But here too, with the demise of the Protestant firm and the advantages it entailed, much of "this different code of honour going back to my youth is gone now." It follows that we must look primarily to changes in religious attitudes to account for the relatively high rate of mixed marriages in the 1970s.

The all-consuming importance of the parish in the lives of Lower Lansdowne's Protestants was reflected in the impressive array of parish activities for a congregation of little more than 900. These included a Mothers' Union, a Men's Society, various youth organizations, table tennis, football and bowling clubs, and a Musical Society. From cradle to grave, this constant round of parish activities was well able to satisfy the social inclinations of even the most socially energetic of parishioners. right up until the 1970s, parish organizations were more widely supported in Lower Lansdowne than in either of the urban, middle-class parishes which I shall refer to as Kilrath and Kingstown. To use one of many examples, active membership in the Mothers' Union of Lower Lansdowne was not much smaller than in the Dublin parish of Kilrath, although Kilrath was almost three times larger. Similarly, the provincial parish of Kingstown, which was half the size of Lower Lansdowne, had a Mothers' Union with only a third as many active members. Support for the Mothers' Union in rural parishes continued to be more widespread than in Lower Lansdowne, but even rural areas could not compete with this Dublin parish in the sheer range and frequency of its many parochial activities.

Before the mid-1960s the parishioners of Lower Lansdowne were also distinguished by the strength of their religious convictions and by the stress they laid on specifically religious matters in parochial organizations. This was evident in the Men's Society, an organization which prospered in only a handful of parishes in the Republic. Whereas a comparatively secular ethos prevailed in most middle-class parishes, the twice-monthly meetings of the Men's Society of Lower Lansdowne were principally concerned with biblical and doctrinal matters, devotional issues, and discussions of moral questions. In a sense, its functional equivalent in the middle class was the Masonic Lodge which was much less directly concerned with the preservation of the members' Protestant faith. So too in its youth organizations, the Boys' and Girls' Brigades, with their compulsory bible studies and regular examinations in religious knowledge, were much more religiously orientated than the typical Scouts and Guides troops of middle-class parishes. The strong religious tenor of Lower Lansdowne, however, was much more pervasive than these two organizational examples imply. Compared to middle-class Irish Anglicans, the middle-aged and older parishioners of Lower Lansdowne were much more likely to speak of the importance of their faith in their lives and to express regret over the passing of the era of "hell fire sermons," when all knew how "our Protestant heritage" differed from that of Rome. During their youth, many recalled, they were not allowed to attend dances or go to a film, while drinking and the frequenting of pubs were even more taboo. Instead, their time was taken up with parish events or with much more consciously evangelical organizations such as Christian Endeavour and the YMCA. Until the late 1940s Sunday evening services at the YMCA were highly popular among the youth of the parish. This was partly because their parents would not allow them to do anything else on a Sunday, but they were also drawn by the YMCA's spirited hymn singing and lively evangelical atmosphere, which was so different from the formal and subdued Church of Ireland liturgy. Some sought additional nourishment in the fundamentalist side of their faith by occasionally attending nearby Plymouth Brethren services, although religious involvement outside the Church of Ireland was never widespread except in the case of the YMCA. But it was most common in parishes like Lower Lansdowne, and it reflected the intense Protestantism that once prevailed in this section of the community.

Their sense of separateness at this time was further strengthened by the strongly held religious convictions of the Catholic majority. Exclusivist, anti-Protestant sentiments were once to be found throughout the country, but in Dublin it appears that they were rather more common among the Catholic lower classes.[16] Before the 1960s, poorer Protestants were much more likely to rub shoulders with Catholics on a daily basis at their place of work, whereas the segregated offices of the middle classes made it far easier for the latter to avoid this potential source of friction. On their crowded and narrow streets, the middle-aged parishioners of Lower Lansdowne recalled, "you could never play much with Catholics because you were always jeered." They soon learned that "there was a strong feeling that our religion didn't count for much," and stories circulated throughout the parish of Catholic clergy harassing Protestants in mixed marriages in order to ensure that they and their children became Catholics. Of course, segregation was never absolute. At an early age, it was not uncommon to have "R.C. pals on the road" or to "meet an R.C. girl" from the neighbourhood. But when they grew older, "it would never occur to me to date an R.C. girl" and "your social life was separate." By and large, the prevailing attitude was that "I didn't interfere with them and they didn't interfere with me."

On the surface, it seemed as if life in Lower Lansdowne in the 1970s was not much different than in former years. Although a few now went down to the pub on Saturday evening, the lives of many married adults still revolved around the parish. Others were no longer involved, but their close friendships were still normally confined to other Protestants whom they had met within the parish. While they agreed that "our Catholic neighbours are very good," most were quick to add that "we don't live in each other's houses – we don't go out socially." And similarly, for the young up to the age of seventeen or eighteen, it was claimed that through school and parish organizations "they are still a crowd" and "we have everyone who is available."

However, in many other respects it was apparent that much had changed. Middle-aged parishioners believed that there was now less of an undercurrent of religious hostility in their relations with their Catholic neighbours, and they felt that they were now less likely to be regarded as "heretics." As relations improved in the 1970s, young boys in the parish began to bring their Catholic friends to the Boys' Brigade. The adult leaders were initially uncertain as to how they should respond, but by 1978 they had admitted six Catholics to the brigade of twenty-eight on the ground that they were providing a Christian rather than a Protestant education. Although other parish organizations remained closed, church attendance and support for the Mothers' Union started to decline after the mid-1960s at a faster rate than the population of the parish. Over the same period, the Men's Society was also halved in size; by 1974 its meetings had been reduced from twice to once a month and its program had been secularized in response to "complaints over the religious emphasis." In addition, though to a far lesser extent, some parishioners became involved in new organizations outside the parish. When a local chapter of the Irish Countrywomen's Association was formed in the area in 1973, a parishioner who was well known for her handicraft skills was invited to become its first president. In the following year, approximately 12 per cent of the membership of 115 were Protestants. In a similar vein, a Ladies' Club connected to the Catholic parish decided to open up its membership after the outbreak of violence in the North. Although only a handful were prepared to take such an obvious step into the Catholic world, one of the few who had made the plunge claimed that its offerings of "records and bingo" were attracting "more all the time." In 1974 these developments had not yet lessened the opposition of married adults to mixed marriages or led them to establish many close friendships with Catholics. But collectively, they do suggest that the strong religious commitment and intense parish loyalties, which had once been so characteristic of Lower Lansdowne Protestants, were on the decline.

Among the teenagers and the young unmarried adults of the parish, the segregationist traditions of the past were being much more thoroughly eroded. This was particularly evident in the recent history of the United Churches Football League. It had been established in the late 1940s with the specific intent of keeping "Protestants together." By charter, Catholics were not permitted to play, and the member clubs were drawn primarily from the poorer, Protestant parishes in the Dublin area. Through weekly practices, matches on Saturday, and the excitement of interparish competition, the league was highly effective in involving young men within the parish and in creating a sense of city-wide unity. In its heyday, there were over twenty teams in the league, but in the 1960s the number began to fall. Some were forced to withdraw because of declining numbers within their parishes, while three others moved into non-Protestant leagues in order to compete at what they considered to be a higher standard of football. Faced with this situation, the league as a whole decided in 1973 to admit Catholic players and teams on the grounds that it was "that or die." Seven new teams were added to the existing fourteen in the league: four were entirely Catholic, and the three which were mixed were former parish teams that had dropped out earlier. In the original fourteen teams, the number of Catholics varied, with the thirty-four-man club of Lower Lansdowne containing four Catholics in 1974. Again we see the difficulties created by the diminishing population of this sector of the community, but this demographic pressure was not nearly as strong as in rural areas where segregated recreational activities still survived. The decision to open the league was not without its opponents, for some of "the older lads" felt that segregation was "the only way to keep in touch with other Protestants." However, "the younger lads couldn't see the point in it."

Of even greater importance was the gradual disappearance of facilities within the parish for young men and women to meet one another. Until about the mid-1950s, the youth clubs of Lower

Lansdowne and similar parishes ran a variety of activities and dances which were attended by most unmarried parishioners between the ages of eighteen and thirty-five. Thereafter, the frequency of their meetings and the age of the members slowly fell. In 1974 the Youth Club of Lower Lansdowne met only on Sunday evenings, and with few exceptions its members were nineteen or younger. Additional parochial dances had been stopped in the early 1960s as the young grew ever more resistant to ball-room music and lack of bar facilities. The Youth Club dances continued until the 1970s, but those who were working – and hence of marriageable age – were more and more inclined to dismiss them as events for "the young ones." Some went on to the rugby club dances frequented by the Protestant middle class, but the working-class members of the parish tended to feel out of place there. Instead, in response to the greater affluence and changed styles of the second half of the 1960s and 1970s, they turned to the discotheques and commercial dances in the centre of the city. In 1974 a youth club leader in his early twenties claimed with some justification that "If they're not doing a steady line with a Protestant girl after leaving the Youth Club, they're a definite loss" to the community. And by 1978 even the Youth Club had been closed because of dwindling interest among older teenagers, a shortage of adult leadership, and uncertainty as to how to handle the growing number of Catholics attending. Youthful rebellion and this gap in the parochial umbrella were the immediate causes of the high rate of mixed marriages. But the fundamental reason was the fading commitment of old as well as young to their religious heritage and to the segregationist convictions of their past. As one middle-aged parent expressed it, "You had the hammer then. Now they don't listen. What can you do?"

THE URBAN MIDDLE CLASS

The parishioners of Kilrath and Kingstown ranged from affluent businessmen and professionals to the less financially secure body of junior managers whose numbers grew during the economic expansion of the 1960s and 1970s. With the social upheaval of these years, the origins and outlook of the top and bottom of the middle class shaded off imperceptibly into the respective worlds of the West Britons and the poorer Protestants of Lower Lansdowne. But as a group, they had a character and a strength all their own. On no other part of the Protestant community did the multiple divisions of the past weigh so heavily. Although they showed few signs in the 1970s of the British leanings of the West Britons, they had always attached much more importance to religious differences and to their parishes. Class-based sentiments and secular associations with segregated traditions were also much more central to their lives than was true of either the rural minority or the Lower Lansdowne Protestants. Furthermore, they were not nearly so troubled by the problems of small and scattered numbers. Kilrath and its suburban neighbours had large and often growing congregations of as high as 2,000 or more; and even the parish of 450 in the provincial town of Kingstown was significantly larger than the average rural parish. The continuing influence of these various insulating forces may be seen in the recent admission of a young teenager from Kilrath that while she did not "think about religion ... most of my friends are Protestant because they're the ones I meet." Nevertheless, mixed marriages had risen to a 33 per cent rate in the early 1970s among the ninety-two brides and grooms of Kilrath and Kingstown. In the light of their protected backgrounds, this not inconsiderable development must seem all the more surprising.

For many years, Masonry was one of the more important secular components in the segregated world of the middle class. Although its rules did not exclude Catholics, the longstanding animosity of the Catholic church toward secret societies and toward Masonry in particular effectively precluded Catholic membership. By 1974 Lord Donoughmore, the Irish Grand Master, claimed that there were "a number"[17] of Catholic members, but they cannot have been very numerous for none of the Masons I interviewed were aware of any Catholic members in the lodges with which they were familiar. In the mid-1970s White estimated that three-quarters of the approximately 4,000 active lodge members in the Republic were resident in the Dublin area.[18] There was a scattering of lodges throughout the midlands, and the border parish surveyed supported an active lodge. But even here, Masonry had a rather urban and prosperous character as it tended to draw upon larger and more progressive farmers and those employed in the towns. All the other avowed Masons I interviewed came from solidly middle-class backgrounds in Dublin and Kingstown. The exclusive Protestant fellowship of Masonry and the security provided by its internal charitable activities both played a part in its appeal, while some may have found that its complex rituals filled a need that was not being met by the rather plain liturgy of Protestantism. And for its predominantly middle-class membership, it would also be remiss to ignore the many opportunities for business and social contacts that inevitably flowed from such a fraternity.

It is impossible to estimate the degree of Protestant support for

Masonry from its official records, and Masons were unwilling to discuss in any detail the affairs of their lodges. Although Dublin Masons usually claimed that "it is dwindling," a few said that their lodges were prospering and the prevailing view in Kingstown was that "we are holding our own." Fortunately, a much more clear-cut picture emerges from the personal accounts of the very small sample of thirty-one men I interviewed in Kingstown and Kilrath. Within these middle-class strongholds, at least three-quarters of their fathers had been Masons;[19] 55 per cent of those interviewed had joined at some point in their own lives; and only 36 per cent continued to be active members in 1974. In that year, 47 per cent of those over the age of forty were still in active membership, whereas this was true of only 21 per cent of those under that age. There are problems in generalizing from such a small sample, but the consistency and magnitude of the trends strongly suggest that Masonry was in decline. Moreover, the current minority of younger men who were still involved often said that they had "joined for my father," and they were inclined to express doubts about "whether I'm completely happy." A few cited "the secrecy," the "jobs for the boys" tradition in Masonry, and the financial costs of membership as the reasons for their refusal to follow in their fathers' footsteps. But with the recent breakup of so many of the old Protestant firms and the erosion of economic aid among Protestants that it entailed, the great majority of younger nonmembers simply claimed that they "couldn't see the point in it."

Over the same years, there was an equally marked transformation in the attitudes of Catholics. During the 1920s and 1930s a number of Catholic periodicals and books by Catholic clergy helped to sustain a strong public antipathy towards Masonry.[20] On religious grounds, it was castigated as an organized, secret, and dangerous foe of Christianity in general and Irish Catholicism in particular. Economically, it was deeply resented for its role in perpetuating Protestant privilege and jobbery. And politically, Fianna Fail in its rise to power briefly took up the theme that Masonry was a powerful, antinational organization capable of subverting the unfulfilled nationalist aspirations of the new state. Although Catholic invective of this sort may have deterred some Protestants from joining the order, it would appear that their support for Masonry did not go into a major decline until much later. However, in subsequent years anti-Masonic propaganda also began to fade as the remaining nationalist issues were resolved, as the economic position of Catholics improved, and as the ecumenical movement took effect. By the 1970s the virulent rhetoric of the past was no longer to be heard in public. The clearest sign of the change was the growing rapprochement between the Masons and the Knights of St Columbanus. The Knights had been initially established in 1922 as a parallel Catholic organization "to counter discrimination against Catholics by Freemasons and others."[21] As their unsuccessful attempt in 1949 to take over the Meath hospital indicated, the Knights could be highly aggressive in their defence of Catholic interests. But by the mid-1970s the two old rivals were having informal talks with one another, were proclaiming that they were not in conflict, were dining together, and were making plans for various cooperative efforts of a charitable nature.[22] No doubt some of the old suspicions survived on both sides, and for the time being Masonry continued to provide a source of exclusive fellowship for a good proportion of older Protestants. But it was less widely supported than formerly, and membership no longer had the abrasive and divisive significance of earlier years.

In the recreational and sports clubs supported by the middle class, the old divisions were being much more thoroughly eroded. The small size of the Protestant community in Kingstown had already led to the complete disappearance of any segregated secular activities by the beginning of the 1960s. In the larger Protestant community of Dublin, some clubs showed much greater resilience, but here too segregation was on the decline. This appeared to be least true of tennis. Of the three clubs mentioned by parishioners in Kilrath, only one had become "mainly Catholic" by the mid-1960s; another was still largely Protestant, although it had been admitting a few Catholics since the late sixties; and the remaining club did not admit any Catholic members as it was tied to the parish. On the other hand, the barrier had broken down much more completely in rugby. Due to family tradition, a few parishioners were members of two clubs which had been no more than nominally Protestant for many years. A third club began to admit Catholics in significant numbers after 1945. While current members insisted that "nobody thinks about religion any more," a committee member estimated that in 1973 about 20 per cent of the players, 25 per cent of the committee, and 40 per cent of the older, nonplaying members were Protestants. The remaining club did not admit its first Catholic member until the late 1960s. With this decision, there were no more closed Protestant clubs left in the Republic. It was still very much a Protestant club in 1973, but the Catholic presence is likely to grow in the future as a sixth of the players and a third of that year's new members were Catholics.

Many of these clubs initially turned to Catholics because they could not find sufficient Protestant members, but this sort of demographic pressure did not apply to the last-mentioned rugby club or to Kilrath's golfing clubs. Traditionally, the area had supported separate Catholic, Jewish, and Protestant clubs. Although there were a few Catholics in the Protestant club before the 1960s, their numbers were static and "well over three-quarters" of the members were Protestants. As was the case in most of the other clubs to which I have referred, Catholics were never officially excluded. However, an applicant usually required the sponsorship of existing members, who rarely had contacts with or the inclination to recruit Catholics; and if a Catholic had applied at this time, as occasionally did happen, "he would have been discouraged." With the greater prosperity of the 1960s, these traditional practices began to change as the number of Catholic applicants steadily rose during the decade. This occurred despite the fact that the Protestant population of Kilrath was also increasing quite rapidly. By 1974 the captain, a third of the committee, and a little over half of the general members were Catholics. There can be little doubt that the northern conflict made Protestants all the more reluctant to reject a Catholic, but fear was not the only force at work, for they insisted that they were already coming to question the propriety of exclusion prior to 1969. By 1974 the great majority had come to believe that "it wasn't right to exclude Catholics" from activities not directly connected with their parishes.

Of course, many of these clubs still provided a substantial measure of Protestant fellowship, which was reinforced by their involvement in their parishes. Like Lower Lansdowne, Kilrath continued to sponsor a wide range of parochial activities in the 1970s, whereas the vitality of Kingstown's parochial life had declined considerably over the previous ten years. The latter's size, its even smaller teenage population, and its loss of a curate were all contributing factors, but more than this was involved. Both parishes now contained a growing body of young married parishioners who tended to be much less involved than their parents. In Kilrath, their comparative lack of interest was reflected in the failure of the parish's Sunday School and other organizations to grow at a rate consistent with the arrival of approximately twenty new families in the parish each year. The result was that a core group of older parishioners was responsible for many overlapping memberships. To some extent this was true of all parishes, but the pattern seems to have been especially marked in these middle-class parishes. The clearest overall indicator was that their rates of church attendance were lower than in either Lower Lansdowne or in the rural parishes.

In short, in comparison with their own past and with all but the West Britons in the 1970s, parish activities and religion generally played a less important – though far from insignificant – part in their lives.

These general observations may be demonstrated more concretely by reference to recent developments in two rather different associations attached to Kilrath and Kingstown. Kilrath, it may be remembered, had long sponsored a Boy Scout troop rather than the more religiously orientated Boys' Brigade. Its parent body, the Scouts Association of Ireland was part of the international and interdenominational organization founded by Baden-Powell. Prior to 1949 it was officially connected with the British founding organization, and its general ethos tended to reflect this link. In reaction to its British, colonial, and interdenominational character, the Catholic Boy Scouts of Ireland was formed in 1927 under the direction and control of the Catholic church. This reinforced the already prevailing tendency for the world-wide Baden-Powell movement to be largely supported by Protestants. At local level, the Protestant character of the Scouts Association of Ireland was additionally strengthened by the practice in many parishes of "sponsoring" their troops, which entitled them to impose denominational restrictions on membership. However, these marked divisions started to crumble after 1949 when the Scouts Association of Ireland terminated its official links with England. By the mid-1960s it had entered into a federation with its Catholic counterpart. Thereafter, the Catholic Association started to participate in international events; cooperative ventures of various sorts between the two groups were initiated; and the possibility of a formal merger began to be discussed by representatives of the two national bodies. In this changing atmosphere, the Scouts Association of Ireland grew so rapidly that its membership was approximately 85 per cent Catholic in 1978.[23] In the sponsored parish troops, there was also a marked increase in Catholic applicants, which led many of Kilrath's middle-class neighbours to give up their sponsored status and to begin to admit Catholics. Although Kilrath remained sponsored and hence segregated in 1978, I was told that it was "one of the last to do so." With the breakdown of formal merger talks in 1978, the institutional divisions of the past are unlikely to disappear in the near future.[24] Nevertheless, the a-religious character of the Scouts Association of Ireland, its rapid growth, and the increasing participation of Catholics all suggest an increasing secular indifference to religious distinctions among Catholics as well as Protestants.

These emerging secular tendencies also lay behind recent developments within the Young Wives' Club of Kingstown parish. Although its active membership of about twenty-five in 1972 was no smaller than that of the badminton and other parish clubs supported by rural Protestants, it began to admit Protestants from mixed marriages during the late 1960s. They were shortly followed by Catholic partners in mixed marriages and then by Catholic acquaintances in entirely Catholic marriages. By 1972 seven of the regular participants were Catholics, although five were from mixed marriages. In the same year, when a Protestant from a mixed marriage was elected president, the issue of formally admitting Catholics was raised. Some felt that "one wants to get away from this closed shop sort of thing," but the issue proved so divisive that attendance at meetings dropped to less than half its former level. As no acceptable solution could be reached, the Young Wives' Club was closed. It was, as one embittered young wife from a farming background put it, "a disgrace to see it finished. Only for it I wouldn't know anybody" in Kingstown. It is clear that a good proportion still wished to keep the Young Wives closed to Catholics. However, those who thought this way were no longer prepared to act upon their views, and in the following year only three joined the Mothers' Union which was widely regarded as dull, as too religious, and as an association "for grandmothers."

Although other parish activities remained closed to Catholics, there was now a substantial degree of integration in the organized social life of the middle class. Of the forty-nine married parishioners in Kilrath and Kingstown who were actively involved in parochial or other secular organizations in 1974, only 37 per cent inhabited an exclusively Protestant world. The remaining 63 per cent encountered Catholics in all or some of their communal activities; 45 per cent were members of traditionally Protestant organizations which were admitting Catholics in the 1970s; while only 24 per cent had become members of Catholic associations.[25] In other words, integration was most common *within* the old social boundaries of the Protestant community. This may be seen in the presence of only a very small number of Protestants in Kilrath's Catholic golf club, which stood in marked contrast to the former Protestant club with its many Catholic members. In the newer suburban areas around Dublin where associational life is less well established, it is possible that Protestants may become more involved in the social world of the majority. In fact, some of the young married newcomers to Kilrath had joined a new, nondenominational community centre, but in 1974 the prevailing trend was still one of Catholic entrance into the traditional social preserves of Protestants. Given the large number of old Protestant associations, their solidly middle-class character, and the shortage of secular associations for the expanding Catholic middle class, Catholic pressure of this sort is hardly surprising. In many ways, it closely parallels the experience of middle-class Protestant schools. And in both cases, it suggests that the traditional community boundaries of the middle class were subject to greater external pressure than that felt by Protestants in either Lower Lansdowne or in rural areas.

These developments did not result in anything like the same degree of close friendships across the religious divide. Even among young couples who were no longer involved in their parishes, their schooling and past involvement in the Protestant world ensured that "through circumstance, it seems wrong, but most of my close friends are Protestants." Of course, through work, their clubs, an occasional close relationship with a neighbour, or "someone I met on holiday," many could point to one or two Catholics whom they regarded as friends. This was much more common in Kingstown, where the smaller and more transient Protestant community made it all the more difficult to sustain complete segregation. As one newcomer who had made a number of Catholic friends explained, he had "lost contact with the birth of my Protestantism – my school"; while another acknowledged that "my best friend is a Catholic, but if I was in my home environment she wouldn't be." But in Kingstown, as in Dublin, the ingrained habits of one's upbringing were not easily discarded, and through the influence of Masonry, the now defunct Young Wives' Club, the parochial school, and the parish itself many found that "the people we go out with are usually Protestants."

Like their elders, the young unmarried adults and teenagers of Kilrath and Kingstown continued to be partly insulated by their schools, and by parish and secular associations. Otherwise, they showed little interest in preserving their separateness. The major functions and dances which they attended were associated with the various secular clubs referred to earlier. For some time, many of these clubs had held public dances from which Catholics could not be excluded, and even their private dances grew less exclusive as the number of Catholic members increased. In Kingstown, the Youth Club and the YMCA, which had once been the major focal points for the youth in the city, were closed because of insufficient numbers and a "lack of interest" among those who still remained. These changes were due to more than simply a growth of indifference, but the same could not be said of the recent history of the youth clubs in Kilrath and its adjacent parishes. As late as 1966 I was assured that the youth club dances were "at least 90 per cent Protestant." In order to restrict admission, tickets were distributed in advance among the surrounding Protestant youth clubs and schools. But by 1973 about half of those attending were Catholics; and ten of the eighty-five participants in the regular activities of the Youth Club were also Catholics, although they were not allowed to become official members. One of the leaders of the Youth Club readily admitted that "the kids know each other well enough" to "keep Catholics out if they wanted," but they refused to do so because they felt "we can't exclude." When parents became aware of this, attendance "dropped by a half," and a number of neighbouring parishes temporarily closed their youth clubs in the face of a similar situation. The following year, parental pressure ensured that the regular activities of Kilrath's Youth Club were "closed tight," but the greatly reduced membership of thirty-one in 1978 amounted to "only a fraction of the young." In the same year a few strictly supervised dances were held, for which tickets were again available only by invitation. However, the curate doubted the effectiveness of these renewed efforts at exclusion, since "a large number" of those attending addressed him as "Father" when they presented their invitation-only tickets.

The increasing indifference of middle-class youth to the segrega-tionist expectations of their parents was closely linked to the diminishing religious commitment of the older generation and to its growing uncertainty as to the propriety of excluding Catholics from its own secular activities. These spreading secular tendencies were also strengthened by the improving economic position of Catholics, which weakened the class motivations behind their separateness. In these changing circumstances, there emerged a new, middle-aged view that "the older folk can become involved but not the young," which was most commonly justified by the claim that "it all boils down to Ne Temere you see." However, younger Protestants were less and less likely to accept this partly integrated view, which they regarded as an outdated double standard. Although they shared their parents' resentment at any suggestion that the Catholic church might put pressure upon them if they married a Catholic, they believed that it was now possible to avoid these traditional pressures. And neither their education nor their day-to-day experi-ence imbued them with the stronger commitment to their own faith and the more deeply rooted distrust of Catholicism that had been instilled in their parents. As one strong churchman whose daughter had just married a Catholic explained, "They feel this is a more enlightened age. They think I am too narrow. It is our Church that is going to the wall. They don't see the importance of this."

CHAPTER EIGHT

Conclusion

Above all else, I have argued that the two most striking trends of the post-independence era were the diminishing alienation and declining marginality of Protestants in relation to the rest of Irish society. It is true that prior to 1922 the institutionalized privileges of the minority had already been undermined by the demise of the penal laws, the disestablishment of the Church of Ireland, the transfer of land from Protestant Ascendancy to Catholic tenantry, and the introduction of democratic principles of government. And yet, important as these developments were in eroding the minority's self-confidence, they did not in themselves reduce the social and psychological isolation of Irish Anglicans. Indeed, in many respects, their sense of marginality was enhanced both by the events leading up to 1922 and by the activities of the newly ascendant Catholic majority during the first twenty-five years of independence. In the latter period, the character of the tensions between the two communities continued to change, but it was not until after World War II that the well-entrenched communal boundaries of the minority began to crumble. The clearest indication of this new development is to be found in the growing rate of mixed marriages after 1946. Of course, these statistics may also be interpreted to mean that some 60 to 70 per cent of the small Church of Ireland community still preferred to marry fellow Protestants in the 1970s. When viewed from this perspective, the mixed marriage data serve as a salutory reminder that there still existed a distinctive, though increasingly porous, community of Protestants at the end of the period dealt with in this study. Nevertheless, barring such unpredictable developments as the active involvement of the Republic in the violence of the North, the trends I have documented seem so well established that they are unlikely to be reversed in the foreseeable future.

Neither of these emerging trends seemed very likely in the early 1920s. After the violence of the previous years, many Protestants believed that their very right to remain in the country was in jeopardy. They were acutely conscious that their colonial heritage did little to endear them to the now ascendant Catholic majority, and some feared that they might suffer because of their still considerable wealth. With their new powers, both of the major political parties did much to strengthen Protestant alienation by enacting legislation which affirmed the Gaelic and Catholic character of the state. The animosities that flared within the remote western parish during the early 1950s, after Church of Ireland spokesmen criticized the Mother and Child scheme, were an indication of how enduring and close to the surface tensions could be. But by and large, the minority met with relatively little overt discrimination or open persecution. And on the few occasions when Protestants did encounter organized Catholic pressure, the Dunbar-Harrison case and the incidents at Fethard-on-Sea and the Meath hospital showed that the government was not prepared to countenance such behaviour.

There were, I believe, three major reasons for this policy. The first, as I have argued, was that the government wished to demonstrate that northern Protestants could expect fair and equitable treatment in a united Ireland. Second, the numerical and political dominance of Catholics was so overwhelming in the south that they had little reason to fear or to suppress the small and powerless Protestant minority. Hence toleration came much more easily to southern Catholics than it did to northern Protestants whose obsessive fear of becoming a minority in a united Ireland led them to be much more restrictive and suspicious in their treatment of their own 35 per cent Catholic minority. Of course, the other side of the equation was that the hope of a united Ireland made northern Catholics all the more intransigent in their opposition to Protestant dominance; whereas southern Protestants, who had no hope of altering their minority status, tended to be much more conciliatory in their dealings with Catholics. Third, despite the many economic advantages of Protestants, the major source of Catholic resentment had already been removed by the land acts which left Catholics in control of the dominant agricultural sector of the economy. Thereafter, the more prosperous supporters of Cumann na nGaedheal had little desire to interfere with Protestants. And Fianna Fail, which drew much of its support from small farmers in the west during its more radical early phase, was not under much electoral pressure to concern itself with the exclusivism of the old Protestant firms in the cities on the eastern seaboard.

However, the generally equitable treatment of the minority by the government did not in any way lessen the underlying tensions between the two communities. The *Irish Times*, the General Synod, and other Protestant spokesmen were sometimes openly critical of government policies, but their outspokenness at the national level was often deeply disturbing for the rank and file of the community. Away from the watchful eye of the central government, they were acutely aware that they were ill-equipped to deal with any confrontation or overt conflict. In large measure, the peaceful relations that normally prevailed were made possible only by social segregation, by avoiding all controversial topics when dealing with "the other side," and by the implicit understanding that the minority bow to the Gaelic and Catholic ethos of the country.

Given this initial state of affairs, even the partial erosion of community boundaries that has occurred in recent years becomes all the more remarkable. In examining the underlying causes and implications of this development, we are inevitably brought back to the question raised in the introduction as to whether we have been observing assimilation or integration. Assimilation, it may be remembered, implies that Protestants have been steadily losing and/or discarding their cultural heritage as they have been incorporated into the larger Catholic community. Integration, on the other hand, suggests that Protestants and Catholics have grown closer together by treating their differences as matters of private and individual choice. Empirically, it is sometimes difficult to distinguish between the two trends, but they differ in two fundamental ways. First, assimilation implies that at some future point Protestants will disappear by being absorbed into the Catholic community; whereas integration suggests that they will survive, although this process would still entail a radical transformation in the relations between the two communities. Second, assimilation implies that it has been primarily Protestants who have changed; while integration suggests that both parties have changed. Unfortunately, the real world rarely fits neatly into the theoretical concepts we construct, and even cursory reflection suggests that we have seen signs of both assimilation and integration. No definite conclusion can be drawn at this early stage, but I believe that it is possible to go some way in clarifying which of the two trends is likely to prevail in the future. In order to do so, we must consider the nature of the forces that weakened the three original divisions of ethnicity, class, and religion.

The British loyalties of the minority were the first of its many differences with the Catholic majority to fall into decline. With the end of colonial rule in 1922, the minority was effectively cut off from the essential sustaining basis of its divergent ethnic allegiance. From this point on, there was considerable pressure from within the Church of Ireland community to suppress its British loyalties which were now regarded as an embarrassing anachronism that served no useful purpose. This development did not occur immediately or easily for few of those raised prior to independence could bring themselves to embrace the new nationalism which they so feared and despised. But under the persistent leadership of the *Irish Times* and the Church of Ireland, the rank and file were exhorted to recognize their Irish nationality, and with the passage of time these appeals slowly gained acceptance. The transformation was in part made possible by the fact that Protestants had long regarded themselves as in some way Irish, even though they were quick to deny any bond with the Gaelic tradition of the majority. Unlike many postcolonial minorities who were racially distinguishable, it was much easier for Protestants to mask, deny, and eventually discard their colonial heritage when independence made it a liability. Moreover, the costs in doing so were minimal, since religious differences enabled them to preserve their separateness and to justify their feelings of superiority without reference to their ethnic heritage.

Behind this partly voluntary shift of emphasis to their religious identity was strong external pressure from the Catholic majority, which was openly hostile to their British loyalties. Under both political parties, the remaining public symbols and rituals connected with Empire and Commonwealth were ignored, decried, and then removed; and when the law allowed such displays, Protestants soon learned to tread carefully, especially after Albert Armstrong was murdered for giving evidence in court against men who had torn down a British flag in front of his place of work. Of much greater importance for the generation raised after 1922 was the new school curriculum, which effectively required the minority to neglect and to condemn its British heritage. Of course, the administrative independence of Protestant schools gave them a certain leeway in interpreting the state's curriculum, and the prominence of the English language in their schools was never seriously threatened. It should be remembered that Protestant schools were not asked to do anything more than was required of Catholic schools. Nevertheless, it was only on the ethnic dimension that the state forced the minority to suppress its own traditions and take up those of the majority. While the government's legislation on divorce and contraception paid little heed to the minority's sensibilities, there was certainly no pressure to convert its members to Catholicism. The constitutions of both 1922 and 1937 expressly prohibited any form of religious discrimination, and in the 1937 constitution the Church of Ireland was at least granted the status of being a "recognized" church. In practice, the state went out of its way to protect the minority's religious rights by creating special rules intended to keep small Protestant schools open and by insisting that no child could be required to take religious instruction without parental agreement. In effect, toleration was extended to the minority as a religious group but not as an ethnic group.[1] In so doing, the state played a major role in hastening the disappearance of ethnic differences between the two communities.

Yet as long as Catholics retained a strong consciousness of their colonial past, the minority could never escape the stigma of colonialism – no matter what changes it initiated or had imposed upon it. However, after the severing of the last of Ireland's constitutional ties with Britain in 1949, there were no longer any political issues in the internal affairs of the Republic around which to organize either British or anti-British sentiments. Just as independence was the crucial blow to the minority's British attachment, so was the Republic of Ireland Act the major turning point for the colonialist obsession of Catholics. With the passing of the revolutionary elite, a less backward-looking, and a less intensely nationalistic climate emerged; the exclusivist concerns of the Gaelic revival were pursued with less vigour; and apart from the current conflict in Northern Ireland, issues of social and economic reform came to dominate the secular side of public life. Throughout the 1960s in particular, the British allegiance and colonial heritage of the minority were neither sustained by nor relevant to the major concerns of Irish society. In this changed environment, members of the minority finally began to regard themselves as simply Irish; and they were now prepared to espouse the appropriately supportive attitudes towards the Irish language. There were, of course, changes on the Catholic side, and over the long haul it was the Gaelic tradition that was superseded by an English-speaking culture. But in the short term, the virtual disappearance of British loyalties among the minority, the radical decline in the number of Protestant politicians, and their early incorporation into the major political parties suggest that assimilation rather than integration best describes the decline in the ethnic division.

In 1969 the Republic's twenty years of freedom from the issue of colonialism were brought to an abrupt halt by the eruption of violence in the North. Once again, public life was caught up in intense debate over the island's relations with Britain and over the political implications of the religious divide. In this climate, the anti-British sentiments of some Catholics probably grew more marked, and the occasional outburst of hostility against Protestants inevitably added to their feelings of insecurity. On the other hand, as noted in chapter 3, the great majority of Catholics continued to distinguish between northern and southern Protestants and to regard the latter as integral members of the Republic. For obvious reasons, the conflict showed no signs of reviving the minority's British loyalties. Nor did Protestants simply shrink back into their shell of embittered marginality. In fact, it was precisely during the 1970s that they grew more outspoken in their demand for recognition of their rights as Protestant Irishmen. As was most evident in the 1972 referendum decision to remove the reference to the "special position" of the Catholic church from the constitution, this greater sensitivity of Catholics to Protestant sensibilities was partly a response to events in the North. The horror felt by both Protestants and Catholics at the daily news of sectarian violence in the North may help to explain the popularity of ecumenical services and the many Catholic efforts to involve Protestants in local community life. Similarly, among Protestants the northern conflict may have been partly responsible for their greater unwillingness to exclude Catholics from their schools and secular associations. There is, I believe, a danger in exaggerating the impact of the North, for as we shall see there were other, equally important reasons for the above developments. Moreover, mixed marriages and other signs of rapprochement were already on the increase before 1969. It does, however, seem clear that the violence in the North did more to foster than to hinder closer relations between Protestants and Catholics in the South.

The second communal division of class was never as absolute as those of religion and ethnicity, since Protestants came from a variety of class backgrounds which created internal divisions within their own community. But as a whole, Protestants were much better off than Catholics; a much smaller proportion of their community could be described as working or lower-class; and their influence at higher levels greatly exceeded their percentage of the total population. These advantages were then compounded and made all the more visible by the existence of separate Protestant firms which gave middle and lower-class Protestants many more opportunities for advancement than were available to Catholics with a similar class background. Initially, their resulting aloofness was reinforced by the colonialist conviction that their breeding and cultural traditions were superior to those of the "mere Irish." Since some Catholics were slow to cast off their ingrained habit of colonial deference, the minority often retained a local prestige and stature in excess of its economic standing – and in spite of the state's hostility to its colonial past. All this put Protestants in a rather different position from that of most other minority groups, which usually found that they suffered from the double impediment of being both economically and culturally subordinate. But in southern Ireland these economic forces were essentially reversed. In fact, for economic reasons alone, Catholics have long been attracted to the privileged social world of the minority. Thus whereas ethnic and religious differences were expressed in mutually exclusive attitudes, the class boundary was rather more precarious because it was primarily sustained by the minority.

As political independence did not usher in any form of economic revolution, it is much more difficult to pin-point a date at which these status and class divisions fell into serious decline. From the beginning, the ever sparser representation of Protestants in public life undermined their traditional view of themselves as the natural leaders of the country; and their self-confidence was further eroded by the hostility of Catholics to their colonial heritage. But in order to explain diminishing class tensions, we must look primarily to the private sector, since it was here that most Protestants were employed. The significant developments were the expansion of the economy, industrialization, and urbanization. These trends were slow to emerge, but even the fitful and limited growth of the 1930s and 1940s brought about some improvement in the position of Catholics in the private sector. In conjunction with the opportunities available in the public sector, these outlets for Catholic aspirations may have helped to lessen their indignation over the tenacious exclusivism of so many of the old Protestant firms. Then, with the introduction of new government policies in the late 1950s, the rate of economic growth accelerated and industry became the country's principal source of employment. A huge increase in motor cars, sprawling suburbs, shopping malls, and new industrial estates were all indications of the magnitude of the change. In the 1970s Ireland was still relatively poor by European standards, and its economy has run into difficulties in the 1980s. However, it is not the degree of affluence that is the major issue here, although there can be little doubt that it increased. What matters most of all is that the economy was transformed by the rapid growth of the last twenty years, and with this change there occurred a huge increase in the size of the middle and upper classes. Since Protestants were barely able to hold their own in view of their dwindling population, the vast majority of these new positions were filled by Catholics who swamped the minority in their upward surge.

In the process, Protestant influence at the higher levels of the economy was reduced; the visibility and hence the social significance of their remaining influence was further obscured by the demise of the segregated Protestant firm; and their competitive edge over Catholics of similar class backgrounds was weakened by the decline of preferential employment practices among Protestant employers. Faced with an increasingly powerful, established, and well-educated Catholic community, the minority's sense of superiority and social exclusivity inevitably declined; and Catholics had less and less reason to feel either resentful or subservient. Many older Protestants regretted the passing of the old days, but neither they nor the younger generation appeared to feel embittered or personally threatened by the transformation. In fact, there was little reason for such feelings since economic growth enabled the rising Catholic majority to engulf – rather than to displace – the minority. Of course, Protestants did lose certain advantages with the decline of segregationist practices in their old firms, but any loss they might have felt was offset by the far greater employment opportunities and affluence of the 1960s and 1970s. In stressing these developments, I do not wish to imply that Ireland was becoming a classless society. In many ways class distinctions now mattered more to Protestants, since their economic bonds with each other across class lines were no longer as strong as formerly. Although they had become somewhat more concentrated in the middle and upper classes, the growing Catholic proportion of these classes ensured that Protestants were now less likely to mix with one another for class reasons alone. All that had really changed was that class had become a less effective means of uniting Protestants and of separating them from Catholics. Under these conditions, neither Catholics nor Protestants were inclined to attach much importance to their remaining class differences.

The combination of economic growth, industrialization, and accompanying urbanization led to many other changes in the nature of Irish society and in the relations between Protestants and Catholics. It is in considering these broader ramifications that the issue of assimilation versus integration becomes more relevant. In the narrower contexts of diminishing class and occupational divisions, the signs of change within both communities suggest that integration best describes these developments. But these narrow economic trends can be regarded as no more than an intermediate stage in a process which may lead to either assimilation or integration. In pursuing this latter theme, we immediately confront the close connection between the social consequences of recent economic growth and the changing significance of religion – the third, the most fundamental, and the most enduring basis of communal division.

Before we consider the major theme of secularization, the ancillary and partly independent growth of the ecumenical movement deserves attention. Its importance lay in its undermining of the exclusivist, anti-Catholic message of the Church of Ireland and in its provision of a religious rationale for greater harmony, toleration, and cooperation between the two communities. Few Protestants had ever been eager for full church unity, and by the end of the 1970s many were disillusioned and angered by the reluctance of the Catholic church to compromise on such matters as mixed marriages. But by and large, they were not prepared to discard the rhetoric and public rituals of ecumenism. Their reasons were numerous, but this support for ecumenism may be best understood as a reflection of their desire to achieve integration and to avoid assimilation. Faced with a declining population, diminishing class and ethnic tensions, the shadow of the northern conflict, and a growing rate of mixed marriages, their old stance of embittered marginality seemed neither attractive nor feasible. At the same time, few Protestants relished the prospect of being absorbed by an unchanging and triumphant Catholicism. In other words, full assimilation was as distasteful as their previous isolation was now impossible. Under the banner of ecumenism, they sought a new and closer relationship with Catholics which might still allow them to preserve an identity and existence in some way separate from the Catholic majority. Thus it was that men like Archbishop McAdoo, who were strongly committed to their faith and community, were equally unprepared to discard the language and weapon of ecumenism. In large measure, the success of this new and dangerous course of integration depended on the nature and extent of secularization among Catholics as well as Protestants.

As previously noted, secularization refers to a contraction in the range of situations in which religious institutions, symbols, and precepts exert a socially binding influence.[2] It does not necessarily imply, as in the everyday use of the term, the growth of religious indifference at the individual or personal level, although the experience of other European countries suggests that indifference is a common consequence.[3] Observers elsewhere have usually attributed secularization to the growth of industrialization and urbanization.[4] I would contend that the beginnings of a similar transformation were evident in Ireland. In education, in social service, in national values, and in communal living patterns, the emerging urban-industrial world subjected old denominational structures to increasing pressure; and new expectations and social arrangements were created which brought Protestants and Catholics together in many novel ways. As a useful though somewhat crude general rule, integration might now be said to depend on the growth of secularization among *both* Protestants and Catholics. Assimilation, on the other hand, would seem to be the likely result if secularization was primarily confined to one of the two parties – and to the minority in particular. The role of economic growth in bringing about integration and secularization within the occupational world has already been examined; there remain to be considered the three crucial areas of politics, education, and communal life.

For the first three decades after independence, Protestants were virtually alone in their opposition to the increasingly Catholic tone evident in the laws of the state. Although their ire was dampened by the purely symbolic character of some of the legislation and by their own conservative views on divorce and contraception, they argued that such laws were discriminatory in their assumption that the entire nation was Catholic. As Protestants, they stressed that they were committed to the ideal of freedom of conscience, and hence they were opposed to any attempt by the state to reflect the views of any one religion. They were soon reduced to an occasional splutter by the futility of their protest, but in the 1970s various committees of the Church of Ireland again became more persistent in their demand that the state be deconfessionalized. Indeed, they were prepared to argue that divorce facilities should be made available, although their own church did not approve of the remarriage of divorced persons. As students of Protestantism in other parts of the world have noted, this long-standing demand for the separation of church and state reveals a deeply rooted secular propensity within Protestantism itself.[5] However, its integrationist implications were not to be fulfilled until the 1970s. At the end of the decade, Ireland was not a fully secular state by international standards. But much had changed as was evident in the restructuring of the Censorship Board, the altering of "Article 44," the passing of contraceptive legislation, and the various surveys which showed that a majority of the population now favoured divorce as well as contraceptive legislation. In effect, it would appear that a majority of Catholics had come to accept the Protestant and secular notions of individualism and freedom of conscience. Such developments surely indicate the growth of integration far more than they do of assimilation.

This striking shift in public attitudes expressed by the opinion polls on contraception and divorce was obviously due to far more than simply a desire to seduce northern Protestants into a united Ireland. However, in the early 1980s there was a brief period when it seemed that the tensions created by the northern hunger strikers might prove to be the catalyst for further legislative changes. In September 1981 the New Taoiseach, Garrett FitzGerald, went on national radio to call upon the country to join him in a national crusade to seek reconciliation and eventual unity with the North by instituting a wide-ranging review of those parts of the constitution to which northern Protestants objected. Not long after, a motion supporting his proposal was hotly debated in the Senate for four days before being passed by a margin of thirty to seventeen.[6] Much of the debate centred on his criticism of articles two and three, which affirmed the Republic's claim to jurisdiction over the entire island – and hence over Northern Ireland. But more than this was involved, for FitzGerald also emphasized the need to reform what he initially described as the "sectarian" character of the constitution. He claimed that he wanted to create a constitution that was no longer dominated by the views of any one religion, so that Protestants, as well as Catholics, would be able to give it their full allegiance. During the Senate debate, he conceded that he was speaking of only a small part of the constitution and that these elements might be better described as "confessional." His supporters went on to raise a host of issues, ranging from mixed marriages to the role of the churches in education, but it was the constitutional prohibition on divorce that emerged as the major issue. And though FitzGerald, as well as many of his supporters, was not yet prepared to sanction the implementation of legal divorce facilities, he later indicated that he was personally convinced of "the propriety and wisdom"[7] of having the constitutional prohibition reviewed.

Protestant spokesman welcomed FitzGerald's initiative. Archbishop McAdoo pointed out that the Taoiseach's proposal reiterated what the Church of Ireland's Role of the Church Committee had been saying for some time,[8] while the Protestant senators who took part in the debate stressed their particular wish to see some movement on divorce. However, there was strong opposition from other quarters, especially when it came to articles two and three. Led by Charles Haughey, Fianna Fail condemned FitzGerald for betraying the united Ireland aspirations of centuries of patriots, and it claimed that his charge of sectarianism was an unjustified slander which only served to strengthen intransigent unionism.[9] On the divorce question, Fianna Fail appeared to be somewhat more open to change in that it agreed to set up a committee of its own to examine the issue; but it was not prepared to join the all-party committee proposed by the government.[10] Indeed, with the government's precarious majority in the Dail, it seemed likely that Fianna Fail would be tempted into complete opposition, as occurred in 1974 when it voted against the Coalition's contraceptive bill. Then in January 1982 a budgetary proposal of the government led to its unexpected defeat in the Dail, and the prospect of immediate political movement on the divorce question appeared to have faded. The fact remains that the North had enabled the Taoiseach to provide a measure of cautious leadership for the approximately two-thirds of the population, if the polls are to be believed, that wished to see the removal of this last remaining symbol of Catholic influence in the constitutional realm. If the various efforts at contraceptive legislation over the previous decade are any indication, further Irish governments may find it difficult to resist these mounting pressures for a more secular state.

In the field of education, successive Irish governments showed no interest in tampering with the principle of denominational control, but here too the pressures of the new urban-industrial order were having their effect. As educational aspirations rose, some 40 per cent of Protestant secondary school children turned to Catholic schools because they were out of reach of a Protestant day school. With the parallel expansion of the Catholic school system, their proportion of lay teachers rose to 78 per cent in 1978, and there was every reason to believe that the trend would continue.[11] At the same time, the new community school system demonstrated the Catholic church's inability to meet the growing educational needs of its laity; and the resulting controversy over the powers granted to the clergy revealed a new opposition to the once unquestioned authority of the church in educational matters. Although the powers of the religious orders were untouched in other secondary schools, the resulting limitations placed on the promotion opportunities of the now preponderant body of lay teachers is also likely to create further pressure for change in the future. Finally, there has been the Dalkey School Project as well as other efforts to establish multidenominational schools in the suburbs around Dublin and in Cork. There organizers claimed that they had no intention of banning religion from their schools, but the demand for full lay control and the insistence that the views of no one religion should prevail were clearly moves in a secular direction. Significantly enough, this new struggle emerged within the heart of the new urban-industrial society. But for the moment these incipient secular developments have not yet altered the fundamentally denominational character of Catholic education. Thus most Protestant parents continued to opt for their own schools whenever possible, since the alternative was to place their children in an overwhelmingly Catholic environment with all the attendant risk of assimilation.

On the Protestant side, two developments stand out. First, the strong Protestant thrust to the religious education of previous generations was replaced by an ecumenical emphasis with far less concern for doctrinal instruction. Second, and more importantly, many schools in the late 1970s were admitting a substantial minority of Catholics who often took part in integrated religious education classes at the secondary level. Approximately 20 per cent were Catholics in Protestant secondary schools, while the average was probably somewhat lower at the primary level, although at one school it ranged as high as 30 per cent. Moreover, this was only the tip of the iceberg, for Catholic applicants greatly exceeded the number accepted. Without discounting the class-based attraction of Protestant schools, which has always existed, I would argue that the recent growth in the number of Catholic applicants reflected their desire for a more secular education than that available in their own schools. With their diminished emphasis on denominational instruction and their religious mixture among teachers and pupils, Protestant secondary schools went a long way to meet this demand. In turn the schools also reflected and fostered an integrationist and secular outlook within their own community. However, it was integration – and not assimilation – which Protestants sought, and hence most schools continued to give priority to Protestants by putting a quota on the admission of Catholic applicants.

Finally, we turn to the last and most crucial development of all – namely, the diminishing social segregation of the minority at the local community level. In rural areas and in the smaller towns, Protestants began to move outside their own communal boundaries by involving themselves in local secular associations which had once been almost exclusively Catholic in makeup. With the greater prosperity of the 1960s and 1970s, there was also an increase in the number and activities of nonsectarian organizations which brought Protestants and Catholics together in many new ways. Similar trends were evident in urban areas, although they tended to be less common in all but the newer suburban areas where the minority's old institutional network was not so well established. By and large, a rather different pattern developed in that it was primarily Catholics who began to be admitted to the golf, rugby, and other recreational activities of the minority. Perhaps the most striking sign of this transformation was the recent revival and growth of the once predominantly Protestant Scouts Association of Ireland, which steadily reduced its links with Protestant parishes as the Catholic proportion of its enlarged membership rose to approximately 85 per cent by the second half of the 1970s. In short, in rural as well as urban areas, there seemed to be emerging among both Catholics and Protestants a new secular conviction that religious affiliation should not be a consideration in recreational and special interest activities not directly connected to their parish churches. At the same time, Protestants continued to mix primarily with one another in the more intimate areas of close friendships, visiting, dinner parties, and the like. Taken together, this combination of greater public intermingling and persisting segregation in the more private areas of social life again suggests the growth of integration rather than assimilation.

However, in the light of the minority's growing rate of mixed marriages, this conclusion may well seem rather suspect. Clearly integration in other areas had its dangers. Whether it was at the office, the rugby club dance, or even the secondary school, young Protestants of a marriageable age were now encountering Catholics more often and in more intimate circumstances than did their parents. Young adults and teenagers were also predictably resistant to the dictum of their parents that "we may mix but you may not." Furthermore, falling rates of church attendance and a general decline in support for parochial activities both indicate that the religious commitment of the minority was not as strong as it had once been. This did not appreciably affect the friendship patterns of adult married Protestants whose outlook and social habits had been formed in earlier years. But for those of a younger age, their fading religious commitment undoubtedly helps to explain their increasing propensity to marry Catholics, and it may well have made them all the more acquiescent to the raising of their own children as Catholics. In contrast, the much higher rates of Catholic church attendance suggest that the personal religious commitment of the Catholic partner was likely to be stronger. In view of the added pressure of the Catholic church's mixed marriage laws, the likelihood that Protestantism will survive at this crucial level would seem all the dimmer.

Nevertheless, I believe it would be equally mistaken to draw unduly pessimistic conclusions. Although the available evidence is slim, the aforementioned signs of secular and integrationist sentiments among Catholics cannot be ignored. This is not to say that all Catholics wished to send their children to Protestant schools or that they all believed that their Catholic faith should no longer shape their political and social life. Neither do I wish to imply that all who shared these views were necessarily indifferent Catholics. But these developments do suggest that some Catholics now viewed religion as a personal and private matter. It is this attitude which surely lies behind the recent indications of a new resistance among mixed marriage couples to the notion that the religion of the Catholic partner would inevitably prevail. Moreover, if there was justification for the fears of the clergy that an increasing number of couples were resolving the conflicting demands of their parents by not allying themselves with either religion, then this secular compromise might still lead them to favour the Protestant school system. Further research on the children of mixed marriages is obviously needed before any definite conclusion can be drawn. With some 60 to 70 per cent of the minority still marrying fellow Protestants, it is apparent that neither full assimilation nor total integration is likely to occur for some time. For the moment, all that can be safely said is that the recent growth of secular tendencies among some Catholics calls into question the assumption of earlier years that mixed marriages would inevitably lead to assimilation and the eventual extinction of Protestantism.

Speculation is always a risky business, but I believe that it is possible to go a little further. Since Catholics so greatly outnumber Protestants, the survival of the minority requires that a relatively small proportion of Catholics be willing to regard religion as a matter of individual choice. As the Dalkey School Project and the many Catholic applications to Protestant schools indicated, the very strength of traditional Catholicism made it all the more likely that Catholics with secular inclinations would be attracted to the Protestant world. Similarly, in the political arena, liberal Catholics and Protestants were often brought together by their shared opposition to the forces of conservative Catholicism. And for reasons of class and status, diminishing segregation in the now dominant urban sector was again characterized by Catholic entrance into the associational life of the minority. In short, I am suggesting that there may now be emerging a new and broader secular movement built on and around the Protestant community. In this alliance with the more secular Catholics, Protestants may find the environment they need to sustain a substantial mixed marriage rate and yet see their numbers stabilize and possibly grow. Such an alliance in opposition to the more conservative Catholics would not be as clearly drawn as the former division between Protestant and Catholic. However, in the light of the many changes that have occurred within the Catholic community over the last decade, there is good reason to believe that this alliance will grow in the future.

In looking ahead in this manner, it would be unwise to underestimate the current strength of traditional Catholicism and the still considerable desire of many Protestants to retain a measure of separation. Nor should it be forgotten that the minority had discarded its British allegiance and thereby assimilated on the ethnic dimension. But now that the last remaining communal division, based upon religion, has begun to be questioned by Catholics as well as Protestants, the prospects for integration and Protestant survival seem much brighter than at any time since 1922.

Notes

CHAPTER ONE

1 R.D. Edwards, *A New History of Ireland*, pp. 33–54.

2 J.C. Beckett, *The Making of Modern Ireland 1603–1923*, pp. 16–39.

3 Ibid., pp. 40–105.

4 J.C. Beckett, *The Anglo-Irish Tradition*, pp. 34–42.

5 J.C. Simms, *Jacobite Ireland 1685–81*.

6 W.E.H. Lecky, *A History of Ireland in the Eighteenth Century*, 1: 136–9.

7 Edwards, *A New History of Ireland*, p. 117; M. Elliott, "The Origins and Transformation of Early Irish Republicanism," *International Review of Social History* 23 (1978): 415.

8 For further discussion of the differences between northern and southern Protestantism, see F.S.L. Lyons, *Culture and Anarchy in Ireland 1890–1939*, pp. 18–26, 113–45.

9 J. White, *Minority Report: The Anatomy of Southern Irish Protestants*, pp. 31–40.

10 J. Lee, "Grattan's Parliament," in B. Farrell, ed., *The Irish Parliamentary Tradition*, pp. 149–59.

11 Comment by Hannay, one of the few nationalist Church of Ireland clergy, in R.B. McDowell, *The Church of Ireland 1869–1969*, p. 101.

12 See E. Larkin's trilogy of articles: "Economic Growth, Capital Investment and the Roman Catholic Church in Nineteenth Century Ireland," *American Historical Review* 72 (1967): 852–84; "The Devotional Revolution in Ireland 1850–1875," *AHR* (1972): 625–52; "Church, State and Nation in Modern Ireland," *AHR* 80 (1975): 1244–76.

13 Lyons, *Culture and Anarchy in Ireland*, p. 8.

14 Larkin, "The Devotional Revolution in Ireland," p. 649.

15 D.H. Akenson, *A Mirror to Kathleen's Face: Education in Independent Ireland 1922–1960*, pp. 1–4.

16 F.S.L. Lyons, *Ireland Since the Famine*, pp. 81–6.

17 D.G. Bowen, *The Protestant Crusade in Ireland 1800–70*.

18 D.H. Akenson, *The Church of Ireland: Ecclesiastical Reform and Revolution 1800–1885*; J.C. Beckett, "Disestablishment in the Nick of Time," *Theology* 63 (May 1970).

19 Quoted in McDowell, *The Church of Ireland*, pp. 3–4.

20 J.E. Pomfret, *The Struggle for Land in Ireland 1800–1923*, pp. 306–8. The remaining large estates were then forcibly sold under the auspices of the Irish Free State. Lyons, *Ireland Since the Famine*, pp. 595–6.

21 See *Report of the Special Meeting of the General Synod 1886; Journal of the General Synod*, 1893, 1912. Hereafter cited as *JGS*.

22 See *Irish Times*, 12 Dec. 1921.

23 *JGS*, 1893, p. 262.

24 *Gazette*, 19 April 1912; *JGS*, 1893, p. li.

25 In McDowell, *The Church of Ireland*, p. 98.

26 Letter by Lord Granard in R.B. McDowell, *The Irish Convention, 1917–1918*, p. 152.

27 P. Buckland, *Irish Unionism I: The Anglo-Irish and the New Ireland 1885–1922*, p. 140.

28 L.P. Curtis, "The Anglo-Irish Predicament," *Twentieth Century Studies* 4 (1970): 46–62.

29 S. Clark, *Social Origins of the Irish Land War*, pp. 182–93.

30 The authoritative account of the Ascendancy's political decline is in Buckland, *Irish Unionism I*.

31 Lord Middleton in ibid., p. 218.

32 Ibid., pp. 146–301.

33 Archbishop of Dublin in G. Seaver, *J.A.F. Gregg, Archbishop*, p. 116.

CHAPTER TWO

1 Unless otherwise indicated, all statistics in the text and the tables of this chapter are derived from the appropriate volumes and years of the *Census of Population of Ireland*, *Report on Vital Statistics*, and *Annual Report of the Registrar General*.

2 P. Buckland, *Irish Unionism I*, p. 30; *Irish Times*, 13 June 1923.

3 *Census of Population of Ireland*, 1926, 10: 46.

4 F.S.L. Lyons, "The Minority Problem in the Twenty-Six Counties," in F. McManus, ed., *The Years of the Great Test, 1926–1939*, p. 93.

5 Capt. R.F. Hibbert, a local landlord, quoted in D. Fitzpatrick, *Politics and Irish Life*, p. 73.

6 L.P. Curtis, "The Anglo-Irish Predicament," *Twentieth Century Studies* 4 (1970): 57.

7 Buckland, *Irish Unionism I*, p. 279.

8 L. Fleming, *Head or Harp*, p. 63.

9 D. O'Sullivan, *The Irish Free State and Its Senate*, p. 104.

10 J. White, *Minority Report*, p. 85.

11 *Irish Times*, 1 May 1922.

12 *Gazette*, 16 June 1922.

13 White, *Minority Report*, p. 89.

14 *Irish Times*, 13 June 1922.

15 Buckland, *Irish Unionism*, pp. 286–7.

16 *Irish Times*, 13 May 1922.

17 Ibid., 8 Dec. 1921, 13 May 1922.

18 Ibid., 30 Apr. 1922.

19 Ibid., 30 Oct. 1922.

20 Quoted in White, *Minority Report*, p. 91.

21 Buckland, *Irish Unionism*, pp. 278–9.

22 Fitzpatrick, *Politics and Irish Life*, p. 78.

23 *Irish Times*, 11 Sept. 1979.

24 The method of estimating these figures closely follows the procedure developed by B.M. Walsh. For details see his "Trends in the Religious Composition of the Population in the Republic of Ireland, 1946–71," *Economic and Social Review* 6 (1975): 543–55; and *Religion and Demographic Behaviour in Ireland*. In interpreting the table, three considerations deserve brief mention: first, in calculating the birth rate, no account is taken of births among emigrants or of the Catholic offspring of mixed marriages, and hence the birth rate is an estimate of the minority's capacity to produce future Irish Anglicans, rather than an index of their biological capability; second, young Anglican immigrants between the ages of 0–2 (and 0–4 in the 1960s) create an exaggerated impression of the minority's real birth rate, a distortion particularly influential in the 1960s when English immigration rose rapidly; third, because death rates are normally lower among the economically privileged, the use of national life tables makes it likely that Church of Ireland death rates are overstated. Thus the minority's real rate of natural decrease is probably somewhat less than indicated.

25 *Report of the Commission on Emigration and Other Population Problems 1948–1954*, table 69.

26 R.E. Kennedy, "Minority Group Status and Fertility: The Irish," *American Sociological Review* 38 (1973).

27 R.E. Kennedy, *The Irish: Emigration, Marriage and Fertility*, pp. 138–172.

28 *United Nations Demographic Year Book 1970* (New York, 1971), table 10.

29 Walsh, *Religion and Demographic Behaviour*, p. 12.

30 S. Leslie, "Conversion in Ireland," *The Furrow* 9 (1953): 132.

31 See *Gazette*, 23 June 1930; 21 July 1950.

32 Kennedy, *The Irish*, p. 10.

33 *Irish Times*, 7 Dec. 1922.

34 *Gazette*, 3 Aug. 1923.

35 Lyons, "Minority Problem," p. 97.

36 Fleming, *Head or Harp*, p. 93.

37 *Gazette*, 21 Sept. 1923.

38 Ibid.

39 G. Seaver, *J.A.F. Gregg, Archbishop*, p. 126.

40 *Irish Times*, 23 Jan. 1929.

41 W.B. Stanford, *A Recognised Church: The Church of Ireland in Eire*, p. 16.

42 O'Sullivan, *The Irish Free State and Its Senate*, pp. 255–56.

43 See "The Irish Free State: An Ex-Unionist View," *Round Table* 16 (1925): 31–32; M.D. Sullivan, "Minorities in the Free State," *Quarterly Review* 258 (1932): 312–26; H. Butler, "Portrait of a Minority," *The Bell* 19 (1953–54): 33–39.

44 J.H. Whyte, *Church and State in Modern Ireland, 1923–1970*, p. 47.

45 *Gazette*, 11 Jan. 1935.

46 C.I.R., "Gigmanity Uprooted," *The Bell* 11 (1944–5): 69.

47 See J. Jackson, *The Irish in Britain*, pp. 25–6.

48 Lyons, *Ireland Since the Famine*, pp. 611–7.

49 *Report of the Commission on Emigration*, par. 504.

50 J. Meenan, "Economic Life," in M. Hurley, ed., *Irish Anglicanism 1869–1969*, p. 142.

51 See chap. 4: Decline of the Protestant Firm.

52 *Irish Times*, 11 Sept. 1979.

53 For details, see Walsh, *Religion and Demographic Behaviour in Ireland*, pp. 27–9.

54 H.W. Robinson, *A Study of the Church of Ireland Population of Ardfert*. My estimate does not include marriages by members of the diocese to Protestants outside the diocese, since it is likely that an equal number of Protestants from outside took part in marriages within the diocese.

55 H.W. Robinson, *A Study of the Church of Ireland Population of Ferns Diocese*. Robinson does not make it clear how many of the mixed marriages took place in Church of Ireland churches. The 16 per cent figure assumes that all mixed marriages took place in Catholic churches. The latter estimate assumes that five of the eight mixed marriages occurred under Church of Ireland auspices. This proportion may be too high, but the next year mixed marriages were divided between the two churches in these proportions. *Irish Times*, 21 June 1975.

56 *Irish Times*, 21 June 1975. If the total number of marriages in Church of

Ireland churches increased by a lesser amount, then the mixed marriage rate would be higher.

57 Personal correspondence: The Most Reverend D.A.R. Caird, bishop of Meath and Kildare.

58 See Whyte, *Church and State*, pp. 169–71; P. Blanshard, *The Irish and Catholic Power*, pp. 171–2.

59 *Irish Times*, 14 Dec. 1978.

60 Source: copy of instructions issued to parish clergy by Irish episcopate following the Motu Proprio "Matrimonia Mixta."

61 J. Fulton, "Intermarriage and the Irish Clergy: A Sociological Study," in M. Hurley, ed., *Beyond Tolerance*, p. 159.

62 Ibid., p. 161.

63 *Irish Times*, 8 Oct. 1979.

64 Ibid., 9 Jan. 1979.

65 Ibid., 21 June 1975.

CHAPTER THREE

1 *Gazette*, 9 Dec. 1921, 13 Jan. 1922; *Irish Times*, 7, 9, and 12 Dec. 1921.

2 *Irish Times*, 7 Dec. 1921.

3 *Gazette*, 20 and 6 Jan. 1922.

4 For details, see B. Chubb, *The Government and Politics of Ireland*, p. 147.

5 Information was derived from sources too numerous to list for each candidate. The printed sources include W.J. Flynn, *The Oireachtas Companion and Saostat Guide*, 1926–1939; *Dail Debates*; *Irish Times*; *Gazette*; J.L. McCracken, *Representative Government in Ireland: A Study of Dail Eireann, 1919–1948*; *Who's Who, What's What and Where in Ireland*; T. Nealon, *Guide to the 21st Dail and Senate*.

6 S.L. Robinson, *Bryon Cooper*, p. 147.

7 *Gazette*, 29 Apr. 1938.

8 Ibid., 1 Feb. 1973.

9 Speech by Lemass, then a prominent Fianna Fail spokesman, quoted in D. O'Sullivan, *The Irish Free State and Its Senate*, p. 232.

10 Catholics outnumbered Protestants at Trinity by the mid-1970s, but this very recent trend is unlikely to have led to as great a change in the older electorate of graduates.

11 *Irish Times*, 27 and 30 May 1927.

12 B. Chubb, "The Independent Member in Ireland," *Political Studies* 5 (1957): 132.

13 P.M. Sacks, "Balliwick, Locality and Religion: Three Elements in a Dail Constituency Election," *Economic and Social Review* 1 (1970): 535.

14 *Hibernia*, 5 Nov. 1976.

15 P.M. Sacks, *The Donegal Mafia: An Irish Political Machine*, pp. 153–63.
16 *Irish Times*, 25 Aug. 1923.
17 Ibid., 12 Feb. 1932.
18 *Dail Debates*, 264: 1100.
19 Chubb, *Government and Politics in Ireland*, p. 152.
20 *Irish Times*, 7 Dec. 1921.
21 *Gazette*, 21 Sept. 1923.
22 Ibid., 19 Aug. 1927.
23 Ibid., 2 Sept. 1927.
24 *Irish Times*, 13 Feb. 1932.
25 Ibid.
26 Ibid., 23 Jan. 1933.
27 Ibid., 7 Nov. 1930.
28 J.H. Whyte, *Church and State in Modern Ireland*, p. 42.
29 *Irish Times*, 6 Sept. 1927.
30 *Irish Press*, 26 and 27 Nov. 1931.
31 *Irish Times*, 25 Aug. 1923.
32 *Gazette*, 16 Dec. 1924.
33 Ibid.
34 "The Irish Free State: An Ex-Unionist View," *Round Table* 16 (1925): 34.
35 *Irish Times*, 13 Feb. 1932.
36 F.S.L. Lyons, *Ireland Since the Famine*, p. 624.
37 D.H. Akenson, *A Mirror to Kathleen's Face*, pp. 35–42.
38 *Irish Times*, 18 Nov. 1926.
39 Ibid., 17 Nov. 1926.
40 C.B. Armstrong, "Education – Secondary," in N.D. Emerson and W. Bell, eds. *The Church of Ireland: Report of the Conference*, pp. 223–4.
41 *Irish Times*, 13 Nov. 1926.
42 *Catholic Bulletin* 17 (January 1927): 7.
43 *Gazette*, 23 Oct. 1926.
44 *Dail Debates*, 26: 1258–64.
45 Ibid., 26: 721.
46 Ibid., 26: 714.
47 Ibid., 26: 1277.
48 Ibid., 10: 162.
49 *Irish Times*, 23 Feb. 1925.
50 *Gazette*, 13 Feb. 1925.
51 *Dail Debates*, 10: 159–61.
52 See M. Adams, *Censorship: The Irish Experience*.
53 *Dail Debates*, 26: 628–65.
54 Ibid., 53: 2017–20.

55 *Gazette*, 19 Mar. 1971.
56 Whyte, *Church and State*, p. 48.
57 For the most thorough analysis of the constitution, see ibid., pp. 51–6.
58 *Gazette*, 7 May 1937.
59 *Dail Debates*, 41: 921–33.
60 *Irish Times*, 24 Jan. 1932.
61 Lyons, *Ireland Since the Famine*, pp. 506–14.
62 *Gazette*, 15 Jan. 1973.
63 J. Whyte, "Political Life," in M. Hurley, ed., *Irish Anglicanism, 1869–1969*, p. 146.
64 *Irish Times*, 30 June 1937.
65 Chubb, *Government and Politics of Ireland*, p. 81.
66 *Gazette*, 11 June 1937; *Irish Times*, 15 and 30 June 1937.
67 *Irish Times*, 30 June 1937.
68 Ibid.
69 For the most detailed account, see Whyte, *Church and State*, pp. 196–272.
70 *Irish Times*, 12 Apr. 1951.
71 Whyte, *Church and State*, p. 232.
72 *Gazette*, 20 Apr. 1951.
73 Ibid., 27 Apr. 1951.
74 *Irish Times*, 18, 25, and 27 Nov. 1948.
75 *Dail Debates*, 117: 439–43.
76. Whyte, *Church and State*, p. 236.
77 *Dail Debates*, 117: 446.
78 *Irish Times*, 30 May 1951.
79 Ibid., 1 Mar. 1951.
80 Ibid., 18 May 1954.
81 *Gazette*, 11 Jan. 1957.
82 Chubb, *Government and Politics of Ireland*, p. 125.
83 M. MacGreil, *Prejudice and Tolerance in Ireland*, p. 419.
84 Sacks, *The Donegal Mafia*, pp. 99, 160–2.
85 Ibid., pp. 196–205.
86 *Gazette*, 11 Feb. 1972.
87 MacGreil, *Prejudice and Tolerance*, p. 208.
88 Sacks, *The Donegal Mafia*, p. 160.
89 D. Thornley, "Ireland: The End of an Era," *Studies* 53 (1964): 8.
90 A. Cohan, *The Irish Political Elite*.
91 J.H. Whyte, "Ireland: Politics without Social Bases," in R. Rose, ed., *Electoral Behaviour: A Comparative Handbook*, pp. 630–7.
92 Lyons, *Ireland Since the Famine*, pp. 624–30.
93 Whyte, "Ireland: Politics without Social Bases," pp. 642–3; MacGreil, *Prejudice and Tolerance*, pp. 403–7.

94 MacGreil, *Prejudice and Tolerance*, p. 125.

95 Ibid., p. 468.

96 Ibid., p. 210.

97 Adams, *Censorship*; White, *Minority Report*, p. 115.

98 Whyte, *Church and State*, pp. 322–5.

99 *Report of the Committee on the Constitution*, 1967, p. 48.

100 Whyte, *Church and State*, pp. 350, 388–9.

101 *Seanad Debates*, 70: 966.

102 Whyte, *Church and State*, p. 405.

103 *JGS*, 1971, p. lxxxviii.

104 Whyte, *Church and State*, pp. 408–9.

105 Market Research Bureau of Ireland, "Religious Practice and Attitudes towards Divorce and Contraception among Irish Adults," *Social Studies* 3 (1974): 282.

106 *Irish Times*, 26 Nov. 1973.

107 Ibid., 17 July 1974.

108 Ibid., 21 Feb. 1978.

109 White, *Minority Report*, p. 123.

110 *Irish Times*, 3 Jan. 1979.

111 Whyte, *Church and State*, p. 405.

112 *Irish Times*, 30 May 1978.

113 Ibid., 5 April. 1978.

114 Whyte, *Church and State*, pp. 415.

115 *Irish Times*, 1 Mar. 1979.

116 Ibid., 29 Oct. and 1 Nov. 1980.

117 *Report of the Committee on the Constitution*, 1967, p. 43.

118 Whyte, *Church and State*, p. 403.

119 *JGS*, 1979, pp. 201–8.

120 Speech by Bishop Armstrong to Synod of Cashel and Emly, Waterford and Lismore, in *Gazette*, 29 Oct. 1976.

121 Speech by the Archbishop of Dublin, in ibid., 3 Dec. 1976; *JGS*, 1978, p. 196.

122 *Gazette*, 12 Mar. 1976.

123 *Report of the Role of the Church Committee*, 1973, p. 13.

124 Archbishop Ryan, in *Gazette*, 12 Mar. 1976.

125 *JGS*, 1977, p. 91.

126 *Irish Times*, 3 Apr. 1978.

127 *Irish Independent*, 18 May 1978.

CHAPTER FOUR

1 J.H. Whyte, "Political Life," in M. Hurley, ed., *Irish Anglicanism 1869–1969*, p. 143.

2 The following analysis of class trends is restricted to males because males in Ireland tend to define the social class position of their families. A similar decision was made in the one major study of the Irish class system. See B.R. Hutchinson, *Social Status and Inter-Generational Social Mobility in Ireland.*

3 J.W. O'Hagen and D.C. McDonald, "The Rationale for, and Extent of, Government Intervention," in J.W. O'Hagen, ed., *The Economy of Ireland: Policy and Performance,* pp. 66–7.

4 On government growth see F.S.L. Lyons, *Ireland Since the Famine,* pp. 610–35, 645–73.

5 See chap. 7: West Britons.

6 J.H. Whyte, *Church and State in Modern Ireland,* pp. 165–6; J. White, *Minority Report,* pp. 164–5.

7 B. Inglis, *West Briton,* p. 37.

8 White, *Minority Report,* p. 162.

9 K.A. Kennedy, *Productivity and Industrial Growth,* pp. 10–34; J. Meenan, *The Irish Economy Since 1922,* pp. 132–6.

10 Meenan, *The Irish Economy,* pp. 132–6.

11 These statistics and a summary of this growth may be found in Kennedy, *Productivity and Growth,* pp. 1–36; O'Hagen, *The Economy of Ireland,* pp. 116–26.

12 *Irish Times,* 31 July and 1 Aug. 1973.

13 B. Hutchinson, *Social Status and Inter-Generational Social Mobility in Dublin,* p. 7.

14 Ibid.

15 Quoted in J. Jackson, "Ireland," in M. Archer, ed., *Contemporary Europe,* p. 216.

16 Ibid.

17 *Gazette,* 13 Oct. 1925, 24 Apr. 1930, 31 Jan. 1947, 19 Oct. 1951.

18 See chap. 7: Urban Lower Classes.

19 *Gazette,* 11 Jan. 1935.

20 White, *Minority Report,* p. 158.

21 M. MacGreil, *Prejudice and Tolerance in Ireland,* p. 395.

22 L. Gorman et al., *Managers in Ireland,* pp. 22–6.

23 White, *Minority Report,* p. 163.

24 Gorman, *Managers in Ireland,* p. 22.

CHAPTER FIVE

1 D.S. Connery, *The Irish,* p. 157.

2 J.H. Whyte, *Church and State in Modern Ireland,* pp. 362–76.

3 C.K. Ward, "Socio-Religious Research in Ireland," *Social Compass* 11 (1964): 26.

4 A.H. Small, "Fellowship Between Catholics and Non-Catholics," *Irish Monthly* 50 (1922): 368–72; S.J. Brown, "Reviews of 'The Catholic Approach to Protestantism' and 'The Spirit and Forms of Protestantism'," *Studies* 45 (1956): 495–6.

5 P. Blanshard, *The Irish and Catholic Power*, p. 137.

6 Whyte, *Church and State*, pp. 18, 305–7.

7 F. O'Donoghue, "Protestants – As We See You," *Focus* 8 (1965): 224.

8 W.A. Phillips, ed., *History of the Church of Ireland*, 1: 4.

9 J. Ryan, "The Church of Ireland and the Celtic Church," *Studies* 23 (1934): 330.

10 This and all other pamphlets quoted in the following pages can be found in the Representative Church Body Library of the Church of Ireland. As they are available in a collected form, they will not be annotated individually.

11 C.B. Moss, "The Disestablished Home Churches," J.W.C. Ward, ed., *The Anglican Communion: A Survey*, p. 265.

12 Ibid.

13 D.H. Akenson, *The Church of Ireland*, pp. 302–9.

14 Archbishop Trench quoted in P.M.A. Bell, *Disestablishment in Ireland and Wales*, p. 190.

15 See *The Book of Common Prayer ... According to the Use of the Church of Ireland* (Dublin, 1949), pp. 713–31.

16 G. Seaver, *J.A.F. Gregg, Archbishop*, pp. 141–58.

17 Moss, "The Disestablished Home Churches," p. 265.

18 A.H. McNeile, "The Anglican Communion: Ireland," in C. Jenkins and R. MacKenzie, eds., *Episcopacy: Ancient and Modern*, p. 142.

19 *Gazette*, 30 Nov. 1956.

20 For a detailed, though somewhat dated, description of the church's governmental structures and its distribution of powers, see W.G. Wilson, *How The Church of Ireland is Governed*.

21 Calculated from the opening pages of the appropriate years of the *JGS*.

22 See Seaver, *Gregg, Archbishop*.

23 Ibid., p. 119.

24 *Catholic Bulletin* 26 (March 1936): 193–202.

25 *Gazette*, 12 Feb. 1936.

26 *JGS*, 1939, p. lxxviii.

27 Ibid., 1949, p. lxxxiii.

28 Ibid., 1939, p. lxxx.

29 Ibid., 1939, pp. lxxviii–lxxx.

30 Ibid., 1949, pp. lxxxiv–v.

31 *Administration 67: Report of the Advisory Committee on Administration*, table k. Figures for table 13 are derived from the appropriate volumes of the census and the *Church of Ireland Directory*.

32 Ibid.; *JGS*, 1978, p. 72.

33 *JGS*, 1979, pp. 12–44.

34 R.B. McDowell, *Church of Ireland 1869–1969*, pp. 128–9.

35 See, for example, *JGS*, 1974, pp. 28–44.

36 Ibid., 1947, pp. lxxxii–iii.

37 Ibid., 1977, p. 12–31.

38 Ibid., 1977, pp. 21–9; 1979, pp. 21–33.

39 *Gazette*, 28 Mar. 1975.

40 *JGS*, 1949, pp. lxxxiv–v; 1954, p. lxxxvi.

41 *Representative Church Body Retirement Benefits Report*, 1974, p. 5.

42 *JGS*, 1978, p. 72–3.

43 Ibid., 1975, p. 89.

44 "Select Committee Report on the Auxiliary Ministry," *JGS*, 1974.

45 *JGS*, 1931. p. 364.

46 Seaver, *Gregg, Archbishop*, pp. 176–9; *JGS*, 1979, pp. 160–2.

47 See *Gazette*, 10 Jan. 1947; 25 Sept. 1974; *Irish Times*, 19 Sept. 1972.

48 C.M. Grey-Stacks, "The Mystery of the Empty Chair," *Focus* 9 (1966): 54–6.

49 *Gazette*, 21 Jan. 1966.

50 *The Furrow* 17 (1966): 477.

51 *Irish Times*, 6 Nov. 1972.

52 Ibid., 27 and 28 Sept. 1973.

53 J. White, *Minority Report*, p. 175.

54 See "Chapter IX of the Constitution of the Church of Ireland," *JGS*, 1974.

55 *JGS*, 1973, p. 249.

56 V.G.B. Griffin, *Anglican and Irish: What We Believe*.

57 *Gazette*, 17 June 1977.

58 *JGS*, 1966, isc.

59 French commentator approvingly quoted in H.R. McAdoo, *Being an Anglican*.

60 M. MacGreil, *Prejudice and Tolerance in Ireland*, p. 168.

61 Ibid.

62 Ibid., p. 169.

63 Archbishop Simms quoted in *Report of the Role of the Church Committee*, 1974, p. 5.

64 H.R. McAdoo, *Marriage and the Community – The Inter-Church Marriage*, p. 7.

65 *JGS*, 1975, pp. 94–5.

66 *Irish Times*, 9 Jan. 1979.

67 *JGS*, p. 92; see also *Gazette*, 10 June 1977.

68 Griffin, *Anglican and Irish*, p. 47.

69 McAdoo, *Being an Anglican*, p. 5.

70 J. Wilson, *Religion in American Society: The Effective Presence*, pp. 424–34.
71 MacGreil, *Prejudice and Tolerance*, p. 392.
72 T. Luckman, *The Invisible Religion*, p. 104.
73 P. Berger, *The Sacred Canopy*, p. 110.
74 Unless otherwise indicated, all information was obtained from doctors and a senior administrator connected with the Adelaide Hospital.
75 *Gazette*, 1 May 1951.
76 Ibid., 20 June 1952.
77 Based on interviews with Service officials and its annual reports. The latter can be found in the *JGS*.
78 MacGreil, *Prejudice and Tolerance*, p. 274.

CHAPTER SIX

1 See D.H. Akenson, *A Mirror to Kathleen's Face*, pp. 93–108; Cardinal Conway, *Catholic Schools*; The Irish Episcopal Conference, *Directory on Ecumenism in Ireland*.
2 *Irish Times*, 13 Oct. 1978.
3 *Gazette*, 28 Feb. 1975.
4 Department of Education, *Rules and Regulations for National Schools*.
5 Source: interviews with the current and past principals of the college.
6 *JGS*, 1923, p. 212.
7 All statistics were obtained from the appropriate years of the *Annual Report of the Church of Ireland Training College*.
8 *Rules and Regulations for National Schools*, nos. 29–36.
9 John Mescal, *Religion in the Irish System of Education*, p. 112.
10 *JGS*, 1932, p. 237; 1933, p. 231; 1934, p. 224.
11 Akenson, *Mirror*, pp. 117–18.
12 In 1955 there were 508 Anglican children attending Catholic schools; 363 did so because no Protestant school was available. *JGS*, 1956, p. 121. For the total number of pupils in Church of Ireland schools, see *JGS*, 1950, 241–69; 1961, pp. 165–94.
13 See *JGS*, 1965, pp. 98–101; *Dail Debates*, 217.
14 *JGS*, 1968, p. 98.
15 *The Education Times*, 25 July 1974; *Irish Times*, 3 Mar. 1975.
16 J. White, *Minority Report*, p. 143.
17 Ibid., p. 144–6.
18 Ibid., p. 145.
19 See *Gazette*, 5 July and 4 Nov. 1977; *Hibernia*, 18 June 1976; *Irish Times*, 3 Oct. 1978.
20 See letter from Fr. Sayers, secretary of the Education Secretariate of the Catholic Church in the *Gazette*, 7 Oct. 1977.
21 *JGS*, 1974, p. 133.

22 *Irish Times*, 18 May 1978.

23 Akenson, *Mirror*, p. 77.

24 J.H. Whyte, *Church and State in Modern Ireland*, pp. 37–8.

25 *JGS*, 1944, p. 174.

26 *Report of the Council of Education*, p. 64.

27 Annual Report of *The Incorporated Society for Promoting Protestant Schools in Ireland*, 1929.

28 *Report of the Advisory Committee on Secondary Education*, p. 16.

29 *Report of the Council of Education*, p. 64.

30 *Report on Secondary Education*, pp. 12–14. In fact there were forty-three schools at the time of the survey, but information for only forty were listed.

31 Ibid., p. 6.

32 See, ibid., pp. 18–22; *JGS*, 1975, p. 124.

33 *JGS*, 1974, p. 146.

34 White, *Minority Report*, p. 152.

35 See Secondary Education Committee reports in *JGS*, 1967–69; and N. Atkinson, *Irish Education: A History of Educational Institutions*, pp. 172–6.

36 *JGS*, 1979, p. 144.

37 See speech by L.F. Jacobs to General Synod, reported in *Gazette*, 23 May 1969.

38 Information on fees was obtained from unpublished records of the Secondary Education Committee and *JGS*, 1975, p. 124.

39 *Gazette*, 21 Apr. 1972; *JGS*, 1975, p. 124.

40 Rev. C. Fox, national vocations director, quoted in *Irish Times*, 3 Apr. 1978. In fact, even during the 1960s the proportion of religious seemed to be falling. See article by John Horgan in *Hibernia*, 7 May 1976.

41 For details of this early proposal and the few Catholic comprehensive schools, see Akenson, *Mirror*, pp. 149–56.

42 *Irish Times*, 22 Apr. and 31 May 1978.

43 Ibid., 12 June 1979. With the acceptance of the new proposal by the Dublin V.E.C., a final signing of the deeds seemed only a matter of time. Ibid., 14 July 1979.

44 *Gazette*, 14 Mar. 1975

45 In order to receive the higher government salary, teachers of other subjects were required to demonstrate an oral competency in Irish, but headmasters claimed that this hurdle could be overcome with a few months' study.

46 *JGS*, 1961, p. 109.

47 See table 14 and the report of one of the headmasters of the Incorporated Society that enrolment in their eight schools rose by 30 per cent between 1948 and 1956. *Irish Times*, 17 Apr. 1956.

48 *Catholic Bulletin* 17 (January 1927): 2.

49 The survey was conducted by the Dublin Diocesan Board of Education. *Irish Times*, 26 Oct. 1978.

50 White, *Minority Report*, p. 143.

51 M. MacGreil, *Prejudice and Tolerance in Ireland*, p. 175.

52 *Report of the Commission on Higher Education 1960–1967*, 2: 435.

53 Whyte, *Church and State*, p. 305.

54 H.R. Chillingworth, "Trinity College Dublin and the Irish Free State," *Contemporary Review* 151 (1937): 305; White, *Minority Report*, p. 154.

55 K.C. Bailey, *A History of Trinity College Dublin, 1892–1945*, pp. 42–3.

56 The above statistics and all those that follow were obtained either from college authorities or from *The Report of the Commission on Higher Education 1960–1967*.

57 Whyte, *Church and State*, pp. 306–7.

58 *Commission on Higher Education*, 2: 443.

59 F.S.L. Lyons, *Ireland Since the Famine*, p. 643.

60 Ibid., p. 77.

61 Akenson, *Mirror*, p. 39.

62 See National Programme Conference, *National Programme of Primary Instruction*; *Report of the Second National Programme Conference 1925–1926*; Department of Education, *Secondary School Programme 1925–1926*.

63 Akenson, *Mirror*, pp. 41–54.

64 Lyons, *Ireland Since the Famine*, p. 626.

65 Irish National Teachers' Organization, *Report of Committee of Inquiry into the Use of Irish as a Teaching Medium*; J. MacNamara, *Bilingualism and Primary Education*.

66 *JGS*, 1941, p. 232.

67 J. MacNamara, "Success and Failure in the Movement for the Restoration of Irish," in J. Rublin and B. Jernudd, eds., *Can Language Be Planned*, pp. 71–3.

68 *Irish Times*, 16 Oct. 1936.

69 MacNamara, "Sucesss and Failure," p. 75.

70 Ibid., pp. 71–5.

71 See D.P. Barrett and C.F. Carter, *The Northern Ireland Problem: A Study in Group Relations*, p. 91.

72 J. Magee, "The Teaching of Irish History in Irish Schools," reprinted from *The Northern Teacher* 10 (1970): 2.

73 See D. Casserley, *A History of Ireland*.

74 Magee, "The Teaching of Irish History," p. 3.

75 *Primary School Curriculum: Teachers' Handbook*, pp. 87–88.

76 Akenson, *Mirror*, p. 123.

77 *Irish Times*, 18 May 1923.

78 Akenson, *Mirror*, p. 123.

79 *JGS*, 1923, p. 215.

80 Ibid., 1927, p. 371.

81 "A 'Day Boy'," *The Bell* 7, no. 2 (1944): 439.

82 All quotes and information can be found in *The Report of the Advisory Committee on Religious Education.*

83 See Church of Ireland Board of Education, *A Curriculum for Religious Education in Primary Schools; Guidelines for a Curriculum in Religious Education for Secondary Schools.*

84 *Report of the Advisory Committee on Religious Education*, p. 21.

85 *Irish Times*, 26 Oct. 1978.

86 Of a total of twelve schools on which some information could be obtained, only the Cork comprehensive had completely segregated classes in religious education with separate curricula. At Newpark, the Dublin Comprehensive, there was a rather odd arrangement whereby pupils studied a common curriculum in separate classes. See *Gazette*, 14 Mar. 1975; *Irish Times*, 3 Mar. 1975.

87 See *Irish Times*, 3 Mar. 1975; 26 Oct. 1978.

88 *Gazette*, 28 Oct. 1977.

CHAPTER SEVEN

1 See chap. 2: Mixed Marriages.

2 See chap. 3: Political Attitudes and Electoral Allegiances.

3 A. Gray, *The Orange Lodge*, p. 258.

4 M. Harris, *Prejudice and Tolerance in Ulster*, pp. 138–9.

5 B. Inglis, *West Briton*, p. 19.

6 Ibid., p. 213.

7 Ibid., p. 16.

8 Ibid., p. 18.

9 Ibid., p. 19.

10 C.I.R., "Gigmanity Uprooted," *The Bell* 11, no. 2 (1945): 690–1.

11 Inglis, *West Briton*, p. 214.

12 Jackson, "Ireland," in M. Archer, ed., *Contemporary Europe*, p. 218.

13 J. Morris, "Anglo-Irish," *Encounter* 15 (1970): 17.

14 J. White, *Minority Report*, p. 29.

15 "A 'Day Boy'," *The Bell* 7, no. 2 (1944): 437.

16 I have no evidence of this in earlier years, but these class differences could still be discerned in Dublin in the early 1970s. See M. MacGreil, *Prejudice and Tolerance in Ireland*, pp. 278–9.

17 *Irish Times*, 18 Jan. 1974.

18 White, *Minority Report*, p. 167.

19 This is a conservative estimate as the few fathers for whom I had no information were assumed not to be members.

20 For a brief description of these sentiments and literature, see T. de Vere White, "Freemasonry," in T.D. Williams, ed., *Secret Societies*, pp. 46–57; J.H. Whyte, *Church and State in Modern Ireland*, pp. 72–3.

21 Whyte, *Church and State*, p. 41.

22 *Irish Times*, 16 Jan. 1974; White, *Minority Report*, pp. 168.

23 *Hibernia*, 11 May 1978.

24 Ibid.

25 The latter two figures of 24 and 45 per cent slightly exceed the figure of 63 per cent because some individuals had memberships in both Protestant and Catholic associations.

CHAPTER EIGHT

1 For a similar argument, see D.H. Akenson, *A Mirror to Kathleen's Face*, pp. 118–19.

2 As used here, the terms secularization, integration, and assimilation are very similar. The key difference is that secularization refers to the declining social significance of religious differences – and only religious differences. In contrast, assimilation and integration are broader terms that encompass the declining social significance of all three dimensions of religion, class, and ethnicity associated with members of the Church of Ireland.

3 H. Mol, ed., *Western Religion*.

4 B.R. Wilson, "Aspects of Secularisation in the West," *Japanese Journal of Religious Studies* 3 (1976): 259–69.

5 P. Berger, *The Sacred Canopy*.

6 *Seanad Debates*, 96: 16–426.

7 *Irish Times*, 11 Dec. 1981.

8 Ibid., 29 and 30 Sept. 1981.

9 Ibid., 29 Sept. and 12 Oct. 1981.

10 Ibid., 11 Dec. 1981.

11 J.H. Whyte, *Church and State in Modern Ireland*, p. 383.

Bibliography

IRISH GOVERNMENT
PUBLICATIONS

Annual Report of the Registrar General. Dublin: Stationery Office 1926–52.

Central Statistics Office, *Census of Population of Ireland*: 1946, vols. II and III; 1961, vol. VII; 1971, vol. IX. Dublin: Stationery Office.

Dail Eireann Debates. Dublin: Stationery Office, 1922–79.

Department of Education. *Primary School Curriculum: Teachers' Handbook*. Dublin: Stationery Office 1970.

– *Rules and Regulations for National Schools*. Dublin: Stationery Office 1965.

– *Secondary School Programme 1925–26*. Dublin: Stationery Office 1925.

Department of Industry and Commerce. *Census of Population of Ireland*: 1926, vol. III; 1936, vol. III. Dublin: Stationery Office.

National Programme Conference. *National Programme of Primary Instruction*. Dublin: Educational Company of Ireland 1922.

Report of the Commission on Emigration and Other Population Problems 1948–54. Dublin: Stationery Office 1954.

Report of the Commission on Higher Education 1960–67. Dublin: Stationery Office 1967.

Report of the Committee on the Constitution. Dublin: Stationery Office 1967.

Report of the Council of Education: The Curriculum of the Secondary School. Dublin: Stationery Office 1960.

Report of the Council of Education: The Function of the Primary School. Dublin: Stationery Office 1954.

Report of the Organization for European Cultural Development Survey Team: Investment in Education. Dublin: Stationery Office 1965.

Report of the Second National Programme Conference 1925–26. Dublin: Stationery Office 1926.

Report on Vital Statistics. Dublin: Stationery Office 1953–74.

Seanod Eireann Debates. Dublin: Stationery Office 1981.

CHURCH OF IRELAND PUBLICATIONS

Church of Ireland Board of Education. *A Curriculum for Religious Education in Primary Schools, 1977.*

– *Guidelines for a Curriculum in Religious Education for Secondary Schools,* 3 vols., 1977–9.

Church of Ireland Directory, 1922–77.

Journal of the General Synod of the Church of Ireland, 1893–1979.

Religious Education: A Syllabus and Handbook for Grammar and Secondary Schools. Belfast: Nicholson and Bass 1965.

Report of the Advisory Committee on Administration: Administration 1967. Dublin: Dublin University Press 1967.

Report of the Advisory Committee on Religious Education for the Church of Ireland, 1972. Dublin: Dublin University Press 1972.

Report of the Advisory Committee on Secondary Education in the Republic of Ireland. Dublin: Dublin University Press 1965.

Report of the Church of Ireland Training College. 1921–22 to 1973–74.

Report of the Incorporated Society for Promoting Protestant Schools in Ireland, 1926–74.

Report of the Role of the Church Committee. Dublin: Dublin University Press 1974.

Report of the Special Meeting of the General Synod 1886. Dublin: Hodges Figgis 1886.

Representative Church Body Retirements Benefit Report. Mimeographed. Dublin 1974.

Representative Church Body Supplemental Report: Retirement and Superannuation of the Clergy. Mimeographed. Dublin 1973.

The Book of Common Prayer ... According to the Use of the Church of Ireland. Dublin: A.P.C.K. 1949.

NEWSPAPERS AND MAGAZINES

Catholic Bulletin
Church of Ireland Gazette
The Church of Ireland Magazine
Focus

Hibernia
Irish Independent
Irish Press
Irish Times

BOOKS, PAMPHLETS, AND
ARTICLES

Adams, M. *Censorship: the Irish Experience.* Dublin: Scepter Books 1968.

Akenson, D.H. *The Church of Ireland: Ecclesiastical Reform and Revolution 1800–1885.* New Haven and London: Yale University Press 1971.

– *The Irish Education Experiment: The National System of Education in the Nineteenth Century.* London: Routledge and Kegan Paul 1970.

– *A Mirror to Kathleen's Face: Education in Independent Ireland 1922–1960.* Montreal: McGill-Queen's University Press 1975.

Armstrong, C.B. "Education – Secondary." In *The Church of Ireland: Report of the Conference,* edited by N.D. Emerson and W. Bell. Dublin: Dublin University Press 1932.

Atkinson, N.D. *Irish Education: a History of Educational Institutions.* Dublin: Allen Figgis 1969.

Babbington, R. *Mixed Marriages.* Dublin: A.P.C.K. 1930.

Bailey, K.C. *A History of Trinity College Dublin 1892–1945.* Dublin: Dublin University Press 1947.

Barrett, D.P., and Carter, C.F. *The Northern Ireland Problem: a Study in Group Relations.* rev. 2nd ed. London: Oxford University Press 1972.

Beckett, J.C. *The Anglo-Irish Tradition.* London: Faber and Faber 1976.

– "Disestablishment in the Nick of Time." *Theology,* 63 (May 1970).

– *The Making of Modern Ireland 1603–1923.* London: Faber and Faber 1966.

– *Protestant Dissent in Ireland 1687–1780.* London: Faber and Faber 1948.

Bell, P.M.A. *Disestablishment in Ireland and Wales.* London: S.P.C.K. 1969.

Berger, P. *The Sacred Canopy.* New York: Doubleday 1967.

Blanchard, J. *The Church in Contemporary Ireland.* Dublin: Clonmore and Reynolds 1963.

Blanshard, P. *The Irish and Catholic Power,* Boston: The Beacon Press 1953.

Bowen, D.G. *The Protestant Crusade in Ireland 1800–70.* Dublin: Gill and Macmillan 1978.

Brown, S.J. "Reviews of 'The Catholic Approach to Protestantism' and 'The Spirit and Forms of Protestantism'." *Studies* 14 (Winter 1956).

Buckland, P. *Irish Unionism I: The Anglo-Irish and the New Ireland 1885–1922.* Dublin: Gill and Macmillan 1972.

Butler, H. "Portrait of a Minority." *The Bell* 19 no. 7 (1954).

Camier, J.W. *The Early Irish Church.* Dublin: A.P.C.K. 1932.

Casserly, D. *A History of Ireland.* 2 vols. Dublin: Talbot Press 1945.

Cave, S.A. *Our Church in History*. Dublin: A.P.C.K. 1954.

Chamberlain, G.A. *The Church of Ireland: What Is It?* Dublin: A.P.C.K. 1929.

Chillingworth, H.R. "Trinity College Dublin and the Irish Free State." *Contemporary Review* 151 (1937).

Chubb, B. *The Government and Politics of Ireland*. Stanford: Stanford University Press 1970.

− "The Independent Member in Ireland." *Political Studies* 5 (June 1957).

C.I.R. "Gigmanity Uprooted." *The Bell* 11, no. 2 (1945).

Clark, S. *Social Origins of the Irish Land War*. Princeton: Princeton University Press 1979.

Clarke, A. *The Old English in Ireland 1625−1642*. London: MacGibbon and Kee 1966.

Cohan, A. *The Irish Political Elite*. Dublin: Gill and Macmillan 1972.

Connery, D.S. *The Irish*. New York: Simon and Schuster 1968.

Conway, Cardinal. *Catholic Schools*. Dublin: Veritas Publications 1974.

Curtis, L.P. "The Anglo-Irish Predicament." *Twentieth Century Studies* 4 (November 1970).

"A 'Day Boy'." *The Bell* 7, no. 3 (1944).

de Vere White, T. *The Anglo-Irish*. London: Gollancz 1972.

− "Freemasonry." In *Secret Societies in Ireland*, edited by T.D. Williams. Dublin: Gill and Macmillan 1973.

Dillon, M. "Douglas Hyde." In *The Shaping of Modern Ireland*, edited by C.C. O'Brien. London: Routledge and Kegan Paul 1960.

Edwards, R.D. *A New History of Ireland*. Dublin: Gill and Macmillan 1972.

An Elementary Catechism. Dublin: A.P.C.K. 1933.

Elliott, M. "The Origin and Transformation of Early Irish Republicanism." *International Review of Social History* 23, pt. 3 (1978).

Fitzpatrick, D. *Politics and Irish Life 1913−1921: Provincial Experience of War and Revolution*. Dublin: Gill and Macmillan 1977.

Fleming, L. *Head or Harp*. London: Barrie and Rockliff 1965.

Fletcher, D. *Home and Marriage: A Warning*. Dublin: Church of Ireland Printing Co. 1936.

Flynn, W.J. *The Oireachtas Companion and Saorstat Guide*. Dublin: Hely's 1926 and various years to 1939.

Fulton, J. "Intermarriage and the Irish Clergy: A Sociological Study." In *Beyond Tolerance: The Challenge of Mixed Marriages*, edited by M. Hurley. Dublin: G. Chapman 1975.

Garvin, T. *The Irish Senate*. Dublin: Institute of Public Administration 1969.

Gorman, L., Handy, R., Maynihan, T., and Murphy, R. *Managers in Ireland*. Dublin: Irish Management Institute 1974.

Gray, A. *The Orange Lodge*. London: The Bodley Head 1972.

Gregg, J.A.F. *The 'Ne Temere' Decree*. Dublin: A.P.C.K. 1935.

– *The Primitive Faith and Roman Catholic Developments*. Dublin: A.P.C.K. 1909.

Grey, W.R. "The Vanishing Protestants." *Focus* 9, no. 10 (1966).

Grey-Stacks, C.M. "The Mystery of the Empty Chair." *Focus* 9, no. 3 (1966).

Griffin, V.G.B. *Anglican and Irish: What We Believe*. Dublin: A.P.C.K. 1976.

Hammond, T.C. *Marriage My Choice: What Shall It Be?* Dublin: Church of Ireland Printing Co. 1936.

Harris, M. *Prejudice and Tolerance in Ulster: A Study of Neighbours and 'Strangers' in a Border Community*. Manchester: Manchester University Press 1972.

An Historical Catechism for the Use of Members of the Church of Ireland. Dublin: A.P.C.K. n.d.

Hutchinson, B. *Social Status and Inter-Generational Mobility in Dublin*. Dublin: Economic and Social Research Institute, Paper no. 48 (1969).

Inglis, B. *West Briton*. London: Faber and Faber 1962.

The Irish Episcopal Conference. *Directory on Ecumenism in Ireland*. Dublin: Veritas Publications 1976.

"The Irish Free State: An Ex-Unionist View." *Round Table* 14, no. 12 (1925).

Irish National Teachers' Organization. *Report of the Committee on Inquiry into the Use of Irish as a Teaching Medium*. Dublin: I.N.T.O. 1941.

Jackson, J. "Ireland." In *Contemporary Europe*, edited by M. Archer. London: Heinemann 1972.

– *The Irish in Britain*. London: Routledge and Kegan Paul 1963.

Johnston, T.J. *The Church of Ireland: Its Continuity in Doctrine and Faith*. Dublin: A.P.C.K. 1955.

Jordon, G.V. *The Reformation in Ireland in the XVIth Century*. Dublin: A.P.C.K. 1932.

Keane, T. "Demographic Trends." In *Irish Anglicanism 1869–1969*, edited by M. Hurley. Dublin: Allen Figgis 1970.

Kennedy, K.A. *Productivity and Industrial Growth*. Oxford: Clarendon Press 1971.

Kennedy, R.E. *The Irish: Emigration, Marriage and Fertility*. Berkeley: University of California Press 1973.

– "Minority Group Status and Fertility: the Irish." *American Sociological Review* 38, no. 1 (1973).

Kinch, F.H. *Should I Join the Church of Rome?* Dublin: Church of Ireland Printing Co. 1937.

Kingsmill-Moore, H. *Ireland and Her Church: A Short History of the Church of Ireland*. Dundalk: Dundalgan Press 1937.

– *The Work of the Incorporated Society for Promoting Protestant Schools in Ireland*. Dundalk: Dundalgan Press 1928.

Larkin, E. "Church, State and Nation in Modern Ireland." *American Historical Review* 80, no. 5 (1975).

– "The Devotional Revolution in Ireland, 1850–75." *American Historical Review* 77, no. 3 (1972).

– "Economic Growth, Capital Investment and the Roman Catholic Church in Nineteenth Century Ireland." *American Historical Review* 72, no. 3 (1967).

Lecky, W.E.H. *A History of Ireland in the Eighteenth Century.* 5 vols. London: Longmans, Green 1892.

Lee, J. "Grattan's Parliament." In *The Irish Parliamentary Tradition*, edited by B. Farrell. Dublin: Gill and Macmillan 1973.

Leslie, S. "Conversion in Ireland." *The Furrow* 9, no. 3 (1953).

Luckmann, T. *The Invisible Religion.* New York: Macmillan 1967.

Lyons, F.S.L. *Culture and Anarchy in Ireland 1890–1939.* Oxford: Oxford University Press 1979.

– *Ireland Since the Famine.* London: Weidenfeld and Nicolson 1971.

– "The Minority Problem in the 26 Counties." In *The Years of the Great Test 1926–39*, edited by F. MacManus. Cork: Mercier Press 1967.

McAdoo, H.R. *Being an Anglican.* Dublin: A.P.C.K. 1977.

– *Marriage and the Community: The Inter-Church Marriage.* Dublin: A.P.C.K. 1974.

– *No New Church.* Dublin: Church of Ireland Publishing Co. 1945.

McCracken, J.L. *Representative Government in Ireland: A Study of Dail Eireann 1919–48.* London: Oxford University Press 1958.

McDowell, R.B. *The Church of Ireland 1869–1969.* London: Routledge and Kegan Paul 1975.

– *The Irish Convention 1917–1918.* London: Routledge and Kegan Paul 1970.

McElligott, T.J. *Education in Ireland.* Dublin: Institute of Public Administration 1966.

MacGreil, M. *Prejudice and Tolerance in Ireland.* Dublin: College of Industrial Relations 1977.

MacNamara, J. *Bilingualism and Primary Education: A Study of Irish Experience.* Edinburgh: Edinburgh University Press 1966.

– "Successes and Failures in the Movement for the Restoration of Irish." In *Can Languages Be Planned?*, edited by J. Rublin and B. Jernudd. Honolulu: University of Hawaii 1970.

McNeile, A.H. "The Anglican Communion: Ireland." In *Episcopacy: Ancient and Modern*, edited by C. Jenkins and R. MacKenzie. London: S.P.C.K. 1930.

Magee, J. "The Teaching of Irish History in Schools." *The Northern Teacher* 1 no. 1 (1970).

Market Research Bureau of Ireland. "Views on Contraception and Divorce." *Social Studies* 3, no. 3 (1974).

Meenan, J. "Economic Life." In *Irish Anglicanism 1869–1969*, edited by M. Hurley. Dublin: Allen Figgis 1970.

– *The Irish Economy Since 1922.* Liverpool: Liverpool University Press 1970.

Mescal, J. *Religion in the Irish System of Education.* Dublin: Clonmore and Reynolds 1957.

Mol, H., ed. *Western Religion.* The Hague: Mouton 1972.

Morris, J. "Anglo-Irish." *Encounter* 25, no. 4 (1970).

Moss, C.B. "The Disestablished Home Churches." In *The Anglican Communion: A Survey*, edited by J.W.C. Wand. London: Oxford University Press 1948.

Nealon, T. *Guide to the 21st Dail and Senate.* Dublin: Institute of Public Administration 1978.

O'Donoghue, F. "Protestants – As We See You." *Focus* 8, no. 10 (1965).

O'Hagan, J.W., and McDonald, D.C. "The Rationale for, and Extent of, Government Intervention." In *The Economy of Ireland: Policy and Performance*, edited by J.W. O'Hagan. Dublin: Irish Management Institute 1975.

O'Sullivan, D. *The Irish Free State and Its Senate: A Study in Contemporary Politics.* London: Faber and Faber 1940.

Phillips, W.A., ed. *History of the Church of Ireland.* 3 vols. London: Oxford University Press 1933–4.

Pomfret, J.E. *The Struggle for Land in Ireland 1800–1923.* New York: Russell and Russell 1930.

The Representative of the Church of St. Patrick, the Church of Ireland or the Church of Rome in Ireland – Which? Dublin: Church of Ireland Publishing Co. 1938.

Robinson, H.W. *A Study of the Church of Ireland Population of Ardfert,* 1971.

– *A Study of the Church of Ireland Population of Ferns Diocese,* 1973.

Robinson, S.L. *Bryon Cooper.* London: Constable 1931.

Roman Claims – An Elementary Catechism. Dublin: A.P.C.K. 1933.

Ryan, J. "The Church of Ireland and the Celtic Church." *Studies,* 23 (Summer 1934).

Sacks, P.M. "Balliwick, Locality and Religion: Three Elements in a Dail Constituency Election." *Economic and Social Review* 1, no. 4 (1970).

– *The Donegal Mafia: An Irish Political Machine.* New Haven: Yale University Press 1976.

Seaver, G. *J.A.F. Gregg, Archbishop.* London: Faith Press 1963.

Seymour, J.D. *The Twelfth Century Reformation in Ireland.* Dublin: A.P.C.K. 1932.

Shearman, H. "Irish Church Finances after Disestablishment." In *Essays in British and Irish History in Honour of James Eadie Todd*, edited by H.A. Crone, T.W. Moody, and D.B. Quinn. London: Frederick Muller 1949.

Simms, J.C. *Jacobite Ireland 1685–91*. London: Routledge and Kegan Paul 1969.

Small, A.H. "Fellowship Between Catholics and Non-Catholics." *Irish Monthly* 50, no. 9 (1922).

Stanford, W.B. *A Recognised Church: The Church of Ireland in Eire*. Dublin: A.P.C.K. 1944.

Sullivan, M.D. "Minorities in the Free State." *Quarterly Review* 258 (April 1932).

Thornley, D. "Ireland; the End of an Era." *Studies* 68 (1964).

United Nations. *Statistical Yearbook 1970*. New York: Publishing Service United Nations 1971.

Wall, M. *The Penal Laws*. Dundalk: Dundalgan Press 1967.

Waller, B.C. *The Pope's Claims and Why We Reject Them*. Dublin: A.P.C.K. 1932.

Walsh, B.M. *Religion and Demographic Behaviour in Ireland*. Dublin: Economic and Social Research Institute, Paper no. 55 (1970).

– "Trends in the Religious Composition of the Population in the Republic of Ireland." *Economic and Social Review* 6, no. 4 (1975).

Ward, C.K. "Socio-Religious Research in Ireland." *Social Compass* 11, nos. 3/4 (1964).

White, J. *Minority Report: The Protestant Community in the Irish Republic*. Dublin: Gill and Macmillan 1975.

White, N.J.D. *The Teaching of St. Patrick*. Dublin: A.P.C.K. 1932.

Who's Who, What's What and Where in Ireland. London: Geoffrey Chapman 1973.

Whyte, J.H. *Church and State in Modern Ireland 1923–1970*. 2nd ed., rev. Dublin: Gill and Macmillan 1980.

– "Ireland: Politics without Social Bases." In *Electoral Behaviour: A Comparative Handbook*, edited by R. Rose. New York: Free Press 1974.

– "Political Life." In *Irish Anglicanism 1869–1969*, edited by M. Hurley. Dublin: Allen Figgis 1970.

Wilson, B.R. "Aspects of Secularisation in the West." *Japanese Journal of Religious Studies* 3, no. 4 (1976).

Wilson, J. *Religion in American Society: The Effective Presence*. New Jersey: Prentice Hall 1978.

Wilson, W.G. *The Church of Ireland: Why Conservative*. Longford: A.P.C.K. 1970.

– *How the Church of Ireland is Governed*. Dublin: A.P.C.K. 1963.

Index